PRAISE FO

'G ry Marcus, one of the deepest
h s given us an entertaining and en
ght about music, learning, and th
teven Pinker**, Professor of Psychol **d on or before**
and author of *The B*

' u can't teach an old dog new tricks, goes the saying, but psych-
ist Gary Marcus disagreed. Here, he shows how he used
scientific knowledge to... play the guitar like a musical
us (well, near enough).' *The Observer*

elightfully inspiring, charming, and detailed musical journey
explodes myths of human limitation, while revealing that
ountain of youth very well may be made of wood and played
ix strings.'

Richard Barone, musician and author of
Frontman: Surviving the Rock Star Myth

d with wonderful insights about music and the human mind.'
Scientific American

cus is one of the smartest psychologists around, a deep
ker and an eloquent writer, and the story he tells is informed
b he best science of perception and learning and evolution;
ta nt and effort, genius and frustration and success. If you have
ever dreamt of becoming a musician, you simply must read
Guitar Zero.'

Paul Bloom, Professor of Psychology at Yale University and

GUITAR ZERO

The Science of
Learning to be Musical

GARY MARCUS

ONEWORLD

A Oneworld Book

First published in Great Britain and the Commonwealth
by Oneworld Publications 2012
First published by arrangement with The Penguin Press, a member of the
Penguin Group (USA), Inc.
This edition published by Oneworld Publications in 2013
Reprinted 2013, 2016

Illustration credits:
Pages 41 and 205: Athena Vouloumanos
Page 140: Gary Marcus
Pages 18 and 218: Meighan Cavanaugh based on sketches by the author.

ISBN: 978-1-85168-962-0
Ebook ISBN: 978-1-78074-100-0

Designed by Meighan Cavanagh

Printed and bound in Great Britain by Clays Ltd, St Ives plc

Oneworld Publications
10 Bloomsbury Street, London WC1B 3SR

Stay up to date with the latest books,
special offers, and exclusive content from
Oneworld with our monthly newsletter

Sign up on our website
www.oneworld-publications.com

ABOUT THE AUTHOR

Gary Marcus is Professor of Psychology and Director of the New York University Center for Language And Music (CLAM), where he studies evolution, language, and cognitive development. He has written three books about the origins and development of the mind and brain, including *The Algebraic Mind*, *The Birth of the Mind*, and *Kluge*, and is also the editor of *The Norton Psychology Reader*. His scientific articles have been published in leading journals, such as *Science* and *Nature*, and his essays have appeared in *Wired*, the *Wall Street Journal*, the *New York Times*, and many others. He lives in New York City and tweets from @garymarcus.

I've been obsessed with the guitar since I was twelve. In many ways my life has been one long conversation about the guitar, interrupted only by the countless hours of deep pleasure I have playing the darn things, as well as some less pleasant time spent doing what needs to be done so that I can get back to playing and chatting about them.

—Perry Beekman, jazz guitarist

First you learn your instrument, then you learn the music, and then you forget all that s**t and just play.

—Charlie Parker

For David and Elaine

CONTENTS

GUITAR ZERO

TUNING UP

What Does It Take
to Become Musical?

Are musicians born or made?

All my life I wanted to become musical, but I always assumed that I never had a chance. My ears are dodgy, my fingers too clumsy. I have no natural sense of rhythm and a lousy sense of pitch. I have always loved music but could never sing, let alone play an instrument; in school I came to believe that I was destined to be a spectator, rather than a participant, no matter how hard I tried.

As I grew older, I figured my chances only diminished. Our lives, once we finish school, tend to focus on execution rather than enrichment. Whether we are breadwinners or caretakers, our success is measured by outcomes. The work it takes to achieve those outcomes, we are meant to understand, is something that should happen quickly and behind closed doors. If the conventional wisdom is right, by the time we are adults it's too late to learn anything new. Children may be able to learn anything, but if you wanted to learn French, you should have started when you were six.

♪

Until recently, science supported this theory. Virtually everybody in developmental psychology was a firm believer in 'critical periods' of learning. The idea is that there are particular time windows in which complex skills can be learned; if you don't learn them by the time the window shuts, you never will. Case closed.

But the evidence for critical periods is surprisingly weak. Consider, for example, the often-cited case of Genie, an unfortunate girl who was locked in a silent room for many years. When Genie escaped at the age of thirteen, she was exposed to language for the first time, and she was never able to become fluent. Her vocabulary was good enough to get her started, but her grammar was a mess, filled with utterances like 'Spot chew glove' and 'Applesauce buy store'. Does this mean that Genie's critical period for language had passed? Most people interpret her case that way, but another explanation, less often considered, is that Genie's inability to learn language may have come in part from the emotional trauma (and perhaps malnutrition) she had suffered early on. Her case is consistent with the critical period hypothesis, but it certainly doesn't prove it.

The more people have actually studied critical periods, the shakier the data have become. Although adults rarely achieve the same level of fluency that children do, the scientific research suggests that differences typically pertain more to accent than to grammar. Meanwhile, contrary to popular belief, there's no magical window that slams shut the moment puberty begins. In fact, in recent years scientists have identified a number of people who have managed to learn second languages with near-native fluency, even though they only started as adults.

If critical periods aren't quite so firm as people once believed, a world of possibility emerges for the many adults who harbour secret dreams – whether to learn a language, to become a pastry chef, or to pilot a small plane. And quests like these, no matter how quixotic they may seem, and whether they succeed in the end or not, could bring unanticipated benefits, not just for their ultimate goals but for the journey itself. Exercising our brains helps maintain them, by preserving plasticity (the capacity of the nervous system to learn new things), warding off degeneration, and literally keeping the blood flowing. Beyond the potential benefits for our brains, there are benefits for our emotional well-being, too. There may be no better way to achieve lasting happiness – as opposed to mere fleeting pleasure – than pursuing a goal that helps us broaden our horizons.

♪

Still, from primary school onward, every musical attempt I made ended in failure. The first time I tried to play guitar, a few years ago, my friend Dan Levitin (who had not yet finished his book *This Is Your Brain on Music*) kindly offered to give me a few lessons. When I came back to him after a week or two of practice, he quickly realized what my primary school teachers had realized long ago: that I had no sense of rhythm whatsoever. Dan offered me a metronome, and when that didn't help, he gave me something my teachers couldn't – a diagnosis: congenital arrhythmia.

And yet I never lost the desire to play. Music hasn't been studied as systematically as language in terms of critical periods, but there are certainly artists who started late and still became first-rate musicians. Tom Morello – guitarist of Rage Against the Machine and *Rolling Stone* magazine's twenty-sixth-greatest guitarist of all time – didn't start until he was seventeen. Patti Smith scarcely considered becoming a professional singer until she was in her mid-twenties. Then there is the jazz guitar legend Pat Martino, who relearned how to play after a brain aneurysm at the age of thirty-five, and the New Orleans keyboard legend Dr John, who switched his primary allegiance from guitar to piano at age twenty-one (after his left ring finger was badly injured in a barroom fight) and won the first of his five Grammy Awards at forty-eight.

Given my arrhythmia, I had no aspiration of reaching such heights, but at thirty-eight, long after I had completed my PhD and become a professor of cognitive psychology, I realized that my desire to become musical wasn't going away. I wanted to know whether I could overcome my intrinsic limits, my age, and my lack of talent. Perhaps few people had less talent for music than I did, but few people wanted more badly to be able to play.

♪

My first ray of hope came, oddly enough, from a video game, which I bought with the idea that it might improve my rhythm. The game I am referring to is, of course, *Guitar Hero,* perhaps the most mindless yet entertaining game I have ever played. In case you haven't seen it, the basic premise is that coloured dots fall from the top of the screen, in time with music, and as a player your mission consists of nothing more than the pressing of matching coloured buttons on a plastic guitar in time with the falling dots.

What makes it fun is that the game plays a snippet of music each time the player presses a button at the right moment, yielding the illusion that the player is actually playing a song.

Or not. If one's timing is bad enough (as mine was initially), you hear a beep instead of the musical snippet, and worse, the crowd begins to boo. Play badly enough, and the crowd boos you off the stage. I know this rather too well, because every time I tried to play the opening song – a regrettable piece of 1970s blues rock called 'Slow Ride', by Foghat – the crowd soon began to boo, louder and louder, until the song stopped midway through, inevitably accompanied by the rather brutal and unimaginative message informing me that I had 'failed'. As the failures piled up, I was brought back to fourth grade – year five – when I had tried to learn to play the recorder (a sort of poor man's flute that was popular in the Baroque era) and was so musically naive I couldn't get past

'Mary Had a Little Lamb'. *Guitar Hero* might be a poor substitute for real guitar, but for a musical dunce like me even *Guitar Hero* seemed out of reach; I soon packed the game away and returned to my ordinary life.

But then a funny thing happened. My wife, Athena, returned home from a trip to see friends and raved about how much fun she'd had playing a counterpart to *Guitar Hero* called *Rock Band*.

♪

Our copy of *Guitar Hero* came out of the closet, and thus my new life began. Trying again, but this time with the benefit of Athena's feedback (telling me when I was pressing the buttons too early versus when I was pressing too late), I finally managed to play 'Slow Ride' all the way through, with nary a boo. I was so excited I could barely speak. My first taste, ever, of quasi-musical success – it was nothing short of intoxicating.

For weeks, I kept practising, and soon I started getting better and better. I never made it to expert mode, but I eventually got through medium and became obsessed with a different question. I didn't want to while away my later years playing a video game, but if I could make progress with a plastic controller, could I learn to play a real guitar? I began to wonder: Could persistence and a lifelong love of music overcome age and a lack of talent? And, for that matter, how did anyone of any age become musical?

It was time to find out.

♪

To an alien scientist, music – and the desire to create it – might be one of the most puzzling aspects of humanity. Any species, for instance, would presumably have a metabolism, and any reasonably intelligent species would likely also have a system of communication; eventually we would expect it to develop systems of government and law, too. But would such creatures also revere patterns of sound that vary over time? I wonder, would they have any desire to make their own music?

Someday, maybe we will find out, but for now, one thing was clear: my own desire to make music was undeniable. I had reached the point where it felt like it was now or never. I began to read up on the scientific literature. How did children learn music? Were there any lessons for adults?

To my surprise, although children had been well studied, there was hardly any systematic research on people my age. Nobody seemed to know much about whether adults could pick up an instrument late in life, and it wasn't just music that we knew little about; the literature on the capacity of adults to learn new skills in general was far sparser than I had imagined. We know something about gradual declines in memory, but the only truly firm result I could find with respect to the late learning of music in particular concerned perfect pitch (the ability to identify a single note in isolation). For that, one must indeed start early, but lucky for me and anyone else starting late, it is also quite clear that perfect pitch is more luxury than necessity. Duke Ellington didn't have it, and neither did Igor Stravinsky (nor, for that matter, did Joey Ramone).

Several other studies show some kind of advantage for music learners who began earlier in life over adults who began later, but most of those don't control for total amount of practice. When it came to other aspects of music, such as the ability to improvise or compose, or even to learn a simple melody, there was almost no compelling literature. Although any number of studies have shown that the more you practise the better you get, startlingly few have compared what happens when people of *different* ages get the same amount of practice.

How could such a basic scientific question remain so unanswered? I wondered about this for months, until Caroline Palmer, a soft-spoken but exceptionally clear-thinking professor of psychology at McGill University in Montreal, finally explained the answer to me. The problem wasn't a lack of scientific interest; it was a lack of subjects. To learn a musical instrument, you need to put in a lot of work – ten thousand hours is an oft-mentioned (if somewhat oversold) number – and to do a proper study, you'd need a reasonably large sample of participants, which is to say a big group of adult novices with sufficient commitment. Nobody has studied the outcomes of adults who put in ten thousand hours of practice starting at age forty-two because most people of that age have lives and responsibilities. Your average forty-two-year-old might go to lessons once or twice a week, but eventually the burdens of a child, a job, or an ageing parent often take over; few adult learners of music are prepared to invest the kind of time that a teenager has. No subjects, no science.

At that point, I decided to become a guinea pig. I couldn't ethically force other adults to practise for ten thousand hours, but I could experiment on myself. As it happened, I had a sabbatical coming up, which would give me more free time than usual, and I decided to see what would happen if I devoted myself to music full-time, for a month or two – or as long as I could stand. If someone as tuneless as I could make progress, perhaps there was hope for anyone.

♪

At the outset of my journey, one study in particular gave a glimmer of hope.

For years, the strongest scientific evidence for critical periods came not from humans but from animals. To properly establish the existence of a critical period, one needs to do an experiment in which young animals are raised in a carefully controlled environment.

In the literature on critical periods, one of the most influential experiments came from raising barn owls. Barn owls, as it happens, are a little like bats: they rely heavily on sound to navigate. At the same time, however, they can see better than bats typically do, and one of the first things they do after hatching is to calibrate their eyes with their ears, lining up what they hear with what they see. This allows them to use sound cues to help them navigate in their dark nocturnal world. But exact mapping between eyes and ears cannot be hardwired at birth, because the navigational function of the auditory information depends on the exact distance between the two ears, and that distance changes as an animal grows.

How do owls manage to calibrate the visual world with the auditory world? The Stanford biologist Eric Knudsen explored this question by raising owls in a kind of virtual reality world, in which prisms shifted everything by twenty-three degrees. This disrupted the owl's normal capacity to see and forced the owl to adjust its internal map of the visual world. The earlier the prisms were installed, the better the owls were able to cope with the altered world. Young owls could easily learn to compensate for the distortion, whereas old owls could not.

If that were the only paper I had read, I would have given up on the guitar right there. But I soon stumbled on a more recent study, less widely known, in which Knudsen discovered that older owls weren't entirely hopeless after all. Although Knudsen's original results still stand – adults definitely aren't as flexible as baby owls – adult owls can often get to the same place, so long as their job is broken down into smaller bite-size steps. Adult owls couldn't master twenty-three degrees of distortion all in one go, but they could succeed if the job was broken down into smaller chunks: a few weeks at six degrees, another few weeks at eleven degrees, and so on.

Maybe I didn't have talent, and maybe I was old (or at least no longer young), but I was willing to take it slow. Could adults like me acquire new skills if we approached them bit by bit, owl-style?

This book is about how I began to distinguish my musical derriere from

♪

my musical elbow, but it's not just about me: it's also about the psychology and brain science of how *anybody,* of any age – toddler, teenager, or adult – can learn something as complicated as a musical instrument.

What does it take to learn to play an instrument? What makes learning new skills so labour-intensive, when learning to talk seems so easy and so natural? Do children really have an advantage? Can adults make up for any disparity with directed practice?

Along the way, I marvel at the wonder that is music and the human desire to create and enjoy it. I take a look at the nature of music itself and how it evolved culturally and biologically. I explore what separates true experts from mere amateurs and debunk the myth of a 'music instinct' yet show that talent really does exist.

At the same time, I ask whether learning music makes people smarter and investigate what it takes to be a good teacher. Should parents encourage their children to play real musical instruments, or should they relax and let their kids play *Guitar Hero* instead?

With a guitar in one hand and a laptop in the other, I set out to understand the limits of human reinvention and how humans, young and old, talented or otherwise, become musical.

TAKE ME TO THE RIVER

Forming a Plan

Between my age and my manifest lack of talent, it was clear that a bite-size approach was in order. Knowing what I do about language from my day job as a developmental psychologist, I also strongly suspected that my only realistic hope of learning to play an instrument was to become completely immersed. I figured that I had no more chance of becoming musical by playing three minutes every other week than I had of learning to fly. Children who learn second languages in immersion programmes do vastly better than children with more occasional exposure, presumably because it takes the human brain a great deal of exposure to learn anything complicated, and we tend to forget the new stuff if we take too long between practice sessions to consolidate what we've learned. It is no accident that popular music education paradigms like the Suzuki method are based on immersion, and there is no reason to expect that adults would be exempt from the need for high doses of regular exposure.

Why is it that skills like music require such profound dedication?

♪

The cognitive psychologist Anders Ericsson, the world's leading expert on expertise, mentions two vital keys to becoming an expert in any domain. The first is a tonne of practice. The oft-quoted figure 'ten years' or 'ten thousand hours' is based on Ericsson's research into experts in domains ranging from chess to violin. This is not to say that one gets nowhere with five thousand hours, but there can be no doubt that there is a strong correlation between practice and skill.

But practice alone is not enough. Hundreds of thousands of people took music lessons when they were young and remember little or nothing.

The second prerequisite of expertise is what Ericsson calls 'deliberate practice', a constant sense of self-evaluation, of focusing on one's weaknesses rather than simply fooling around and playing to one's strengths. Studies show that practice aimed at remedying weaknesses is a better predictor of expertise than raw number of hours; playing for fun and repeating what you already know is not necessarily the same as efficiently reaching a new level. Most of the practice that most people do, most of the time, be it in the pursuit of learning the guitar or improving their golf game, yields almost no effect. Sooner or later, most learners reach a plateau, repeating what they already know rather than battling their weaknesses, at which point progress becomes slow.

Ericsson's notion of practising deliberately, not just fooling around but targeting specific weaknesses, bears some relation to an older concept known as the 'zone of proximal development', the idea that learning works best when the student tackles something that is just beyond his or her current reach, neither too hard nor too easy. In classroom situations, for example, one team of researchers estimated that it's best to arrange things so that children succeed roughly 80 percent of the time; more than that, and children tend to get bored; less, and they tend to get frustrated. The same is surely true of adults, too, which is why video game manufacturers have been known to invest millions in play testing to make sure that the level of challenge always lies in that sweet spot of neither too easy nor too hard.

♪

My own journey began with what we call in my trade a pilot study – a relatively small-scale exploratory study to see whether further investment might plausibly pay off: two weeks, at the end of August. My wife's family owns a lakeside cottage in Canada, which we visit nearly every summer, and I decided that this summer I would devote those two weeks to music and nothing else. Fresh from my modest success with *Guitar Hero,* six months shy of my thirty-ninth birthday, I decided that now was the time.

To our annual summer retreat I brought nearly every piece of musical equipment I owned. Just because I couldn't play didn't mean I couldn't buy. I had a Casio keyboard, a cheap acoustic guitar (an eBay special), and a small pile of books on music, including *Play Piano in a Flash!* and *The Complete Guitar Player,* along with a pile of ear-training applications on my mobile phone. And I was serious about the immersion: I practised every day, two, three, four, even six hours a day, roughly half on piano, half on guitar. Because I was a complete beginner, my goal was simply to become acquainted with some of music's most basic elements, individual notes and, especially, chords, which are combinations of three or more notes played together.*

♪

The rudiments of piano came relatively easy; guitar was brutal. On piano, it's easy to find the notes and form the basic chords. Every

---

* As I was to learn later, some guitarists extend the definition of *chords* to include certain pairs of notes, such as the 'power chords' (see glossary), neither major nor minor but somewhere in between, that give rock and heavy metal their aggressive feel.

twelve keys the same fundamental pattern repeats. The white keys play the notes C, D, E, F, G, A, and B before repeating; the black keys in between play the so-called sharps and flats, such as C-sharp and B-flat. Place your fingers on C, E, and G, and with those three notes you've formed your first chord, the C major triad. With a pair of simple rules it became relatively easy to play any of the major and minor chords. One can always form a major chord, for example, by starting with some particular note, known as the root, and then counting four keys (both black and white included) to the right, and then heading up three more.

C major, for example, is formed by starting with C, heading to E, and ending with G.

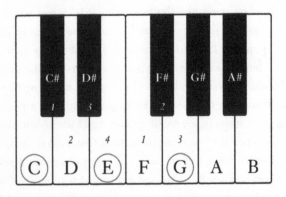

Following the same rule but starting from D, one counts up to F-sharp and A, yielding the three notes in the chord of D major: D, F-sharp, and A. It seemed so simple.

As straightforward and mathematical as piano is, I knew it wasn't the instrument for me. I had spent enough of my life at a keyboard already. Something about the physical intimacy of plucking guitar strings called to me. The guitar was obviously going to be harder to break into, but within a week or two I was convinced that it was the instrument I really wanted to play.

♪

At first, I regretted my decision. Everything, even something as simple as playing a single note all by itself, seemed harder on the guitar. Whereas playing an isolated note on a piano requires nothing more than striking a key, playing a single note on the guitar (unless it's a so-called open string) generally requires two actions, one from each hand, coordinated in synchrony.

For a right-hander such as myself, the left hand does the job known as fretting, which means holding down the right set of strings at the right time at the right place along the neck of the guitar. Frets are the thin metal wires that run across the narrow width of a guitar's neck. The left hand's mission is to clamp the strings down, close to the upper side of a given fret – not halfway between frets, as a beginner might imagine – so as to minimize extraneous vibrations. Meanwhile, the other hand (right for a right-hander) has the job of plucking or strumming the strings. (At first this all seems backwards, since the weaker hand has to contort itself into all sorts of rapid shapes; it's only when you start fantasizing about playing flamenco that you see how hard the job of the right hand can become.)

Playing a chord is even more complicated, in part because you can play only one note on any given string at any one time; forming a chord requires you to form weird left-hand shapes that span across several strings. Even if you know the four-up/three-up mathematics of how to form a major chord on a piano, it's often not at all immediately obvious where to find the requisite notes on the guitar; instead, the beginner has little choice but to memorize an obscure series of shapes. And even once one memorizes where one's fingers are supposed to go, there is the by no means trivial matter of holding them all down at the same time, each perfectly aligned, without creating a foul noise known as fret buzz. For the first several weeks, that challenge alone seemed almost insurmountable; the idea of shifting my hand from one chord to the next in time with a song seemed almost comical.

Yet somehow I remained undeterred. The weather by the lake was nice, and much to the amusement of my in-laws, I kept at it, practising every day – rarely appearing as if I had the slightest idea what I was doing.

♪

My first real breakthrough came a couple weeks later, when, on a road trip to a family reunion in a small town in Vermont, I stopped in a music store and poked through its section of beginning guitar books. And it was there that I discovered David Mead's *Crash Course: Acoustic Guitar*.

For the next seven days, Mead's book became my bible; I worked through it exercise by exercise. Mead had no magic bullets; the contortions of the hand that the guitar required remained difficult, but his 'crash course' broke guitar down into just the sort of bite-size morsels that an old owl like me could easily digest. It gave me a better sense of the basics of rhythm and helped me move beyond simple chords and isolated notes to grasp the significance of larger units, such as scales.

Scales are ascending (or descending) sets of notes that fit together naturally, conveying a particular mood or feel, such as the happy major scale or the sadder minor scale. The most famous scale is the C major scale, represented by the white notes on a piano keyboard: C, D, E, F, G, A, B, and back to C (think do-re-mi-fa-sol-la-ti-do). As I was to discover later, different scales elicit different moods, in part because of the different relationships between notes and in part because each scale has its own set of strong cultural associations with different scales. The song 'Happy Birthday', for example, is an arrangement of notes from the major scale, while the haunting melody of the Rolling Stones' 'Paint It Black' is an arrangement of a scale known as the harmonic minor.

Among the scales a beginner might learn, one of the simplest is the bluesy minor pentatonic, which consists of just five notes. The minor pentatonic, I soon found out, is a mainstay of rock and roll and the blues, used in countless guitar solos, from Jimi Hendrix's 'Hey Joe' to Dire Straits' 'Money for Nothing'. Soon it became a staple of my musical life – and a first hint that I might someday be able to make up my own music. Once I began to be comfortable with my first scales, my fumblings started to become faintly musical. My mother-in-law looked up. When she listened to my playing for the first time, even if it was only for a few seconds, I felt I was finally on to something.

♪

Thus encouraged, I set aside all the books I was reading, stopped watching television, and devoted myself full-time to the pursuit of music. I committed myself to practising every day, even buying a travel guitar so that I could keep practising when I was on the road to give lectures, trundling it through train stations and airports from New Zealand to Abu Dhabi.

And loved every minute of it.

Learning about music soon became, for all intents and purposes, an addiction. Each new note, each new chord, each new scale, and each new rhythm brought me closer to something that I desperately longed for: the capacity to make my own music. Even basic observations like 'the snare drum usually comes on the two and four' came as revelations. When I read some new neuroimaging studies that suggested that new knowledge can bring the same sort of surge of dopamine one might get by ingesting crack cocaine, I could only nod my head in agreement. Pressing plastic buttons in time with someone else's song was one thing; creating my own music another, an adventure that seemed to bring me into a new place altogether: meditative, beautiful, intoxicating.

♪

Along with all that beauty came something else: a first step in what was to be a long process of rewiring my own brain.

One of the first studies to examine the effects of musical practice on the brain came when a team of neuropsychologists led by the German neuroscientist Thomas Elbert combined an array of different brain-imaging techniques together in order to investigate what happens to the brain's representation of fingers as a person learns to play an instrument.

If you have taken a class in psychology or neuroscience, you may recall a famous picture that looks like this:*

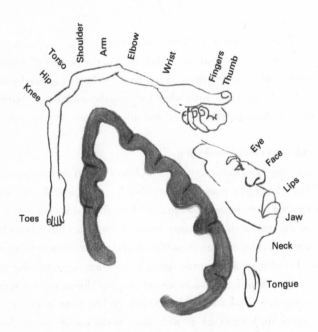

---

* The careful reader will note the absence of genitals in this G-rated version of the sensorimotor cortex. Luckily for the reproduction of our species, the genitals receive considerable coverage in the neural representation of haptic space.

The point of the illustration is twofold. First, the picture makes clear the fact that each part of the body has a specific piece of neural tissue assigned to it in the area of the brain known as the primary motor cortex; second, it also illustrates the fact that the exact amount of cortical real estate allocated varies from one body part to the next, with more sensitive areas getting more brain tissue. Fingers and lips get a lot, the back of the knee hardly any. (You can confirm this with the aid of a pin and a trusted friend. Close your eyes as the friend gently pokes you with the pin. In areas with heavy cortical representation, you will be able to easily discriminate closely spaced pinpricks; in areas with light cortical representation, you will sometimes be unable to distinguish two pinpricks that are close together but not identical.)

Earlier work by Michael Merzenich and others had shown that the boundaries between these areas aren't entirely fixed; a monkey that lost its middle finger, for example, might reallocate some of the primary cortex that was assigned to its middle finger to an adjacent finger. Similarly, in people who are born congenitally blind, the brain sometimes winds up taking some of the neural tissue that would normally be used for vision and using it for hearing. Could music practice similarly rewire the brain?

Indeed it could. Focusing on nine string players (six cellists, two violinists, and a guitarist), Elbert and his team discovered that string players dedicated an unusually large amount of cortical representation to the fingers of their note-selecting left hands, likely yielding two benefits. First, it gives string players greater control of their fingers, and second, it may make them more sensitive to the feedback that their fingers receive, allowing them a more precise mental picture of where their fingers are, and even of how taut a given string is – vital for playing with the correct touch.

Since then, dozens of studies have furthered Elbert's basic conclusion, that the brains of musicians differ from those of nonmusicians, and not just in the sensorimotor cortex but also in other brain areas such as the planum temporale (an area just behind the auditory cortex that is implicated in pitch perception), the cerebellum (implicated in rhythm), and the anterior (frontward) part of the corpus callosum, the thick set of fibres that connects the two sides of the brain, perhaps because of its role in coordinating the left and the right hands.

In keeping with these physical differences, the brains of musicians respond more sensitively to slight deviations in musically relevant parameters such as pitch, rhythm, and timbre (the sonic properties differentiating one instrument from the next, such as the sound of a violin versus the sound of a flute). The differences between musicians and nonmusicians depend in part on a musician's instrument of choice; the brains of violinists are especially sensitive to the sounds of violins, and the brains of trumpeters appear to be specialized for trumpet. Opera singers show specializations in the part of the primary somatosensory cortex that represents vocal articulators and the larynx. (One can only wonder about Prince, who has been known to play guitar, keyboards, bass, drums, saxophone, and harmonica.)

♪

These studies all raise an important question, especially salient for a beginner like me: Are musicians' brains different because they are born that way or because of all the hours they put into practising? With respect to initial differences (which could represent a physiological basis for what is colloquially known as talent), nobody yet knows for sure, but one recent study made it very clear that practice does indeed at least contribute to neural differences.

A team led by the Harvard neuroscientist Gottfried Schlaug tracked two groups of children for two years, starting at the age of five, half of whom were taking lessons in a musical instrument (piano or violin) and half of whom weren't. At the outset, there were no apparent differences between the children who took lessons and those who didn't.

Just fifteen months later, there were already clear neural changes: children who took lessons – especially those who had practised extensively – showed greater growth in the brain regions that control hand movements, in the corpus callosum, and in a right primary auditory area known as Heschl's gyrus. Practice might not make perfect, but it definitely has an effect on the brain.

Of course, evidence for practice is not evidence against inborn talent. Schlaug might have the best evidence for the importance of practice, but he still leaves room for talent, too. When I asked him about his own children, he didn't hesitate. Practice matters, he said, but it was still important that each child find a musical instrument that was a good fit to his or her innate talents. In all likelihood, the brains of musicians differ from those of less musical counterparts for two reasons, not one: both practice *and* talent.

Brain studies have, of course, reflections in behaviour. It's not just that musicians have thicker corpora callosa; it's that their brains are better at comprehending music, in processes such as detecting differences in pitch and slight variations in rhythm. In the brain-imaging study of five- to seven-year-olds, the magnitude of children's brain changes correlated with the size of behavioural changes. In tests of motor skills and melodic and rhythmic discrimination, children who took music lessons quickly overtook children who didn't, and the children who showed the most improvement on these tasks were the ones whose brains changed the most.

♪

All told, aspiring musicians must master at least three distinct sets of skills. They must develop their ears and brains so that they can recognize melodies (the basic tunes that serve as a song's foreground) and harmonies (which serve as accompaniment). They must master time, tempo, and rhythm. And they must harmonize their muscles, coordinating their two hands together at a rate that on a piano can approach eighteen hundred notes in a minute (in complex chords, wherein every digit of both hands works full-time). The kicker is that ultimately all of these skills must be so well integrated that they can all be performed simultaneously, and continuously, throughout the course of any individual piece of music.

Engineers might call this taxonomy a task analysis; I'd call it a gigantic challenge. The sheer amount of brain rewiring that must be done is almost overwhelming. I wished desperately that there were shortcuts to all that neural rewiring, but as a cognitive psychologist I knew better. Playing smoothly would entail rewiring my whole brain, from my temporal lobes to my prefrontal cortex, and there was no way around that. It was time to get cracking.

LEARNING
TO CRAWL

Is Music Built into the Brain?

Even before a baby first sees the light of day, he or she is likely to have been surrounded by music for months. To be sure, the sound quality is kind of dismal. Bass sounds are relatively audible, but most of the treble gets lost in the amniotic fluid that surrounds the growing foetus; it is almost as if the baby were listening to music from the bottom of a swimming pool. Still, lo-fi is better than no-fi. The process of learning about sound and music starts long before the baby begins to breathe on its own. Even putting aside whatever filtered sounds pass through from the outside world, there's plenty to listen to: heartbeats, breathing, and the regular modulations of the expecting mother's voice, which travels on the inside in part through bone conduction. And by the end of the final trimester, the growing foetus begins to take in at least some of what comes through.

Whether as a product of genes or early experience, or (more likely) both, some of the precursors of human musicality emerge very early in life. But how much of music is wired into our genomes? And how much of our musicality is hard-won, through lessons, practice, and listening?

♪

It is very popular these days to talk about humans as if we were born with a 'music instinct', akin to the language instinct that Noam Chomsky and Steven Pinker suggest we are born with.

But what is popular is not always true. At first glance, the notion that we might be born with a music instinct seems pretty plausible. In one study, for example, the Hungarian neuroscientist István Winkler showed that the brains of sleeping newborns could make a first step toward recognizing so-called relative pitch, in which music is understood not in terms of exact frequencies but in terms of the gaps between notes. When infants heard large musical leaps amid a series of smaller leaps, their brains displayed a common measure of surprise.

In another study, Winkler and his associates showed that the brains of awake newborns responded differently to the sudden absence of bass kick drum in an otherwise repetitive four-beat-long drum pattern. In a third study, they found that infants' brains appear to recognize changes in timbre, or when a single pitch is played by more than one instrument. We also know newborns can distinguish consonance (in which the notes of a chord blend together smoothly) from dissonance (in which the notes of a chord clash). But these rudiments aren't the same as a genuine understanding of music, which unfolds more slowly, over the weeks, months, and years that are yet to come.

Another early milestone arrives by about the age of two months, a first aesthetic preference: by then, infants have begun to *prefer* listening to consonance rather than dissonance, and not just to distinguish between the two. (Intriguingly, one study suggests that infant chimpanzees, too, may prefer consonance to dissonance, even though their overall interest level in music is low, perhaps suggesting that the difference between consonance and dissonance has more to do with the dynamics of how primate brains work than with anything intrinsic to music per se.)

By around six or seven months, infants start to become sensitive to the shapes of melodies. Given enough exposure, they can detect when a note has changed, recognize a short melody even when it has been transposed upwards or downwards in pitch, and sometimes remember melodies for weeks.

In some ways, young infants can even find themselves ahead of adults, especially in making fine auditory distinctions. One study, for instance, suggests that ten-month-olds are better able than adults to notice deviations in rhythms that aren't common in their own culture, a finding that has a direct parallel in language, where young infants are sensitive to some linguistic distinctions that adults in their cultures can't recognize. Young Japanese children, for example, might distinguish the sounds of *l* versus *r* where their parents can't.

A few researchers have even argued that babies are born with perfect or absolute pitch, that is, the capacity to recognize the exact frequency of any given note, at least in relatively unmusical sequences of notes. But such observations are controversial, and babies certainly don't have absolute pitch in the sense that some trained musicians do. Trained adults with absolute pitch can not only recognize a note but name it; no infant can do the same. (And of course many infants grow up to be tone-deaf or rhythmically impaired, perhaps because of a confluence of genes and inadequate musical experience – whereas virtually all normal children manage to master their native language.)

♪

Where does all of this leave the idea of a music instinct? Although for most children, most of the time, the rudiments of both rhythm and pitch are in place by the end of the first year of life, a small initial sensitivity to rhythm and pitch does not a symphony make. When it comes to the notion of humans being born with a 'music instinct', there are in fact several reasons for scepticism.

First and foremost is the fact that no matter which rudiments of music might be inborn, for most people it is a long, hard slog from there to anything recognizable as systematic music. Even if it takes your average baby only a few months to recognize some of the basic rhythms of his or her own culture's music, most children don't really work out the fact that there are discrete notes until they are at least two – if then. Notwithstanding the occasional five-year-old prodigy who possesses the rare phenomenon of perfect pitch and manages to learn to play piano by ear, most children struggle early on.

When it comes to singing, for example, toddlers often warble between notes without landing in any particular spot, yielding a kind of out-of-tuneness that sounds a bit like a beginning violinist. Eventually, most (but not all) children start to grasp the general contours of songs, such as when a song starts high and ends low, but even then most children often miss many of the individual notes. (In my own case, pitch was a complete mystery; I remembered songs by their lyrics, but I was largely oblivious to the tune.)

It also takes our ears years to develop. Even basics, like recognizing that major chords tend to sound happier and minor chords sound sad, can take many children until the end of the nursery years. More subtle capacities, like detecting chords that are merely unexpected rather than blatantly out of key, develop at an even slower pace. Children also have trouble paying attention to a background harmony that looms behind a foreground melody and may not even notice if the background harmony is dissonant.

Rhythm is no easier, as anyone who's ever been to a nursery school performance can attest. Although babies can bop along to music by the time they're seven months old, they can't bop *in time* to music until a few years later. In the final analysis, children's first efforts to sing, which is often their first attempt at producing music, are often admirable but rarely especially musical. Even when children reach primary school, about half still understand only the broad contours of songs, rather than seeing songs as collections of specific pitches; a precise sense of melody comes late, in primary school for many children (and much later, if ever, for people less gifted). Mastering the ability to stay in key often takes years. In the polite but damning words of one academic article, 'children enter school with a clear disposition towards learning the words of songs [that] is not matched by an ability to learn and reproduce the melodic components of [those] songs'. And for some of us, these struggles persist well into adulthood. When I started this whole project, my wife described my efforts at singing as 'cute but tuneless'. (As I later discovered, I was not alone: at least 10 to 15 percent of the population never learn to sing in key.)

Compared with some other creatures, such as songbirds like the zebra finch, human beings just aren't that impressive in their early years. By the time a young zebra finch reaches the age of ninety days, it has learned to sing its own song, styled on one it hears from a tutor, with a solid sense of rhythm and pitch – and the young zebra finch manages all of this without any obvious correction or feedback. Few humans can say the same. Whereas nearly every three-year-old masters his or her native language, there are plenty of thirty-three-year-olds who can't sing their way out of a paper bag. There is also some evidence, for example, that birds have a better sense of pitch than most humans. At the same time, humans can lead perfectly normal lives without being musical. Theodore Roosevelt, twenty-sixth president of the United States, is said to have been amusical, and Sigmund Freud may have been, too. A male zebra finch that was unable to sing would be hard-pressed to find a mate.

All of this is a bit bad for the hypothesis that we are born with a music instinct. Even worse is the enormous challenge that most of us face in our efforts to master musical instruments. Although there are legions of six-year-olds trying to play violin, the vast majority don't sound that good to anyone but their blood relatives. Drummers typically take years to learn to move their limbs independently, and guitarists (as I was starting to realize) take many moons to learn to change chords smoothly. Humans clearly have much more innate interest in music than do chimpanzees or monkeys, but compared with your average starling or mockingbird, human children are nowhere near the front of the class.

Where we excel is later; if we humans set our minds to it, we can do almost anything intellectual better than our animal kin. Drawing on our gifts of language, culture, teaching, and leisure time, we can get really good at something if we work hard at it; no songbird will ever compose the symphonies of Mahler or Beethoven. But saying that the most talented among us can produce great works of art if they devote their lives to that pursuit is not the same thing as saying that the average Joe is genuinely born with a gift for music. A good analogy might be skiing: human beings can surely learn to zip down bumpy snow-covered hills at high speeds – if they put the practice in – but that doesn't mean we are born knowing how to carve around moguls.

♪

In hindsight, the idea that the conventions of music are largely learned rather than hardwired shouldn't entirely come as a surprise. In linguistics, there are many candidates for detailed and specific aspects of language that might be cross-culturally universal, like parts of speech. In music, by contrast, universals are few and far between – and often very weak. Most music may, for example, revolve around some sort of central sound, but the Western notion of 'tonality' is hardly typical. Scales generally contain no more than six or seven notes (possibly as a function of human memory limitations), but the common chromatic scale has twelve, and some composers have experimented with dividing the scale into nineteen equal divisions. Most music is organized around steady metrical rhythms, but recitatives are not. Even something as seemingly basic as a melody in which notes change from one pitch to another over the course of a song is not common to all forms of music; some music is based almost entirely around rhythm, with pitch at most an afterthought. Indeed, some of the things that modern listeners take for granted – like major and minor chords, and harmony – are absent in many of the world's musical systems. There's a case for a strong universal grammar, but there may be little that is specifically innate about music.

♪

If music is something that we learn, rather than something that falls directly out of a hardwired instinct, that still doesn't mean that babies must start their musical voyages from scratch. Among all the species on our planet, humans are special in many ways; we may not be the strongest or the fastest, but we are exceptionally good at repurposing old bits of brain tissue towards new tasks. Reading, for example, is not innate, and was not directly selected for over the course of our evolution; it's only about five thousand years old, and our species has a history that goes back millions of years. But reading *draws on* a set of circuits that predate reading itself, like circuits for detecting the sounds of words, recognizing fine visual detail, and drawing connections between different senses.

When we listen to music, we start with circuits in the temporal cortex of the brain (more or less behind the ear) that we share with virtually all other primates, ranging from monkeys to chimpanzees. Whether you are predator or prey, a good sense of pitch and of how sounds change over time can help you navigate and identify danger. Consistent with this notion of our brain repurposing old circuitry for music is the fact that the brain's tools for acoustic differentiation are far more precise than would be necessary for music alone. The upshot is that even if we aren't born to listen to music, we are well stocked with tools that can help make that job manageable.

In all probability, humans' capacity for acquiring music probably derives not just from good ears but also from a trio of other talents. The first is a general ability to soak up knowledge through culture and teaching, accompanied by a sometimes leisurely lifestyle that allows us the time to master new skills – from making stone tools (as our ancestors did) to playing Tetris to driving cars with a manual transmission. The second is a neural architecture, shared with other mammals, that inherently seeks links between different types of sensory information, such as sound and motion. Babies, for instance, can recognize when a vowel that they listen to matches (or fails to match) the mouth movements of an accompanying face.

The third? Our gift for language.

Language, like music, depends heavily on rhythm, and also on the ability to compensate for differences in pitch. We need to recognize words, for example, at whatever pitch they are uttered, whether in a low baritone (think Darth Vader) or in a Mickey Mouse falsetto. Our ability to transpose music – to recognize a melody sung in two different keys – could well be a by-product of our inborn capacity to recognize speech, rather than a direct product of some sort of musical evolution. The same may turn out to be true for rhythm and pitch.

♪

A logical question, then, is about which comes first in the lifetime of an individual child, does language precede music or the other way around?

Surprisingly, only two studies have directly asked this question. The first showed that, given a choice, infants prefer their mother's voice to instrumental music. The only other study comes from my own lab and equally attests to children's chief attraction being to speech rather than to music. In our experiments, we had an ongoing project studying seven-month-old infants and how they come to recognize abstract patterns, such as the *abb* pattern that is present in a string of syllables like *la ta ta*. When it comes to speech, infants are quick learners: after just two minutes of hearing a *la ta ta, ga na na* soundtrack, they can easily distinguish *wo fe fe* (same old *abb* story) from *wo fe wo* (new *aba* structure).

But after a series of studies looking at speech, we tried music and, somewhat to our own surprise, discovered that babies weren't nearly as good at detecting comparable patterns in music. Sequences of musical notes like C, D, D thoroughly engaged the infants, but nonetheless infants couldn't grasp the patterns when they consisted of musical notes, unless they'd had a chance to hear the speech syllables first. Speech, not music, appears to be the sound that holds the greatest initial interest for infants.

If there is one part of music that might be pre-wired and specifically tied to music, it would probably be the connection between rhythm and motion. When we hear music, our bodies want to dance, and that's true even for some of the youngest children anybody's studied. In one fascinating study, the developmental psychologist Laurel Trainor bounced seven-month-old babies at regular rhythmic intervals and discovered that they paid more attention to rhythmical patterns that coincided with patterns of bouncing than to rhythmical patterns that didn't coincide with the bouncing. But even here, it's not clear that what's going on is genuinely special to music, as opposed to being part of a more general tendency that I alluded to before, known as cross-modal matching: no matter what the stimulus, babies like it when information in any two senses goes together (such as when a set of sounds click in synchrony with a set of flashing lights). The coupling between music and motion may just be one more specific instantiation of this broader tendency, rather than a reflection of any sort of special-purpose hardware for music.

♪

The proof lies in the pudding of the human brain. If humans really were born with a specific instinct for music, we might expect to find a specific hunk of brain tissue to be tuned to music and nothing else, much as a spot near the bottom of the brain known as the fusiform gyrus responds more to faces than to any other kinds of stimuli.

Instead, the many brain-imaging studies of music done in the last decade all point to a rather different direction: not toward a single specialized music area, but toward a vast mélange of brain regions – the prefrontal cortex, a portion of the temporal lobe known as the superior temporal gyrus, Broca's area, the planum temporale, the amygdala – not one of which appears to be dedicated full-time to music. Instead, virtually everything that plays a role in music has a separate 'day job'; when the brain listens to music, it moonlights in a second career for which it did not originally evolve.

Broca's area, for example, is a key player in music, but if that area has a principal function, it's as a centre for language. Ditto for the planum temporale, which lies within Wernicke's area. The superior temporal gyrus is indispensable in music, but it is essential for all kinds of auditory analyses, whether we are listening to speech or music or the blips and bangs of a video game. The cerebellum clearly plays a role in musical rhythm, but it's been known for years that the cerebellum is a key player in all kinds of movements, musical or otherwise. The amygdala matters for the perception of musical emotion, but you don't need to have music to have an amygdala; the amygdala is implicated in everything from fear to lust and anxiety, in a vast range of (mostly nonmusical) species. Unexpected chords might trigger the amygdala, but so will electric shocks. In no way is the amygdala, or any of the other regions I just discussed, specifically tailored to music; if there is a music-specific region in the brain, nobody has yet been able to identify it. Every brain area that I have mentioned – the amygdala, the superior temporal gyrus, the planum temporale – evolved long before human beings did and is found in many nonmusical species.

The same kind of argument can be made if you look at the development of the brain, rather than its anatomy. People develop more grey matter when they develop skill in music, for example, but grey matter has also been shown to increase as people learn to juggle or learn to type. Grey-matter increase is a diagnostic of learning in general, not a specific sign of learning music in particular. The brain can certainly acquire a facility for music, but that doesn't mean it specifically evolved for that purpose.

♪

The bottom line is that some parts of our biology are all but inevitable, like the branching part of our lungs and the fact that we have two eyes. But the musical mind is not. A musical mind develops only if we put in years of hard work, or at least active listening, in which parts of the brain that evolved for other purposes such as language, skill learning, and auditory analysis are gradually co-opted into doing something new.

To the degree that we ultimately become musical, it is because we have the capacity to slowly and laboriously tune broad ensembles of neural circuitry over time, through deliberate practice, and not because the circuitry of music is all there from the outset.

IT DON'T COME EASY

The Trouble with the Human Brain

Music, as we have seen, is more like a lifelong journey than a few weeks' project, more chess than draughts. Although many of the rudiments of music fit naturally with the human mind, mastering the detail is an ongoing project. As I soon discovered, every new chord and every new scale took significant amounts of practice; I also started talking to professional musicians and discovered that they too see mastering music as an ongoing pursuit. Virtually every musician I met professes to still be learning; not one claimed to have fully mastered his or her craft. Pat Metheny, for instance, is one of the most accomplished musicians I had the pleasure of meeting; he is widely acknowledged to be one of the world's leading jazz guitarists, yet even after four decades, he has no doubt that he is continuing to develop his craft. For all his accomplishments (eighteen Grammy Awards as of this writing), he still keeps studying; every time Metheny plays, for instance, he keeps a diary – typically six to eight pages long – analysing what worked, and what didn't, in order to make subsequent shows (and recordings) even better.

In a later chapter we'll delve more deeply into what it is that experts know that beginners don't, but before we can even consider what it takes to be a true master, it's important to understand the challenges that confront the musical novice.

♪

One of the first things I struggled with was the aggravating musical alphabet, which I like to think of as the Tyranny of Twelve Against Seven. Every octave is, in Western music, divided into exactly twelve notes, but the Western musical alphabet contains just seven basic letters, C, D, E, F, G, A, and B. That fundamental – but nearly inescapable – juxtaposition poses one of the first challenges for any aspiring musician, and it's monstrous.

In addition to the so-called natural notes of C, D, E, F, G, A, and B, every octave contains five – not seven – interlopers known as sharps: C# (pronounced 'C-sharp'), D#, F#, G#, and A# – but (in the vocabulary that beginners must learn) no E# or B#.

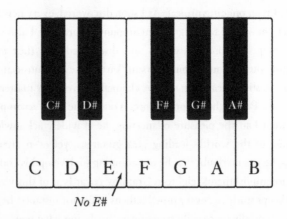

No E#

From start to finish, the rather confusing alphabet of the octave runs C, C#, D, D#, E, F, F#, G, G#, A, A#, B, before returning to C. (The student must also cope with the fact that each of the sharps is synonymous with a flat; C-sharp, for instance, is also known as D-flat.*)

For a machine, that somewhat peculiar alphabet would be no big deal. For the human mind, though, it's a disaster: we see an alphabet that runs from C to C#, D to D#, and we can't help but imagine that E will go to E#. Every time E goes to F, the novice gets confused.

If it weren't for that Tyranny of Twelve Against Seven, learning the musical alphabet might be easy. Instead, the irregularity of the sharps and flats turns the entire adventure into a nightmare.

♪

You can't really appreciate the novice musician's pain unless you try, at least briefly, to play along.

So here goes:

What's one semitone (another way of saying one note) above A?
  (Answer: A#.)
What's one semitone above C? (Answer: C#.)
What's one semitone below B? (Answer: Bb, pronounced 'B-flat.')
Now, quick, what's one semitone below C?

If you're like most people, you were at least initially tempted to say C-flat, but the 'correct' answer is B.

All of this gets even harder when you start dealing with chords and intervals, and thus must count across gaps of several notes. Which note is seven semitones above a D – is it an A or an A#? Even after months of study, I found doing this sort of exercise ridiculously hard, like trying to multiply 712 by 47 without the benefit of a sheet of paper.

---

* Advanced students in the classical tradition have to confront even greater complications, such as the way in which D can also be referred to as C## in certain contexts, or the precise set of circumstances under which it is okay to refer to the note above E as E# rather than the more conventional F.

♪

For my PhD thesis, I studied how children acquire language, working with Steven Pinker on what we often thought of as the Past Tense Project. The idea was to use the past tense of English as a kind of crucible for understanding how language development worked more broadly. Children were known to make a certain kind of error, known as over-regularization, as in 'breaked' instead of 'broke', 'goed' (or even 'wented') instead of 'went'; my mission was to work out why.

One popular theory at the time was that children were simply memorizing the relations between different bits of sounds; the 'ing' at the end of 'ring' was correlated with the 'ang' at the end of 'rang', just as the 'ing' at the end of 'sing' was correlated with the 'ang' at the end of 'sang'; the more verbs there were following a particular pattern, the better the analogy. Could the relation between 'break' and 'breaked' be the detritus of an ill-considered analogy between 'fake' and 'faked'?

As Pinker and I pored over tens of thousands of examples of children's speech, we discovered that the most popular theory wasn't quite right. Children were indeed influenced by similar irregular verbs – a child was more likely to get 'ring' correct if he or she knew other verbs like 'sing' and 'drink' that followed similar patterns – but not by similar regular verbs; the chance that a child would say 'breaked' didn't depend on how many regular verbs like 'fake' he or she happened to know, undermining one of the main predictions of the analogy theory.

Instead, even relatively young children (past about two and a half years old) seemed to treat regular verbs and irregular verbs differently; irregulars were something that they pulled out of their memory – when they could – while regulars were produced by a rule ('add "-ed" to form the past tense') whenever they didn't already remember a specific irregular form. Overregularizations (like 'breaked') turned out to be much rarer than anyone had imagined, but when they happened, they seemed to be something that children created on the spur of the moment, using a simple rule.

Children seem to learn that rule almost overnight. Within a matter of weeks, English-learning children go from frequently leaving their regular past-tense verbs 'uninflected' (saying things like 'I walk yesterday') to systematically inflecting just about all of them ('I walked yesterday'). Overregularizations are a kind of collateral damage: sometimes children know the correct irregular past-tense form ('I broke the glass'), and sometimes they don't, in which case they treat the verb as if it were regular, and overregularization ('breaked') results. The rule to add '-ed' is easy to learn, but the irregular exceptions take forever; it takes children (and adult learners of English) years to fully master the past tense of infrequent irregular verbs like 'flee' ('fled') and 'bear' ('bore').

Rules are easy; idiosyncrasies are hard. Infrequent idiosyncrasies are exceptionally hard. (For anything that is not perfectly rule governed, the more often we hear it, the easier it is to remember, which is why it is easier to remember the melody to 'Happy Birthday' than to a song you just heard for the first time last week.) Worse, although children somehow manage to master their irregular verbs automatically, without explicit instruction and deliberate practice, music's irregularities, and all the complications that ensue from the Tyranny of Twelve Against Seven, can only be mastered with hard work.

♪

Until I started learning guitar, I thought that the worst possible example of irregularity was the German plural system. One says *ein Kind* ('one child', singular) but *zwei Kinder* ('two children', plural), adding *er; ein Auto* (one car), *zwei Autos* (two cars), adding *s*. In all, there are, depending on how you count, at least nine different ways of forming plurals, and the learner has little choice but to memorize them all. As Mark

Twain once put it, in an essay called 'The Awful German Language':

> A person who has not studied German can form no idea of what a
> perplexing language it is. Surely there is not another language that is so
> slip-shod and systemless, and so slippery and elusive to the grasp. One
> is washed about in it, hither and thither, in the most helpless way; and
> when at last he thinks he has captured a rule which offers firm ground
> to take a rest on amid the general rage and turmoil of the ten parts of
> speech, he turns over the page and reads, 'Let the pupil make careful
> note of the following exceptions.' He runs his eye down and finds that
> there are more exceptions to the rule than instances of it.

♪

Guitar, like German, is filled with maddening irregularities. One problem has to do with how the notes are laid out. On a piano, there is what
is known as a one-to-one mapping between notes and keys. Each note
(middle C, for example) corresponds to exactly one key, no more, no
less. What's more, once one knows the basic alphabet, the entire piano
keyboard becomes clear: C, C#, D, and so on, repeating over and over
again from the left edge of the piano to the right.

The aspiring guitarist, in contrast, has to memorize a diagram that
looks like this:

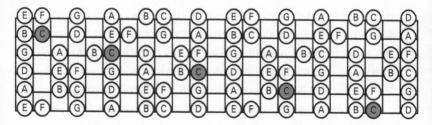

Notes on a guitar, with middle Cs highlighted.

These notes, which run along a wood strip that runs the length of the neck of the guitar, are collectively known as the fretboard.

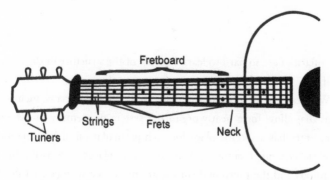

The top row of notes corresponds to the so-called first string, the second row to the second string, and so forth. Reading the top row from the left, the first note – what you get if you play the string 'open', without holding any frets – is E. If you hold down that string just above the first fret, represented by the second column in the diagram, the guitar produces an F note; if you hold the string down just above the third fret, you would have a G.

What makes all this particularly complicated is that any given note can be played in many different places. This greatly expands the advanced guitarist's options in forming chords – but bewilders the poor beginner, who has to learn them all. Whereas the pianist has only one middle C, smack in the middle of the keyboard, the guitarist has four choices and must master all four: not just the second string, first fret, but also the fifth fret of the third string, and for that matter the tenth fret of the fourth string, and in many guitars the fifteenth fret of the fifth string. (Electric guitars generally have at least twenty frets, which leaves room for a bonus C on the twentieth fret of the sixth string.)

Got that? I certainly didn't. This challenge became especially poignant when I tried to learn to read music; even when I could manage to remember that the upper line on the treble clef stood for the note F, I wouldn't know which of the many Fs on the guitar I should actually be playing.

♪

Irregularities are so hard to learn because of the structure of the brain itself.

Whereas computers are endowed with random-access memory chips that allow for a neatly organized system of memory (in which every entry has a specific place for each particular bit of information to be stored), our memories, scattered across places such as the hippocampus and the prefrontal cortex, are more like shoe boxes full of photographs, crammed to the gills but not particularly well organized. Instead of relying on numbered locations, as machines do, we rely on 'cues' or 'reminders' that hint at the information we need, without telling us specifically where we can find it.

The consequence is that we can't always find what we need. Any given cue is often associated with many different memories, and the memory we need may blur together with other memories we don't want, as when we try to remember where our car is parked, only to get confused by where it was yesterday rather than where it is presently. Irregular verbs are difficult to learn because they come in families that tend to blur together – 'sing' goes to 'sang', but 'bring' goes to 'brought'. Any skill that makes heavy demands on our imperfect memories is necessarily hard for us humans to learn, and guitar is no exception. Chess masters must memorize the openings; musicians must memorize reams of details.

And the fretboard's six rows of twelve note names quickly blur together. When you realize it takes your average child five or six years to master irregular verbs, you start to appreciate why the fretboard is so demanding.

♪

Of course, even if I knew where every note was, I wouldn't be close to being a decent guitarist. Beyond the sheer demands of memory – not just for the individual notes but also for the melodies, lyrics, and sequences of chords (known as chord progressions) that accompany them – at least three other things can make any given skill hard to learn. A skill may require precise perceptual mastery, such as recognizing particular sounds or shapes; it may require precise coordination in time between multiple muscles; and it may require development on the part of the muscles themselves.

Music, as it turns out, requires all three. Music shares with virtually all sports the need for carefully coordinated muscle control. Like chess (and many team sports), music demands rapid pattern recognition (especially when improvising live with an ensemble), and it even requires insanely strong fingers. For a beginner, coordinating all that into a song played at a recognizable tempo is close to impossible. The first twenty or thirty times I tried 'Blowin' in the Wind', I missed every other chord and couldn't play in anything like a regular rhythm.

Memory, perception, coordination, strength: guitar is just plain hard.

♪

On the perceptual side, guitarists need exquisitely trained ears and a good sense of where their fingers are at all times. The best guitarists also exploit the tactile sensations they get from their fingers, easing up or placing more pressure as circumstances require. On the auditory side, perfect (absolute) pitch is not a requirement, but a keen sense of so-called relative pitch, which essentially consists of being able to reliably recognize the precise magnitude of the musical steps known as intervals, is essential.*

Consider the opening phrase to the song 'Yankee Doodle' ('Yankee Doodle went to town'). Different people might sing the song in different registers; a child might prefer to start with a G, with the net result being that the opening phrase of the song would now be rendered not as C, C, D, E, C, E, D but as G, G, A, B, G, B, A – a completely different set of notes. Yet it would be immediately recognizable as the same song.

Why? Because the intervals between the notes are the same in both cases. To a trained musician, the melody of 'Yankee Doodle' consists of a particular series of intervals, or steps of precise magnitude.

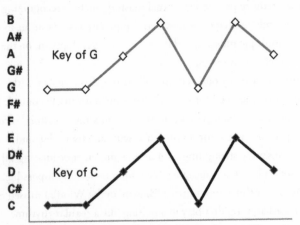

The opening notes of "Yankee Doodle," sung in two different keys

---

* To some extent, most people, even untrained listeners, actually have a bit of both: a mental system that represents songs in terms of abstract relations between notes (relative pitch), and a kind of virtual tape-recording, akin to absolute pitch, that allows us to sing highly familiar songs at close to their recorded pitch. The latter differs from what is technically known as absolute pitch, however, in that the vast majority of people can't actually name the individual notes they are listening to or recalling.

This language of intervals provides the blueprint for the melody of any given song, and it does so in a way that is independent of the key of the song – so that different singers with different pitch ranges can all sing the same song in a recognizable way. It is only when a musician can reliably recognize the exact size of musical intervals that it becomes possible to play 'by ear'.

For many people (except those with perfect pitch), the recognition of intervals is initially quite challenging. Both children and untrained adults have only a rough sense of the size of the musical leaps from one note to the next. Absent training, most listeners can only discern something fuzzier, such as the general direction a melody is going (for example, up versus down) and maybe the difference between big leaps and smaller leaps, without any particular precision. That level of vagueness suffices for speech, where we need only notice broad differences like the contrast between rise in pitch in a question versus the fall in a declarative statement, but it is far too imprecise for music.

As I soon learned, the challenge of precisely distinguishing musical intervals is among the hardest of rapid categorization problems that human beings routinely perform. Using an 'ear training' program that I got for my iPhone, I spent hours trying to distinguish between intervals like perfect fourths and perfect fifths, cursing my lousy ears and rarely getting much above 60 percent correct – among the least pleasant video games I ever played. And all the while, I realized that the ear trainer was making things easier for me: each interval was played in isolation, whereas in real music every new note forms a new interval, in juxtaposition with the note that precedes it, several hundred times over the course of a typical song. A skilled musician might need to recognize several intervals every second; I was lucky if I could identify one on its own. What I was setting out to do was comparable to what a child must do when he or she first learns to recognize letters on a page, long before facing the greater challenge of reading words and sentences. And to my ears the differences were as inscrutable as the *b*-versus-*d* difference that plagues many children early on.

One musician I interviewed, the son of a church organist, said he learned intervals not just by hearing them but by feeling them, sitting in the swell of a church organ as his father played and huge volumes of air swept by. A more common trick (for people who already have a decent sense of pitch) is to associate specific intervals with the opening notes of specific songs. But nobody is born being able to label them, and many people never master them. Some people never even notice that 'Twinkle, Twinkle, Little Star' and 'The Alphabet Song' follow the same melody (and hence consist of the same sequence of intervals).

'Ear training' – the process of refining one's auditory cortex so as to be able to precisely identify specific musical elements – is a fundamental need for most musicians that takes serious effort and considerable brain reorganization.

♪

Our ears – and the brain tissue that evaluates what passes through the ears – are only one part of the equation. Another is sheer physical dexterity, be it in controlling the wrists as a guitarist strums a guitar; in the exact placement of the lips, tongue, and vocal cords in a vocalist; or in controlling the force and dynamics of arms and calves as a percussionist coordinates four limbs in time.

For the beginning guitarist, the first and most evident challenge – one I faced every single day – is contorting one's fretting hand (left for a right-handed guitarist) into the precise shapes required for forming chords. Not one of the hand shapes initially seems natural, yet every one must eventually be made with great precision and speed. And, as I noticed over and over again, close isn't good enough: a finger that is misplaced by even a millimetre can lead to a buzzy noise or a note out of tune. As a beginner, I was happy when I could form a chord at all, but ultimately, the guitarist must be able to create – and move – each shape with essentially no margin of error.

The simplest version of the F major chord, for example, requires the player to simultaneously hold down the first fret of the first two strings with the index finger, while the middle finger must clamp down the third string on the second fret, and the ring finger must maintain pressure on the third fret of the fourth string. To properly sound the lowest bass note, one must also wrap one's thumb completely around the guitar's neck in order to clamp down the first fret on the sixth string. Other chords, even more complex, require the pinkie to get involved as well. Developing this dexterity is taxing; I soon developed calluses, my shoulder tensed, and my fingers ached. Eventually, I ordered a grip strengthener online.

Finger strength is only one part of the equation, though. The process of forming chords is further complicated by the fact that one's fingers don't naturally move independently. (Try, for example, to bring all of your fingers together, with your palm facing down, and then slowly move your pinkie back and forth; your ring finger, and possibly your thumb, will be tempted to go along for the ride.)

Pianists, too, must form enormously complicated hand shapes at an instant's notice, and singers and players of wind instruments need to do similar things with their lips, teeth, and tongues.

One of the biggest problems with learning skills that demand such precision is what computer scientists sometimes call the problem of 'blame assignment': when something goes wrong, it's sometimes difficult to figure out exactly why. The tennis player who misses a return must wonder whether the problem lies with the elbow or the wrist; the guitarist must wonder whether it is the elbow, the wrist, or the joint just below the fingertip. World-class musicians and athletes so often hire coaches because even the best performers sometimes can't diagnose their own limitations. Guitarists may not need big muscles, but playing the guitar is truly an athletic endeavour with the same rigorous demands for efficient and accurate performance.

♪

In virtually every aspect of music, sheer physical speed is crucial. Here the aspiring chess master gets off the hook – except possibly in lightning chess, the physical speed at which one moves one's queen is not really an issue – but the aspiring musician does not. The guitarist must move his or her hands with the precision of a surgeon and do so in perfect time, reshaping his or her hands frequently, often many times a second, each time landing on exactly the right strings, at exactly the right time, placing just the right amount of pressure, and then moving on to the next position as efficiently as possible.

Worse than that, musicians don't just have to be quick; they also have to perform each movement at precisely the right time – another feat that the human brain is not naturally prepared for. Whereas computers and microwave ovens all come from the factory with clocks that are accurate to the millisecond, timing at that level of precision is for human beings a lifelong pursuit. If you, a human being rather than a digital clock, try to count out exactly twelve seconds, you will find considerable slippage; one time you may get it right, the next you may be too fast, the third too slow. We are naturally endowed with circadian rhythms that allow us to keep track of the general time of day, but tracking time in milliseconds poses serious challenges.

To develop that level of precision, aspiring musicians often spend hundreds or thousands of hours playing along to the steady tick-tock-tick-tock of a metronome. Their goal is not just to be able to play each beat exactly when the metronome clicks but to master the time in between the metronome's beats – to play, for example, eighth notes exactly in between the metronome's quarter notes (or, harder still, to divide the period between quarter notes into smaller divisions like triplets or sixteenth notes); in many musical traditions, musicians do something even more challenging, which is to deliberately play ahead of or behind the beat (each of which creates a different rhythmic feel). Split-second timing comes naturally to computers, but human brains never fully master it. Even trained musicians sometimes fall prey to auditory illusions. To take one example, temporal intervals that are filled with subdivisions (for instance, audible sixteenth notes) sound subjectively longer than temporal intervals that aren't filled with comparable subdivisions.

Mastering time can literally take years. One professional musician friend I know tells a story of how, a decade into his career, he went to a master class with a famous jazz musician, hoping to gain great insight into improvisation. 'Sure', his teacher said, after a first interview, watching my friend play. 'We can fix your problems.' But not a word was said about improvisation; instead, the great master said, 'Listen to anything by [the timekeeping legend] Art Blakey and play along to the groove. That'll fix your sense of time.'

♪

Even harder for ordinary mortals is counting two or more things at once, something that is required in all but the simplest music. A cheap app on my phone gives me access to a dozen countdown timers, all perfectly precise, each one independent of the next. The human mind strains when we have to keep as few as two time sequences straight. Try, for example, to count out a cyclical rhythm of three beats with your left hand against two with your right, starting first at a slow speed and gradually increasing the tempo. Most nonmusicians find this hard, at least at first. And even once you get the hang of it, whether or not you are a trained musician, you will almost surely find that as you go faster and faster, you soon reach a speed at which the rhythm breaks down. Three beats against two eventually 'devolves' (to use the technical term) into two beats against one, and one goes faster still; it eventually devolves into one against one.

As another exercise, try alternating between your left hand and your right, first once per second and then gradually increasing the speed. What happens? (Try it!) Eventually, the hands of most people who are not trained musicians go from being out of phase (left hand up while right hand is down, and vice versa) to being in phase (both hands up at the same time, in direct contradiction to the instructions). More complicated ratios, like 7:5 (way outside the range of what a beginner like me could cope with), are even harder; the human mind finds 1:1 easy, but almost everything else is hard, particularly as we try to play at a rapid tempo.

The nature of music requires performers to execute many different actions on different time schedules, but we appear to have only one master clock in the head. As we try to produce complex ratios, we often overburden that clock. The goal of every drummer is to achieve 'independence' between his or her limbs – a noble goal, but one that runs directly counter to our natural tendencies.

In fact, our natural challenges with coordinating our limbs independently are present early in life. Babies frequently make something called overflow errors, in which they pointlessly move one hand in symmetry with the other, lifting their right, for example, when they try to grab something with the left. Current evidence suggests that the brain never achieves true independence at all, but rather learns increasingly intricate ways of grouping (or 'chunking') the separate actions of the two hands (or two hands and two feet) together, yielding an illusion of independence where none actually exists. The faster we go, the more likely that illusion is to break.

IT DON'T COME EASY

♪

Ultimately, every aspect of an aspiring musician's performance must become automatic, achieved with as little effort as possible, like the process of an experienced driver coordinating the steering wheel and the brakes in turning a corner. The same happens with music; initially, each element takes immense concentration. My teeth would clench as I struggled with the dreaded F chord, and more than once I would forget to keep the beat altogether when I tried to make a complicated chord change.

Yet another challenge stems from the fact that the brain is ordinarily bound by what is known as the speed-accuracy trade-off: for virtually anything we do, the faster we go, the more likely we are to make errors. Haste really does tend to make waste. In order to be effective, musicians must circumvent this law, playing both quickly *and* accurately. (A beginner might alternate between the E minor chord and the A minor chord at forty beats per minute, but a rock song could require triple that, with no mistakes, in perfect tempo, and a punk song or heavy metal song could require all of that at speeds of over two hundred beats per minute.)

Alas, the only known way to defy the speed-accuracy trade-off is through practice, using the only technique that the brain can bring to bear, a process known as automatization or proceduralization, in which the brain makes a transition from explicit or 'declarative' knowledge, which can in principle be verbally articulated (albeit slowly), to implicit or 'procedural' knowledge, which can be executed rapidly. As knowledge becomes proceduralized, we sometimes feel as if we know something in our fingers or muscles but lose the capacity to explicitly explain what is going on.

During this process, simple steps get combined or 'chunked' into more efficient, larger units. For instance, when I first learned to drive,

I knew that taking a left turn consisted of several different individually articulated elements ('apply brake pressure', 'use turn signal', 'turn steering wheel', 'look both ways', 'resume gas', 'monitor car to stay in lane'), but it was hard to coordinate them all. In the rush to simultaneously control the steering and the brakes, I'd sometimes forget to flip on the turn signal or, worse, forget to look both ways. Fortunately, my brain eventually managed to re-encode the whole complex set of actions into a single ensemble or 'procedure' ('make a left') that could be executed effortlessly. Much the same happens for any skill; eventually, some of the skills that initially required a great deal of effort become so automatic they take up less conscious focus and leave room for other tasks.

Deliberate practice can presumably make this happen faster, by ensuring that what gets proceduralized is the right set of habits. When practice regimes aren't selected with care, the learner may wind up automatizing bad habits and thus enshrine sloppy or inadequate procedures, in a way that impedes future progress.

At the neural level, proceduralization consists of a wide array of carefully coordinated processes, including changes to both grey matter (neural cell bodies) and white matter (axons and dendrites that connect between neurons). Existing neural connections (synapses) must be made more efficient, new dendritic spines may be formed, and proteins must be synthesized. Often, mental representations that are initially stored in the prefrontal cortex (which we associate with conscious cognition) shift to new parts of the brain such as the hippocampus, associated with memory, and the motor cortex and the basal ganglia, which are in charge of the more immediate control of our muscles.

Until all that practice-spurred brain growth starts to happen, you might be able to enjoy music, but you certainly won't be able to play it. As I struggled to form my chords and change smoothly between them, I was reminded of this, every time I sat down to play.

TALKING HEADS

How Music Is – and
Isn't – Like Language

Language and music have a lot in common, and as I, a lifelong student of language, now immersed myself in music, I couldn't help but constantly reflect upon the relation between the two.

Both language and music are, in the terminology of my trade, 'formal systems'. Languages are made up of words arranged into sentences; songs are made up of notes arranged into melodies. In neither case can the arrangement simply be random. There are rules that govern music, just as there are rules that govern language. Both are 'finite systems' with infinite possibilities; the English alphabet has just twenty-six letters (finite), from which spring everything from Shakespeare to Jackie Collins and whatever else future generations of authors may write (infinite). Likewise, to a first approximation, Western music relies on the same twelve notes, over and over again, in new combinations, in everything from Mozart to Britney Spears.*

---

* 'The same twelve notes' is actually a bit of an exaggeration. Although the piano keyboard is limited to the same twelve notes (C, C#, D, and so on, recurring in higher and lower octaves), many other instruments, including the guitar and the human voice, have the capacity to generate intermediate possibilities. On the guitar, such 'between notes' can be played by physically

Both music and language emerge early in life; children start practising syllables by the time they are five months old, and many start singing by the time they are a year and a half. Newborns can tell the difference between their mother's native language and a different language, and, as we saw earlier, they can discriminate between consonant and dissonant chords. But it's not just that music and language appear to lead parallel lives; to some scholars, language and music are actually twin reflexes, composed of different elements but assembled in the same way.

Is it coincidence that the most musical creatures – humans, songbirds, whales, and dolphins – are among the creatures with the richest systems for communication? Or that the only creatures that can dance in time – humans, songbirds, and at least one elephant – are all vocal mimics? Is music a form of language? Or is language a form of music? Or are the two just fellow travellers? Because of the striking parallels between language and music, sorting out the relation between the two is a vital first step in understanding where music came from.

♪

Just about every possible relation between language and music that you could imagine has been championed. Some have seen music as a special form of language; others have seen music as sui generis, its own independent entity separate from language, all apparent resemblance merely coincidental.

It doesn't take a genius to realize that music and language can't literally be identical. One doesn't automatically become musical by learning to talk, for instance (nor the other way around). Most people speak a native language fluently, but few (aside from trained musicians) manage to fully master relative pitch. Even speaking a tonal language

---

bending the strings, most famously in the service of creating so-called blue notes, such as the slightly flattened third that is common in the blues.

– like Mandarin Chinese (in which the meaning of a word is defined in part by its pitch contour, such that, for example, the word that means 'to drink' when uttered with a high flat tone means 'river' when it is said with a rising tone) – is no guarantee. There are plenty of conservatory-trained musicians who speak tonal languages yet still fail to acquire perfect pitch. Although music may well draw on language, it clearly has its own independent elements, too; the whole notion of musical key, for instance, seems to lack any direct counterpart in language.

Such considerations have led some to argue for the opposite extreme, for a view in which language and music might be physically and psychologically distinct 'modules'. One of the first arguments for this sort of view came nearly two hundred years ago, from Franz Joseph Gall, who in 1825 described a patient with brain damage who had impaired musical abilities but otherwise seemed normal, suggesting that musical faculties could be separated from those pertaining to language. Since then, many more intriguing patients have been found – some with musical impairments (such as amusia, a profound impairment in pitch that often includes the inability to recognize differences between melodies) alongside normal linguistic abilities, another with impaired language abilities (aphasia) yet largely preserved musical abilities. People in the late stages of diseases like Alzheimer's sometimes show markedly impaired linguistic function yet still manage to recognize songs learned long ago. In his book *Musicophilia,* Oliver Sacks described a patient who went in something of the opposite direction, an orthopaedic surgeon who became obsessed with piano after being struck by lightning, with no apparent changes to his linguistic abilities.

♪

As we saw earlier, nobody has yet found a spot in the brain that is tuned exclusively to music and nothing else. Broca's area is implicated in both language and music, and the same can be said for the prefrontal cortex, which has been implicated in everything from sarcasm to pitch perception, orgasm, and jazz improvisation. Music – like language – is an activity that draws on a wide range of the brain's resources. Many of those resources are shared by the two skills. As a recent review by the neuroscientist Aniruddh Patel shows, literally dozens of studies have pointed to some degree of overlap between the brain mechanisms that contribute to language and those that contribute to music.

Similarly, some patients with brain damage show selective impairments for language or music, but many patients who show impairments for one also show impairments for the other. In the most systematic review of brain damage studies that I could find, nearly a third of all patients with musical impairments also had impairments with language.

The neural overlap between music and language is echoed in a growing psychological literature that shows correlations between musical and linguistic abilities. One set of studies shows that people who speak tonal languages like Mandarin are better able to discriminate musical pitch. Another, a study of Japanese speakers learning English, found that people who were better able to sing back melodies and tell how many notes were in a chord were better at recognizing the linguistic difference between the sounds *l* and *r* – further evidence that language and music are tapping into some of the same circuitry.

Another set of studies required native English speakers to listen to sentences like 'The cop that the spy met wrote a book about the case,' sung to melodies that did or did not contain an out-of-key note, and found that in more difficult sentences, the out-of-key notes interfered with people's sentence comprehension – a result that would be hard to explain if language and music were processed by entirely separate brain mechanisms. Still another line of inquiry has shown that the process of training children in musical pitch helps them to better identify the emotions in speech.

♪

Different parts of the brain are specialized, but not in the way we anticipated. Rather than allocating a distinct region for each content area
(say, language versus music versus motor control), each mental ability draws upon a broad range of brain areas, perhaps used in unique
combinations. Broca's area, for instance, may be used whenever the
brain needs to combine smaller units into larger units, whether it be in
combining the sounds of language into words, in combining the notes
of music into a phrase, or in the planning of motor actions that allow
us to use tools. Similarly, the hippocampus plays a recurring role as
an engine for memory, not just in the memory for details like phone
numbers or historical dates, but also in subtle ways in virtually any skill
that demands the development of so-called muscle memory. Language
might use a different constellation of brain areas than music does, but
neither depends on entirely unique neural real estate.

One metaphor I find helpful is that of a tool kit. If one builds, say, a
table or a chair, a certain set of tools tends to get used repeatedly, such
as hammers, screwdrivers, saws, and spanners. Although one might
need the occasional special-purpose tool (like the spoke key in a bicycle
shop), many tools get used over and over for a wide variety of tasks.
This is to say not that a hammer should be used to perform the function
of a screwdriver, or that a screwdriver may substitute for a hammer,
but rather that the end products often draw upon a broad collection of
tools that get used in particular ways for particular projects.

Language is similar in many ways to music because both are products
that emerge from the same fundamental collection of brain tools. Both,
for instance, draw heavily on our neural resources for memory, whether
for storing and recognizing specific words or phrases, or for storing
and retrieving specific melodies or motifs. Although to a certain extent
our long-term memories for words and melodies may be stored in

physically separate places, both sets of memory circuits are likely built by the same genetic code. As a consequence, memory breaks down in comparable ways in both cases. A sentence like 'People people left left' is hard to parse for the same reason that a minimalist composition by Philip Glass with numerous repetitions of generally similar motifs with slight variations can be hard to memorize. As I discussed in my book *Kluge,* our memories lack the neat tabular form of memory that computers have, and the more similar two things we aim to remember are, the more likely we are to confuse them. Listeners get lost in 'People [whom] people left left' because they get confused about which instance of the noun 'people' goes with which instance of the verb 'left'; musicians learning Philip Glass pieces can equally get lost in sequencing which variation on a given motif goes where.

♪

As the pendulum swings back towards the view that there is some important overlap between music and language, an old hypothesis of Darwin's has come back into vogue. After his seminal *On the Origin of Species,* Darwin realized that music and language posed similar puzzles: If all modern species descended with modification from their predecessors, why was it that language and music had so few obvious counterparts in the animal world? Could their emergence be linked? Darwin proposed in *The Descent of Man* that a musical 'protolanguage' might have come first, with language emerging from music.

One of this hypothesis's most cheerful exponents is the archaeologist Steven Mithen, author of *The Singing Neanderthals*. In Mithen's view, music entered the hominid lineage long before language did, and language (or some protolinguistic precursor of language) emerged from music.

In defence of the proposition that music might somehow precede language, Mithen points to the putative universality of motherese, a musical register of long vowels, high pitches, and exaggerated pitch contours that characterize how adults talk to babies. But even if it is universal (a matter that is in dispute), motherese may not be truly innate. Individual parents might work out the idea (or borrow it from their elders) simply because infants pay more attention to it, perhaps because it is easier for the infants to hear or because the high pitches of motherese intrinsically sound happy or fall close to an auditory sweet spot.

Another of Mithen's arguments for the idea of a musical protolanguage derives from his own personal experience. Mithen notes that as an adult he was able (for the first time) to develop some skill at singing – taking a year's worth of singing lessons after being musically idle for thirty-five years – and a functional MRI (fMRI) revealed that there were changes in his brain as a consequence. From this Mithen concludes, 'In effect, I began to release potential musicality that has been placed there by millions of years of evolution, [heretofore] neglected and . . . dormant'. Well, maybe. But the brain changes anytime we do anything; one recent study showed changes in the brain associated with developing skill at golf, another at learning the tango, but one would hardly want to infer from that fact that golf was a direct reflection of our dormant evolutionary heritage.

In the final analysis, as far as I can tell, there really isn't any good reason to think that music preceded language, beyond the true but troubled intuition that music is (arguably) more prevalent than language in the animal world. Birds and whales, for example, have 'musical' communicative systems that depend on ordered sets of pitches with varying temporal durations, but only humans exploit the ordered sets of phonemes that we call words and sentences. Still, sheer prevalence tells us little; many aspects of physiology, ranging from circulatory systems to the defining mammalian characteristic of bearing live young, are far more prevalent than music, yet obviously of little direct relevance to language. Tellingly, music is almost entirely absent in the line of creatures from which we most directly derive. Although gorillas do beat their chests rhythmically, just like in the original *King Kong,* the vast majority of nonhuman primates show almost no interest in music. If some early vertebrate creature was musical, giving rise to songbirds and whales, that musicality was long lost in the ancestral branch that gave rise to primates – which means we still had to have developed music anew. In all likelihood, the communication systems of birds and whales evolved largely *independently* of ours, perhaps sharing some general properties of audition that trace further back to some common ancestor, but still leaving humans to do a lot of reinvention.

Meanwhile, language is ubiquitous, acquired by essentially every normal human being, yet nearly 5 percent of the population is tone-deaf, and many people can't reliably sing on pitch. When one considers the trouble that children – and untrained adults – face in extracting even simple musical intervals as opposed to the gifts that toddlers have in stringing syllables together, the story in which music served as a direct precursor to language seems deeply implausible.

Furthermore, the earliest known musical instrument – an ivory flute found in a cave in Germany – is only about thirty-six thousand years old, and most scholars place the advent of language considerably earlier: at least fifty thousand years ago (some place language as far back as a few million years). Of course, our ancestors may have sung before they made instruments, but there is no particular reason in the archaeological record to think so. In fact, our ancestors were making other kinds of tools far earlier, for at least a million years, suggesting that the lack of musical tools by our early ancestors wasn't due to a lack of toolmaking ability.

Indeed, as we will later see, although most scholars would agree that language is likely a direct product of natural selection, there is good reason to think music is not, but is more akin to a culturally acquired activity (like reading or hang gliding) than anything directly wired into the brain through evolution.

Meanwhile, whenever melody and lyrics clash, lyrics tend to win. As we saw earlier, infants would prefer to hear speech to instrumental music, given the choice, and several studies have shown that for people without musical training, lyrics are more easily remembered than melodies. Another shows that four-year-olds consider two songs to be the same if they have the same lyrics (even if the melodies change), but not if two songs have the same melody (if the lyrics differ). A more recent study has shown a precursor of the same phenomenon with eleven-month-olds. Music and language may draw to some extent on the same parts of the brain, but it is very likely that the parts of the brain they share first arose in the service of language and only later became recruited in the service of music.

♪

If language came first, as seems more likely, does that mean music is nothing more than a special form of language? Not at all: the two may share a lot, but each still stands on its own. By far the most sober and qualified perspective on this debate that I have seen comes from Ray Jackendoff, a well-respected linguist (trained by Noam Chomsky), an accomplished clarinettist, and one of the world's leading contributors to the scientific understanding of music theory (co-author, with the composer Fred Lerdahl, of the enormously influential book *A Generative Theory of Tonal Music*).

Language, Jackendoff suggested to me during a visit to his suburban Boston home, is no more similar to music than it is to the sorts of complex hierarchical planning processes involved in making a cup of coffee. At first I thought he was kidding, but in fact he had a very good point to make. In an academic article, Jackendoff broke down the process of making a cup of coffee into a hierarchy of twenty-three events and subevents, such as 'put pot under faucet' (a lower-level subevent, perhaps akin to a word or a musical motif) and 'put water into machine' (a higher-level subevent, perhaps akin to a sentence or a section of a song), set into the same sort of technical machinery that linguists use for describing language (and that Jackendoff himself used for analysing music). In Jackendoff's view, this so-called compositionality is essential for music and for language, but it is hardly unique to either domain. Language really does share a lot with music, but the question should be not so much 'What do language and music share?' as 'What do language and music share *exclusively* with each other but with nothing else?'

Jackendoff's point (which fits with what we saw earlier about Broca's area being reused in both language and music) is that virtually every aspect of cognitive architecture that is shared by language and music is also shared with other aspects of the mind; both simply draw from a wide range of important cognitive resources. Compositionality, for instance – the putting together of smaller elements into big elements that form still larger units – is a hallmark of language and equally a hallmark of music. But we also exploit compositionality when we put together individual scenes to make larger stories, or plan a trip to the shopping centre. Experimental evidence shows that even mundane activities like making the bed or doing the dishes can be broken down into hierarchies of subevents that are mentally represented in similar ways from one individual to the next.

Likewise, both language and music represent an interesting mix of the universal and the culturally acquired, but that mixture itself is not unique. You can see the same sort of juxtaposition in religion, which is also nearly universal yet instantiated in different ways in different cultures, and in dietary preferences (every culture has some, but as foods like sushi and grasshoppers show, one culture's taboo may be another's delicacy).

Music is like language, but it isn't language; it's just one more wondrous skill that a suitably motivated human brain can acquire.

The American comedian Martin Mull once said, 'Writing about music

♪

is like dancing about architecture.' Although one can certainly use language to describe music, it is painfully obvious that words at best offer only a distinctly limited window into the true nature of music, akin to the underpowered adjectives like 'dry', 'flinty', 'grassy', 'chewy', and 'rounded' that vintners settle for if asked to describe their wares in verbal terms. Even words that we take for granted aren't universal; pitches that we describe as 'high' and 'low' are described as 'light' and 'dark' in Norwegian.

Perhaps the single most vivid description I have ever read of a piece of instrumental music is Alex Ross's elegant description of George Gershwin's *Rhapsody in Blue,* a piece that was itself once described as 'the most popular of all American concert works'. In Ross's words, *Rhapsody*

> begins with a languid trill on the clarinet, which turns into an equally languid upward scale, which then becomes a super-elegant and not at all raucous glissando. Having reached the topmost B-flat, the clarinet then saunters through a lightly syncopated melody, leaning heavily on the lowered seventh note of the scale. The tune dances down the same staircase that the opening scale shimmied up, ending on the F with which the piece began – a typical Gershwin symmetry.
>
> ... The *Rhapsody* plays out as a dizzying sequence of modulations; the Rachmaninovian love theme at the center of the work ends up being in the key of E, a tritone away from the home B-flat.

As I read Ross's description, it is easy for me, as someone who knows the piece well, to bring the Gershwin piece to mind, but it requires a fair bit of musical background knowledge (about modulations, syncopation, scales, and tritones). Even so, the language still falls far short of genuinely conveying what music really sounds like. To someone who has not heard *Rhapsody in Blue* before, much is lost.

You can't even cheat. Even if you were to replace Ross's technical-yet-poetic description with a note-by-note verbatim reading of the sheet music, you still wouldn't capture the beauty of the opening two-and-a-half-octave slide. In fact, the glissando that practically defines the piece isn't even in the original sheet music. Instead, in print, a single whole note is followed by seventeen brief individual notes, ascending a scale. The smooth slide that defines the song developed not out of that notation per se but out of the interpretation and imagination of the clarinettist Ross Gorman (who played it, some say as a joke, in one of the piece's early rehearsals). Capturing the nuance there is so challenging that three physicists wrote an entire article about how professionals play it.

As the composer Aaron Copland put it, in his justly famous book *What to Listen for in Music:*

> Music expresses, at different moments, serenity or exuberance, regret or triumph, fury or delight. It expresses each of these moods, and many others, in a numberless variety of subtle shadings and differences. It may even express a state of meaning for which there exists no adequate word in any language.

Amen.

BACK TO SCHOOL

The Teacher Becomes a Student

By February, after six months of on-and-off practice, my labours begin to pay off. I'm no rock star, and I can see that I won't be fronting David Letterman's band anytime soon, but I'm thrilled to finally be able to play some basic chords in tempo. The A major and D major chords have started to come fluently, and even the pesky F major finally seems within reach. People born with the right combination of innate motor and rhythmic skills might have gotten here a lot sooner – it's taken me six months to do what some people might have done in a week – but I'm positively ecstatic.

Still, I've been able to work on music as much as I have only because I had the year off from teaching. I start to panic when I realize that in another six months, my sabbatical will be over. I suddenly realize that the time has come to get a teacher. If I am to seize the moment, I need help!

I head to my neighbourhood music shop and ask for a recommendation. The people there point me to a teacher named Don. Through Google, I discover that Don definitely seems to know what he's doing; he's been teaching for thirty years and has written several books about guitar. What's more, he has a 'recession special' going and charges only fifty dollars an hour, eminently reasonable for New York City. Hoping not to reprise the trauma of my childhood recorder lessons, I open my wallet and revisit the world of music education.

♪

Why do we need teachers at all? The most obvious answer is that teachers know things that their students don't, be it the most efficient fingering for a sequence of notes in Beethoven's Ninth or the difference between a diminished chord and an augmented chord. Another reason, of course, is that teachers can serve as motivators, either through carrots (gold stars and stickers) or through sticks (mortification, shame, or bad grades). For an adult learner, teachers also likely provide incentive: most of us probably practise less than we should, and then race to catch up when our next lesson is coming up. Good teachers can also impose structure, helping us to know what to practise and when. It is not enough to say, 'Go home and practise'; a good teacher says what to practise, and how: the most skilled teachers aim to help their students practise efficiently. But beyond all this, the most important role of a teacher may be to help the students pinpoint their errors and target their weaknesses; beginning students, especially, are often too busy trying to make music. They don't really hear what they are playing. As one sage academic of music teaching put it, '[Often, too much of a student's] attention is devoted to the production of the music, not [enough] to monitoring the result of the sound.' Teachers can be brilliant in this regard.

♪

When I first speak to Don, I can see he obviously knows his stuff, and he shares my philosophy, which is to understand the tools of music, how songs are written and played, rather than concentrating on simply memorizing particular songs. Rote knowledge is often very brittle, and from the outset I have tried to gain a conceptual understanding, rather than just learn so many songs by heart. As Don puts it, his approach as a teacher has been 'to get people to play, express themselves, and understand what they are playing in order to eventually progress on their own, rather than just "parrot" someone else's musical ideas' – exactly what I am looking for.

Still, Don adds, some songs do have pedagogical value. 'Like a Rolling Stone', he says, is good practice for chord changes, and it can be played with open chords (none of those nasty barre chords, where your index finger has to hold down several strings simultaneously) in the straightforward key of C. Good for beginners.

I promise to practise that before we meet, and as I hang up the phone, he says, 'Of course Jimi Hendrix played it with all barre chords, but that's a story for a different day.' I thrill at the knowledge I may soon acquire. All he wants me to bring is a lined spiral-bound notebook; guitar optional.

♪

On the day of my first lesson, as I'm leaving my apartment, worrying about whether I have spent enough time doing my homework, I see a silver-haired woman in the elevator – my mother's age, maybe a little older – with what looks like a guitar case on her back, same as me. Struck by the coincidence, I break the code of elevator silence. 'Are you a musician, or going to a lesson?' I ask. The latter, it turns out. The instrument she's toting – it's not a guitar but a viola da gamba – is a mystery to me. But it's nice to know that I'm not the only person over twenty going for music lessons on a Thursday afternoon.

At my lesson, Don and I immediately get into a discussion of the sheet music for 'Like a Rolling Stone'. One of the things I've already discovered in my musical quest is that no two songbooks seem to notate any one song in a consistent way. I've brought along the two versions I have at home, and Don looks them over, shaking his head. 'I just don't hear the D minor seventh in this [transcription]. I hear a D minor, but not a seventh.' I wonder to myself whether my ears will ever be that precise.

Don then warns me that he'll want me to play a simplified version he thinks will be good practice. Sometimes, when teaching beginners, he says, he 'takes liberties' in the interest of pedagogy. In the recorded version, there's a whole band playing – keyboard, bass, drums, guitar, and so forth. Don's aim, in teaching a beginner, is not to reproduce the guitarist's particular part but to convey what he calls the 'conglomerate,' the overall sound, in a way that can be captured by just a single instrument. I've looked at enough songbooks to know that some people want exact transcriptions that sound precisely like the original recordings, but I know I'm not ready for that, and I'm not aspiring to be an exact mimic: if I want to hear Dylan, I'll put on a CD. Don plays the version he wants me to learn, and it sounds great.

I discover, to my shock, that Don's overall view of my playing is remarkably positive. He tells me that I 'look relaxed' (news to me) and that I play with a light touch. I show him my primitive efforts at playing barre chords, even attempting a dreaded B minor, and somehow it comes out right, each note clean, not a hint of fret buzz. Emboldened, I show Don the other main skill I've been working on: playing scales.

All in all, Don likes what he hears. He thinks my sense of time – what I have been thinking of as my biggest weakness – sounds okay; I doubt my arrhythmia has completely vanished, but practice is definitely helping somewhat. Don also thinks that my hands work together well (something I hadn't even thought about) and says that the position in which I hold my pick is good. He wants me to use my pinkie more – I kind of cheat with my ring finger when playing some distant notes on the minor pentatonic – but overall the news is good, a better report than I was expecting.

♪

For some people, music lessons are entirely optional. When I asked Tom Morello, one of the best guitarists in recent memory, about this, he told me that he had taken exactly two. Both were when he was thirteen years old. In the first, his teacher taught him to tune his guitar ('What a waste of five dollars', young Tom thought to himself); in the next, Tom eagerly reported to practice, 'all chuffed' that he'd learned to tune the guitar and ready to learn 'Detroit Rock City' and 'Black Dog'. Instead, the teacher taught him to play the C major scale ('do re mi' and so on, but on guitar). This, too, struck young Tom as a complete waste of time, having nothing (or so it seemed) to do with the music that was meaningful to him. Indeed the gap between lessons and the songs Tom wanted to play was so great he gave up entirely, stuffing his guitar in the closet, where it collected dust for the next four years. Since then, he has been largely self-taught. Some of the other highly accomplished musicians I spoke to are also largely self-taught. Sterling Campbell, for example, is a drummer who has played with David Bowie, the B-52s, Cyndi Lauper, and Duran Duran; he credits his skills mainly to learning to play by ear from record albums, not any formal lessons.

Others give a great deal of credit to their teachers. Doug Derryberry, lead guitarist for Bruce Hornsby (and official guitarist for the television programme *Sesame Street*), fondly recalls Phyllis Dye, the piano teacher he had in a small town in Tennessee as a child. 'It wasn't just like, "Learn your piece, play your piece, good, gold star, move on." It was like, "Learn your piece, play your piece to tempo and whatever", but also every week we had a workbook with a theory lesson. So it was like, "This is a theory concept [perhaps something about the logic of a particular type of sequence of chord changes], and here is a little quiz", and I loved those things. I ate it up. I really credit her teaching method as giving me the first tools that helped me decode whatever else I have managed to decode in music.'

♪

What makes a good teacher, or a good lesson? The science of music education (or music pedagogy) is surprisingly thin. Although over 40 percent of affluent American parents send their children to music lessons, comparatively little is known about what makes music teaching effective.

Many teachers, especially of adults, have relatively little training as teachers: many music teachers are musicians who never quite got famous and who need the money; no licence is required. Anyone who knows how to play a piano or a guitar can put up an ad online or a hallway notice board. An aspiring student, especially a young student, may however not be in a position to pick a good teacher. For all I know, my third-grade recorder teacher may have been the greatest recorder *player* in Baltimore, but in hindsight she had no clue how to teach beginners. She lacked two of the most important traits that any teacher could have: patience and the ability to diagnose problems. It didn't take her long to see that I wasn't making progress, but she didn't have the inclination to stick with me, nor the perspicacity to see what it was that I didn't get. In retrospect – and this was what Dan Levitin immediately recognized, years later – I simply didn't understand the nature of rhythm. I knew that 'Mary Had a Little Lamb' had notes that were sequenced in a particular order, but I didn't realize that the notes were supposed to vary systematically in duration. A skilled teacher would have seen that, urged me to set 'Little Lamb' aside for a week or two, and come up with some simple games to increase my sensitivity to rhythm – all without letting on how inept I really was. With support and a proper diagnosis, I might have made progress, rather than giving up in despair.

A good teacher is not just a good diagnostician, of course, but also a

good motivator. Had my teacher urged me to go home and simply practise alternating short notes and long notes, I would no doubt have been
bored out of my mind, as annoyed with that exercise as Tom Morello
was with the C major scale. The truly talented teacher diagnoses the
problem and then proposes a treatment that is both fun and rewarding.
In the larger literature on teaching and training (not just in music, but
in any domain), studies consistently point to the abilities of teachers to
motivate their students, to understand their particular needs, and to
come up with exercises that are neither too easy nor too hard (shades of
the principle of proximal development that I mentioned earlier).

As I began immersing myself in music, I sat in on all kinds of lessons, some as student (in everything from guitar to singing to songwriting), others as spectator, many aimed at children (of all ages, as young as
twelve months old). The differences in the approaches and capacities of
the teachers were mind-boggling. I saw some great teachers and saw, or
at least heard about, some terrible ones. The worst was an über-macho
type who told a friend that 'capos [clamp-like tools that temporarily
shorten a guitar's strings in order to change musical key] are for sis-
sies' – not quite realizing that capos can not only change key but also
add extra resonance to notes that would otherwise need to be played in
a less resonant fashion, in ways that have proven useful for everyone
from Dylan to the Eagles, Johnny Cash, and the Beatles.

♪

The single most gifted teacher I encountered was a jovial woman in
Brooklyn, New York, named Michele Horner, who got her first guitar
at age two. Michele is a devotee of the famous Suzuki method, which
emphasizes (among other things) learning by ear rather than learning
from sheet music. Michele herself is world renowned, often invited to
teach workshops around the globe. When I first saw Michele, she was
giving a small private lesson to two children, one of whom was named

Shiloh, the six-year-old daughter of a friend of a friend. Suzuki is probably best known as a technique for teaching violin, but there are in fact Suzuki curricula for a range of string instruments, including not just orchestral instruments (cello, viola, and so on) but also my instrument of choice, the guitar. As young Shiloh sat attentively, Michele subtly got her students to focus on their posture, by telling them, 'Your mission is to keep your thumb [up] where everyone can see how great it is. Okay?'

Different sections of the day's song had fun labels like 'bread' (for the first section of a song) and 'cheese' (for the second section), hence a song with the form *aba* would be a 'bread cheese bread' sandwich. Rhythmic variations were taught with entertaining syllables: straw-ber-ry for a set of triplets, jell-y for a pair of eighth notes, wa-ter-mel-on for four sixteenth notes, and so on. Shiloh played a short passage, tentatively but almost perfectly. Michele gushed, 'You did a bread, you did a cheese, you did a cheese, you did a bread – you get four stamps for that!' Shiloh was thrilled. By the time Michele turned to me and said, 'We try to make everything fun. 'Cause if it's not fun, who wants to do it? Not even me,' I knew I was in the presence of a master teacher.

At least four characteristics made Michele a great teacher. First, she had the eyes of a hawk: the instant a student tilted a finger from a perfect position, or slouched, or otherwise deviated from ideal classical guitar posture, Michele noticed. Second, no matter what a child did, virtually every utterance Michele made was positive, if not downright ebullient. By being perpetually upbeat and never sounding remotely judgemental, Michele helped instil what the psychologist Carol Dweck would call a 'growth' mind-set. Instead of making some students feel as if they might not have enough natural ability, Michele helped them all feel as if anything was achievable, so long as they worked hard and practised every day. Third, Michele was a master at maintaining her students' attention. Over the years, she's learned all there is to know about the currency of the six-year-old girl's mind. From stickers to the way in which she pronounced the word 'challenge' (as if it were French, as in 'Are you ready for a ... shallenge?'), Michele knew exactly how to keep her charges motivated and focused through a forty-five-minute lesson (long even for university students, as I know only too well).

Fourth, and perhaps most important, Michele knew that life outside the classroom was far more serious than life inside the classroom. Like all Suzuki teachers, she knew that you couldn't learn guitar by playing for an hour or two a week; to be effective, most of a student's learning needs to take place during practice at home, and she knew that children would only practise at home if doing so was pleasurable. What most impressed me about Michele was the immense pains she took to make sure her students' *parents* were well instructed, especially in the art of making practice a happy and regular part of every day's routine. The single point that Michele was most adamant about was a rule for when parents should correct a child's mistake: never, ever, until the child had made that error at least three times. Wisely, Michele saw that her role as teacher was to guide children into developing proper habits; parents who corrected their children could easily wind up destroying their kids' motivation. If practice with Mum or Dad got to be a drag, the whole game was lost. Michele made sure that never happened, sprinkling her weekly parents-only night classes with sound techniques for how parents could navigate the tension between wanting their children to excel right away and being patient enough to foster a happy learning environment.

Six months after I first saw Shiloh take a class, I sat in on her end-of-year recital and was absolutely floored by the precision with which she (now age seven) played; she had graduated from 'Twinkle, Twinkle, Little Star' to the 'Meadow Minuet'. According to her dad, Shiloh had by this point practiced for 126 consecutive days. Her foundation was rock solid, her posture was perfect, and each and every note was played with perfect tone, in perfect time. A lot of learning is about breaking bad habits, and Shiloh had none.

♪

Although Michele is clearly a gifted teacher, the Suzuki approach itself is not without its drawbacks. It works for many children – any number of famous orchestral players had Suzuki training from an early age – but it also risks losing children who aren't steeped in the classical tradition. The basic repertoire of ten volumes (nine for guitar), progressing from 'Twinkle' to Vivaldi, Bach, and Mozart, is incredibly rigid, essentially the same now as when Shinichi Suzuki developed it in the mid-1950s, and focused entirely on music from an earlier era, music that may not speak to many modern children. A newcomer might spend a year learning to play 'Twinkle, Twinkle, Little Star' (in many rhythmic variations), and I could see that a kid who really wanted to rock out to the Beatles or Miley Cyrus might give up and feel (as Tom Morello did) that the gap between what he or she wanted to learn and what was going on in class was too great.

Likewise, the Suzuki method's noble emphasis on perfect form (Michele has a motto: 'It's better to review than to learn something new') might be lost on many children. It takes a special child (like Shiloh) to have the patience to focus on perfection, achieved through a series of almost invisibly small steps. (This is part of why a gifted teacher is so indispensable to the approach. In Michele's capable hands, the method works; in the hands of someone less patient, tempers might fray.)

Another drawback of Suzuki instruction is that it typically tends to teach children little or nothing about improvisation. Much as in the classical conservatory tradition, the emphasis is largely on playing the great works as the great musicians played them, rather than developing a student's own ideas, and while there is indubitably value in that, there is also considerable value in each individual student learning that he or she can make his or her own music. In my own case, the discovery of the joys of improvisation have outweighed virtually all else, yet many musicians trained in the classical style (be it through Suzuki or lessons at Juilliard) feel that they have never learned to improvise. I can't help but feel that they are missing out on some of the greatest joy that music can bring. Another common complaint about Suzuki, which worries me less, is that children trained in that method often don't learn to read music; true, but to my mind not as essential (as I will explain later).

In this respect, I am a big fan of another music-teaching approach (less well-known in the US, but somewhat better known in Europe): the Émile Jaques-Dalcroze method. In Scarsdale, New York, Ruth Alperson, dean of the Hoff-Barthelson Music School, is one of the leading contemporary disciples of the Dalcroze method, and she was kind enough to allow me to sit in on several classes, including two that were geared toward toddlers still in (or barely out of) diapers, one class filled with two-year-olds, the other with children as young as one. Here the emphasis was not on playing a guitar with perfect posture, which would presumably be well out of the motor coordination capacities of most of the students, but on simply developing a sense of music, especially rhythm.

Sitting in with the toddlers immediately confirmed for me the fact that for many human beings music doesn't necessarily come all that naturally: most of the younger kids only dimly grasped the notion formally known as 'entrainment', which is to say moving along to music in synchrony with a beat. Virtually all got the idea of tempo – move faster if the music is faster, move slower if the music is slower. But in the younger group of eight or ten kids, only one – who happened to be the daughter of a professional pianist who worked at the school – could really sway and walk in genuine synchrony with the music.

One clever insight of the Dalcroze method was that with toddlers it might be better for the teacher to come to the student than the other way around. In older age groups, a teacher might set a metronome and ask the student to play in time with it; in the classes I saw with toddlers, Alperson generally let the students set the time. Children, either individually or with the aid of a hand-holding parent or grandparent, walked or loped around the room, and Alperson played in time with them, improvising a melody and rhythm to match the children's movements. The Dalcroze method is also sometimes known as eurhythmics, from the Greek roots *eu* (harmonious) and *rhythm* (motion), and it was easy to see why. The chief emphasis was on gently encouraging children to connect music and motion. For your average two-year-old, banging on a drum in time with music may be too challenging, but music comes from the body first, even before children can play instruments, and the Dalcroze method seemed to be effective in helping bring out that connection. Annie Lennox, founder of the (slightly differently spelled) band the Eurythmics – most famous for their song 'Sweet Dreams (Are Made of This)' – took Dalcroze lessons as a child; I only wish that I had, too.

♪

Another music teacher who impressed me – without teaching a musical instrument at all – was Cirt Gill, a secondary school teacher at Weaver Academy, a school for the performing arts in Greensboro, North Carolina. At one time, Gill was a professional trumpeter who had played as 'juke joint musician' in the film *The Color Purple*. Since 2003, he has been teaching a class in music production, which is to say in the art and science of using recording equipment and computer software to arrange, record, and develop music. When he began, Gill's production class may have been the only one of its kind for school students in the US. Gill was given little more than a classroom and a modest budget for recording equipment and left to his own devices to figure out what should be taught and how he should teach it.

In Gill's class, students compose soundtracks (to children's books of their own devising), create podcasts, and learn about microphone placement in live recording sessions. On the day I sat in, I saw something that looked completely different from anything I remember from my secondary school: originality, inspiration, and students who were genuinely self-motivated. No lecturer standing at the front of the room, but something more akin to a writers' or artists' workshop. Students worked individually or in pairs on compositions while Gill circulated throughout the room, critiquing their compositions and making suggestions, both musical and technical, about their work: adding some percussion here, or encouraging the student to try out a new tool, Melodyne, sort of like Auto-Tune (a popular computer program that corrects the pitch of out-of-key singing) but in certain ways more flexible.

In my school, we couldn't wait for lessons to end so that we could go outside and play Ultimate Frisbee; in Gill's class, many students seemed manifestly disappointed when the lesson ended. Instead of being asked to regurgitate some set of memorized facts for a final exam, the students in Gill's class build their own projects. And instead of competing, they were collaborating. The most skilled student, a seventeen-year-old with a lovely singing voice, was busy mixing her own track with Spanish lyrics and Brazilian rhythms. I wouldn't be surprised if she became a star someday – and not the sort of singer who would sit around passively being told what to do, but the sort of total musician who would have the know-how to serve as her own producer.

With computers on the scene, and traditional instruments being replaced (in some instances) or at least supplemented by machines, it is hard to know exactly what shape music education will take twenty-five years from now, but Gill's classroom struck me as an excellent model.

♪

Another teacher who impressed me immensely, and who takes a very different approach, was Jamie Andreas, a classically trained guitarist who lives in Woodstock, New York, and makes her living giving lessons online (mainly via video Skype). I first discovered her through a classmate from university, Michael Dorfman, who was living in Norway. Dorfman, who had played guitar since childhood, had an accident with his wrist, and that accident had led him to develop an interest in the physical side of playing guitar; he knew the notes and what he wanted to play, but because of the injury his hands could no longer do what his brain wanted them to do. Jamie is one of the few teachers who seems interested in that sort of question, the relationship between muscle and brain, and how to use one's body efficiently. Swimming coaches and golf teachers consider such questions all the time, but it's decidedly rare in the field of music instruction.

Later, I got to meet Jamie in person, and the more we talked, the more impressed I became. Jamie's students are often adults who come to her because they get stuck at a plateau that they'd like to move past. Her main emphasis wasn't on riffs or scales or arpeggios or songs or any of the other things you'd find in a standard guitar book or your average guitar lesson. Instead, her emphasis was almost entirely on the mechanics of proper motor control – on getting one's muscles to do what one wants, as efficiently as possible, with as little tension as possible (reminiscent, for those who know it, of the Alexander technique, but applied to guitar); everything centres around perfect posture and smooth motion. Although Jamie had never taken a formal class in cognitive psychology, she had devoured a textbook on human motor control some years earlier and developed an excellent understanding of how the brain takes in information, incorporating it into her approach. She'd also spent years closely examining where students tended to get stuck. She viewed guitarists the way auto mechanics look at cars: she recognized a host of common problems, had a set of tools for diagnosis, and had a matching set of tricks for making things right.

Jamie didn't claim she could teach true inspiration; her goal wasn't, say, to teach songwriting, and she placed relatively little emphasis on exotic techniques. Her aim was only to teach the basics really, really well. Anyone who wants to be a true artist needs to start with sound fundamentals, and Jamie's lessons (or her cult-classic book *The Principles of Correct Practice for Guitar*) would be a fine place to start, maybe the closest an adult could come to developing the kinds of habits that are instilled in Suzuki training.

♪

A final teacher who impressed me in yet a different way was Terre Roche, middle sister in an influential trio known as the Roches; their self-titled debut was the *New York Times*' 1979 Album of the Year. Terre, too, had no formal training in cognitive psychology, but she took her teaching responsibilities seriously and thought deeply about where her students might get stuck and how to help them. She herself had learned mainly through playing, rather than through formal lessons (only taking formal training years after she had become a professional). Terre has been playing for so long and with so many superstars (Paul Simon, Laurie Anderson, Philip Glass, Robert Fripp, and so on) that she has loads of techniques to impart, especially for advanced players, but what impressed me the most about her teaching style was a set of flash cards – dubbed Fretboard Vitamins – that she created.

Flash cards themselves, of course, aren't remotely new, but Terre rethought how and why they were used. The cards she showed me were aimed at teaching students about the dreaded fretboard and featured two innovations. The first was that the cards themselves were decorated in a way that initially seems goofy but is actually carefully considered. Each card, about five by seven inches, contains a fretboard that highlights a particular musical relationship (for example, the interval of a perfect fifth), surrounded by a fun (and slyly informative) fringe of crazy and colourful tarot-card-like drawings. The student is encouraged to look at a given card for three minutes but also permitted to let his or her eyes wander around freely, within the confines of the card, both on the fretboard diagram and at the surround. The cards allow students to pace themselves without getting saturated, but without zoning out altogether. Proper studies haven't been done yet, but my thinking, which is based on recent studies about the dynamics of processes by which memories solidify over time, is that the cards may be quite effective, because they allow for a period of consolidation, in which memories firm up, interleaved with study.

The second innovation in Roche's deck of flash cards is that rather than requiring students to memorize scales as unanalysed wholes (à la the famous do-re-mi-fa-sol-la-ti-do), each card focuses on a specific interval on the scale (for example, minor third, perfect fifth), illustrating the geometry of where that interval can be found on the fretboard (for example, all the places where one can find a major third relative to some starting note). The cards help instil a good sense of relative pitch early in a student's career and also make it easy for students to begin to improvise fresh melodies, simply by dealing out random sets of cards (major third, minor second, perfect fourth) and choosing among the options that become immediately visible. Because each card illustrates the geometry of a single interval (or, more technically, 'scale degree'), students can focus on the music rather than on the difficult-to-remember geometry. The cards aren't yet commercially available, but the minute I saw them, I wanted a set.

Teachers like Jamie and Terre are great because they take the time not just to figure out the sets of skills their students need to learn but also to anticipate their students' likely stumbling blocks and help them to avoid them.

♪

In studies of musical achievement (typically done in the context of classical music rather than rock music), the one factor besides amount of practice that consistently predicts achievement is not whether you go to Suzuki school, or study under some other method, but parental support, presumably because most young children can't apply themselves sufficiently without external motivation.

Ultimately, motivation can come from without or within – from parents or teachers offering encouragement or from an internal desire to control, even dominate, an instrument. Pat Martino, considered by many to be the greatest jazz guitarist of his generation, took up guitar as a way to impress his parents. Tom Morello, starting at seventeen, did it purely for himself, as a way of gaining power over his own life. His parents probably weren't too thrilled by the heavy metal racket, and he wasn't doing it for a teacher, either – he didn't have one. When I asked Tom whether he had instead learned to play for the girls, his immediate answer was 'Hell, no!' He then paused for a minute and added, more softly, 'Well, maybe, but not in the way you might think. Diving headlong into this obsessive guitar practice was a way of compensating for social lapses. Dating, as the only black kid in Libertyville, Illinois, was harrowing . . . out of my control. The world of practising guitar was all completely *in* my control.' Morello had turned to guitar not because it would lead him to girls but because it led him away from the challenges of interacting with girls, and the social awkwardness and rejection that often came from pursuing them. One of Jimi Hendrix's biographers writes something similar about Hendrix: 'It had not taken him long after his guitar arrived that all [Hendrix] really wanted to do in life was to play guitar. It was his sister, his woman, his muse, his release.' Hendrix, shy and awkward in his teenage years, spent so much time with his guitar that he literally brought it to bed with him. Morello, similarly obsessed, said, 'I didn't choose playing guitar; it chose me.'

Later in his career, as Morello went to competitions known as shred-offs, he began to see the famous racehorse Secretariat as a role model. By the end of university, the goal was not just to win, but to make the other competitors give up and go home. If he was going to achieve this outsize goal, he realized, he had enormous ground to make up. Taking up guitar only at seventeen, Morello had started later than virtually all of his guitar idols (and most of his competitors). To make up for lost time, he began by practising an hour every day. Then two, then four, six, and eventually eight. In his four years as a student at Harvard (where he simultaneously completed an honours degree in political science), Morello estimates that he missed practice on maybe three days. 'If I had a fever of 102 and an exam in the morning, I still got in my six hours.'

I'm not sure any teacher or parent can instil that level of drive in a student – it most likely must come from within – but it is hard to imagine anything of more value.

♪

In the world of music education, one of the most inspiring figures is Marienne Uszler, co-author of the widely regarded *The Well-Tempered Keyboard Teacher*.

When Uszler was first trained – as a pianist, not an educator – the field of music pedagogy scarcely existed; one could study pioneers in cognitive development like Jean Piaget and Jerome Bruner, but few researchers specialized in music education.

Until the mid-twentieth century, most method books 'had a list of things that you had to memorize at the front of the book', and they were really geared to people who already knew how to play to some degree; they were guides for what we might now call intermediate students, not novices; someone like me would have been entirely out of luck. As Uszler put it, 'In the days of [Carl] Philipp Emanuel Bach, the ordinary kid down the block didn't take music lessons', and there wasn't much thought as to how to ease a novice into a life of music. In the old days, it was a master-and-apprentice model, with virtually everything learned by rote, for music as for so much else in education. What books did exist focused mainly on things like scales, and eventually études and exercises; the notion that a student might be better motivated by compositions that were fun to play apparently hadn't dawned on the field yet (or indeed on educators at large).

It also took until the 1920s or 1930s before teachers and writers began to move beyond rote memorization to a broader background in the mechanics of music, towards aspects such as harmony (the coming together of multiple voices or instruments), chords, and theory.

Another innovation, driven perhaps by findings in psychology, was the realization that reinforcement of previously learned concepts was important. In one famous book, *Teaching Little Fingers to Play* (still in use), advertisements vaunted the fact that there was something new on every page – without considering that the human mind needs some degree of repetition in order to fully encode what is learned. 'Something new on every page' sounds good in the abstract, but if what is to be learned shifts too rapidly, consolidation may never occur, and too little may stick (hence Michele's 'It's better to review than to learn something new'). The ideal teacher must balance the old and the new: enough of the old to reinforce good habits, enough of the new to keep lessons from becoming tedious. Uszler is a pioneer in a new generation of music educators, a generation as concerned with the underlying psychology of learning as with the music itself.

♪

The pioneering twentieth-century music educator Edwin E. Gordon has placed particular emphasis on what he calls audiation, or 'the process of assimilating and comprehending (not simply rehearsing) music'. The casual listener merely hears music, without any explicit understanding of how that music is constructed, and the same can happen even for many performers, who learn simply by routine, rather than at a deeper level. As Gordon puts it, 'Memorizing music on an instrument is [ordinarily] primarily related to fingers and other technical matters', and not to a more abstract understanding. Gordon's intention has been to train students to engage more actively, to interpret what they hear in terms of constituent parts like musical scales, chord progressions, and more sophisticated notions such as modulations in musical key, so that they are as comfortable singing a piece – or hearing it on the inside – as they are playing it on their own instruments. In Gordon's words, 'Just as a calculator becomes a crutch for students who cannot multiply or divide, so music instruments [can] become a crutch for students who cannot audiate.'

In striving to help aspiring musicians move beyond mere rote knowledge, Gordon has recommended that students develop audiation skills in a strict sequence of steps that progress from simply listening to familiar and unfamiliar music, to learning to read music, to writing it, to recalling music from memory, and ultimately to creating and improvising music. I have some issues with the details – in my view, Gordon overemphasizes the logical progression in the stages; many early jazz musicians managed, for instance, to become skilled improvisers without ever learning to read or write music. But Gordon's general point – that there is considerable value in understanding a piece of music in terms of its inner structures rather than just as a sequence of notes – is profound. A musician who can merely reproduce what he or she has learned by rote will never match one who understands the logic of music from the inside.

In the final analysis, it may not matter so much whether teachers are trained in the Suzuki method, the Dalcroze method, or others I haven't discussed, such as Orff or Kodaly; instead, what may be more important is whether they are equipped to listen well and give feedback that is simultaneously constructive and enthusiastic. It's not about the technique; it's about the teacher.

SCHOOL OF ROCK

Man Versus Teen

Towards the end of June, about ten months into my musical quest, I got an offer I couldn't possibly refuse: a chance to visit DayJams, a summer camp where kids ages eight to fifteen learn to play and compose rock and roll. The stakes were immediately raised when I spoke to the camp's director, Tobias Hurwitz, who told me, in a kind of pre-interview, 'You're welcome to sit in on the classes, but to get the full experience, you'll want to be in a band.' (Definitely, I thought to myself, half-excited, half-terrified.) 'And if you want to be in a band, it's probably best if you play bass guitar, because there are never enough bass players.'

Um, bass? I'd never played bass. I didn't own one, and in fact the only time I'd ever even touched one was my first year at university, when my friend Alex graciously tried (with no luck whatsoever) to teach me the nine-note opening riff to the Talking Heads song 'Psycho Killer'.

♪

This time, I was determined to have a better attitude. I may have been musically clueless then, but I'd made huge strides on guitar; how hard could bass be?

I stayed up half the night reading online about how to choose a bass to buy for my very own. Hurwitz generously offered that the camp has 'loaners', but a loaner struck me as a terrible idea: I needed to start immediately. If I was to persuade some of the teenagers to let me be in their band, I would have to do it in the first hour of the camp. If I couldn't play at least a few decent licks coming in, it was hard to see how even the lamest, most desperate band of beginners would let someone of their parents' age join in. I found a purple Ibanez online and paid the big bucks for overnight shipping.

For the next three weeks, bass became my life; everything else, even guitar itself, got pushed aside. I learned the opening lick to 'Another One Bites the Dust', memorized the bass's fretboard – which turns out to be a lot easier and more logical than a guitar's, essentially equivalent to the four strings on the guitar that follow a consistent pattern, without the bother of the two that confuse – and prayed that I could find my way into a band.

♪

On the way over to camp the first day, I am, not for the first time in my journey, anxious. Will I have to audition onstage? Will I be any good?

I arrive earlier than I've arrived at anything in years and find my way to Hurwitz. With bulging biceps and curly shoulder-length hair, he looks more like a rock star than a camp director. Luckily, he is unpretentious, and right away he does his best to make me feel comfortable. He tells me that he'll introduce me at the opening assembly but hastens to add that it is up to the campers to decide whether to include me in their band.

After a brief chat, someone gives me a bag containing a beginner's bass textbook, written by Glenn Riley, one of the camp's instructors, and some bass strings, and then Tobias sends me off to a small classroom/ holding pen in which the campers are collecting. Mostly I talk to Ben, a sociable twelve-year-old who's been coming to DayJams since he was seven and who clearly knows far more than I ever will.

Just after 9:00 a.m., the camp officially opens; the fifty or so campers, a few stray parents, and the counselors are led to a huge auditorium, where the instructors are playing 'Message in a Bottle' by the Police. There's another song after that, and then Hurwitz makes half a dozen announcements, my favourite of which is 'No drumming on anything that isn't a drum.'

Tobias eventually calls me up onstage, introduces me as a professor and an author, and tells the audience that I'm there to be a camper and write about it. He says I'd like to be in a band (and not just sit around and watch) and sweetens the pot by mentioning that some of the campers might have their names mentioned in a book. Still, it's up to them, and all I can do is wait; by mutual agreement Tobias will start calling out the names of various instructors and who will be in their respective bands, and it's only once all the kids have already been organized that we'll get to see if there is room for me. While I wait, all I can think of is my days at primary school, hoping to get picked for a kickball team, praying desperately: Pick me, pick me, pick me!

♪

Finally, everything else is organized, and Tobias brings me to one of the youngest bands, which, as it happens, is directed by Michael Raitzyk, who is one of my mother's neighbours and the son of a family friend. He's also one of Maryland's leading jazz guitarists, and happens to be the person who told me about the camp in the first place. Half a dozen campers, all around ten or eleven years old, are fooling around with guitars and drums, one on a keyboard, and they take little notice of me.

Tobias asks if they'd like to have me in their band. Michael puts in a good word: 'Gary's a nice guy, and it'll really help the band to have a bass player.' Three of the kids shrug and say sure; nobody demurs. With that, I'm in a band, my first gig as a bass player.

♪

Three of my bandmates, Ryan (lead guitarist), Riley (drummer), and Greer (keyboardist), have clearly played before; there are also two complete novices, Sarah and Peter, on guitar. By the time I arrive in class, Ryan's already playing a catchy riff that he made up at home. Most of the first forty-five minutes of class time is spent learning his riff; I try to match him on bass, but the lick is too fast and I can't really keep up.

From there, it's off to bass class; this time there are about eight of us (guitarists, keyboard players, and percussionists have all gone elsewhere) and a slightly grouchy teacher named Jamie. Right away Jamie notices that with my right hand I am picking notes with my thumb (rather than the customary index and middle fingers). In his view, this is a bad idea. 'It's not imperative that you play with your fingers . . .' he intones, without ever quite finishing his sentence. His implication – that I'd be an idiot if I kept playing with my thumb – is clear enough. (Only months later do I realize his reasoning – with two active fingers on your right hand instead of one, it's a lot easier to play faster.)

Jamie's chief assistant, Jonathan, is only thirteen and an obvious prodigy; he can already play nearly as well as Jamie can, even though Jamie is a professional musician who started playing long before Jonathan was born.

We start easy, with information I've already more or less mastered in the previous weeks, during my crash course on bass, such as the name of each note on the bass guitar's four strings. As I soon discover, this sort of book learning is about the only thing I know that my classmates don't (I even notice an error on the blackboard). But when it comes to actual playing, I'm miles behind most of the other students, but I can't tell whether that's my age or their experience – all but one have been to the camp before, and many have been playing for years. Will my adult savvy be of any help in trying to close the gap? Or will I fall further and further behind?

♪

Jamie teaches us a relatively simple lick – two notes on the first string, one on the second, two on the third. One of the more experienced campers immediately plays it, and plays it well. Five minutes later Jamie calls me to the centre of the classroom and asks me to play the lick. I've managed to learn the order of the notes, sort of, but definitely haven't mastered their timing. I play tentatively, too embarrassed to make eye contact with the class.

The highlight of the day comes during the final period, listed on our schedules as 'Stage'. The six of us in my band, plus our instructor, Michael, get up on the stage, plug our instruments into professional-grade amplifiers – which are taller than my bandmates – and begin to work out our song. There's no audience – and, to be honest, we wouldn't deserve one – but it doesn't matter. This is only the second time I've ever played with anything resembling a band (the other was with an old friend who came to town and gave me a lesson), and never before have I played alongside a live drum kit – the visceral feel of the kick and snare up close is thrilling.

We start with Ryan's lick, and more or less get it down. The notes are easy – G, A, B, and A again, all on the lowest E string – but I keep getting varying reports on how many times to hit each note. Ryan plays so fast that the two novice guitarists and I have trouble keeping up (though the keyboardist and drummer seem perfectly content).

Michael then calls for suggestions, and I suggest a simple bass lick that's kind of an echo of the main guitar lick (though played in a higher pitch, on the G string rather than the E). Suddenly I find myself stuck with the responsibility of playing a short solo, two bars long, in the middle of the song, and I feel almost overwhelmed by the timekeeping responsibilities I've consequently acquired, especially since I can't quite figure out how to make my five-note lick fit neatly into two bars of four beats each. I try to back out, or at least suggest that my bass solo go at the end of the song (where nobody else would rely on me), but Michael's having none of it. I'm stuck with a burden of my own making.

We practise our composition so far: guitar lick, played four times through, then my two bars, then four more repeats of the whole riff. And most of the time, something or other goes wrong: somebody starts too soon, somebody comes in too late, somebody (often me, because I can't keep up) gets lost altogether. I'm a relative newcomer, and Sarah (and Peter, who would end up leaving the band) literally never played before; only Ryan, Greer, and Riley really seem to know what they are doing, but even they aren't entirely used to playing together as a band. If a perfect band, a band that plays in synchrony, is called 'tight', we're somewhere between 'loose' and 'wandering'. The scary part is that by Friday afternoon, we'd have to pull it together: we would be performing onstage in front of all the campers and their parents – including mine. Would we be able to pull it together?

♪

Much of what we work on over the next few days is structure and timing – when to change from one section of the song to the next, how many times to repeat each riff. None of this comes easily for me, especially at the speed at which my band is playing – more like a Ramones song than a slow ballad. The hardest section – just before my entrance – is when I have to count sixteen consecutive notes of G, all played (by me and everyone else) at full speed, just before my own brief solo. I have *no* idea how I am going to get this right on the night of the show.

Ryan, on the other hand, knows instinctively just how long a measure is. I don't know whether he's come by that instinct naturally or from experience (he's been playing at least since last summer, maybe longer), but I watch agape later in the afternoon. Michael teaches Ryan the notes in the scale of G major and asks him to construct a solo out of those notes, arranging them in whatever sequence he likes. The key is that Ryan has exactly sixteen beats to fill, and somehow he gets it just right, marvelling out loud afterward, 'I don't know how I did that; I just knew.' I may know about algebra, calculus, and statistics, but when it comes to the simple arithmetic of counting beats, these kids are light-years ahead of me.

♪

To a certain degree, how a thing is learned depends on the material itself, independent of who is doing the learning. Neither children nor adults, for instance, could have any hope of learning to play melody without learning the alphabet of music first: melodies are composed of ordered, rhythmical sets of notes; harmonies are composed of sets of notes that combine to form elegant wholes. Anyone learning guitar, whatever his or her age, must become accustomed to the fretboard and the strange shapes it requires. Equally essential is a sense of rhythm and time (ever my Achilles' heel); nothing sounds good if it is not fluid and regular.

But lots of studies suggest that the brains of children and adults are different, and differences in brain structure could in principle lead to differences in learning style. Physiologically, grey matter (consisting mainly of neural cell bodies) increases in density through adolescence, and then gradually begins to decline. At roughly the same time, white matter (consisting mainly of the axons and dendrites that form connections between neurons) begins to increase, presumably a product of all the learning that is taking place. Behaviourally, at least when it comes to learning a second language, perhaps a model for acquiring music late in life, adults are certainly on average less apt than kids. Any number of studies have shown that learning a language early in life clearly beats learning one late in life, even if the decay is not nearly as abrupt as once widely believed.

♪

Nobody really knows why. Are adults at a disadvantage because their memories are weaker? Because some brain module shuts down around the time of puberty? Or simply because they don't try as hard as their younger counterparts? The scientific literature is surprisingly mixed. There is no solid evidence that windows of cognitive opportunity close at clearly defined moments. One recent study of over two million subjects found a linear decline with age – people starting English at age fifty did worse than those starting at age forty, who did worse than those who started at age thirty, and so on – but no firm break in the curve, no decisive moment beyond which a second language could not be learned. Indeed, some recent studies have found that some adults are able to fully master second (or third) languages acquired later in life.

My own reading of the literature is that our memory skills slowly decline from the mid-twenties onward but that there is also a serious issue of interference and habits: the stronger your habits are with your native language, the harder it is to do something different in a second language. And of course the longer you've been speaking your first language, the more ingrained and habitual it has become; if you are used to putting the verb in the middle, it's hard to learn to put it at the end in German.

Children are likely at a further advantage in learning many things because of how they allocate their time and attention, often enduring endless repetition that adults would find tedious. Partly because they are typically saddled with other responsibilities, adults are often in a rush to get the big picture; children are willing to practise a single element – a word or even a syllable – over and over until they get that detail right. In the words of the psychologist Elissa Newport, it may be that sometimes 'less is more'. Bulgarian children learning to play complex folk songs, for example, have been known to focus closely on the details of a performance – learning all the ornaments along with the melody instead of just learning the melody first. Adults might focus first on the overall melody and add the finer details later.

Another difference that applies to all skill acquisition is, as Marienne Uszler pointed out to me, that 'generally speaking, the younger the learner, the greater the willingness to experience something unknown'. It is easier to take risks at fifteen than at fifty.

♪

Many people probably imagine that children are simply quicker learners, but laboratory research suggests otherwise. In the few direct comparisons of 'procedural' learning in children and university-aged adults, adults actually tend to be quicker learners than children. In the most recent, most careful study I could find, six-year-olds, eight-year-olds, ten-year-olds, and adults all did a similar button-pressing task, kind of a simplified version of piano, in which (to balance the playing field) everyone had to learn new patterns that were unfamiliar. Surprisingly, for anyone who imagined children to be quick studies, especially on a button-pressing task that might feel a bit like a video game, adults were systematically better, acquiring the new patterns in significantly fewer trials than children.

If children outshine adults, it's probably not because they are quicker to learn but simply because they are more persistent; the same drive that can lead them to watch the same episode of a TV programme five days in a row without any signs of losing interest can lead a child who aspires to play an instrument to practise the same riff over and over again. Although adults initially learn the patterns more quickly, with enough practice children are ultimately able to achieve the same level of accuracy. The ten-year-olds get there sooner than the eight-year-olds, who are more adept learners than the six-year-olds, but they all manage to get there in the end, and in the long run, if children practise more, they may just overtake their elders. But except in contexts like recognizing fine acoustic differences in pitch, there's no evidence that learning late is an absolute deal breaker.

♪

What really governs the speed of learning is probably not so much age as experience. Factoring out my complete lack of native talent, the single element that seemed to make the difference at any age was sheer practice. The kids who were the quickest studies were, by and large, those who had spent the most years practising. Fifteen-year-olds were better than thirteen-year-olds, and thirteen-year-olds were better than eleven-year-olds. The rare thirteen-year-old wizards (like Jonathan) had generally started very early (at four, in his case). Another thirteen-year-old had never played before, and he was struggling just as much as I was.

Why does practice matter as much as it does? As we saw earlier, when we master any domain, be it guitar or algebra or squash, our brains get better at two things: recognizing what the pieces are (known as chunking) and knowing where to look (known as attention).

To a beginner, any song (or riff) is more or less just a random collection of notes. To an expert, those same notes will be instantly familiar: 'That measure is just like a descending D major scale, except that the F-sharp note is skipped!' Suddenly seven notes become one easy-to-remember block; the more blocks we recognize, the faster and more efficiently we can play. As the guitarist acquires a vocabulary of riffs and scales, everything new becomes easier to remember in relation to the old. Chess players can think further ahead once they can break positions down into familiar chunks, and aspiring London taxi drivers plan their routes more efficiently once they learn the ins and outs of individual neighbourhoods. (All of which has a reflection in the brain: as we saw earlier, our grey matter tends to get denser as we learn new things.) In the same way, expert musicians can better understand music as a whole once they begin to encode bigger and more abstract musical chunks.

♪

As a member of the band, I couldn't maintain the manic energy of my much younger bandmates, but I did have one thing I could contribute: a sense of the dynamics of songs as a whole. My lifelong struggles with arrhythmia hadn't kept me from being an active listener, and now my years of listening started to come in handy. Moreover, for months, I'd been actively thinking about song production and arrangement, through experiments with Apple's GarageBand (a program that allows users to compose their own music), and reading and thinking on the science of aesthetics; relative to my young bandmates, I had a stronger sense of composition as a whole. After Ryan introduced two basic riffs, much of the effort in actually assembling our song wound up in my hands. I ended up suggesting a way for us to begin the song (essentially a joke, with Greer playing the intro of a complex classical prelude – interrupted abruptly by Riley slamming on the drums, at which point the mood changes from a gentle piano recital to hard-rocking mayhem). I also worked out the ending and suggested an organizational scheme in the latter part of the song wherein each of the more experienced members might take solos (or near solos, with everyone but the drummer dropping out). I wasn't pushy about it – I made each suggestion as gently as possible, and never with insistence (especially since I always felt like a guest) – but my bandmates were glad to have them; high-level considerations about composition simply weren't on the kids' minds. The campers would rather polish their riffs than think about the ensemble as a whole. Which left me, as representative of an older generation, a rare place in which to shine.

A few months later, I found myself at a holiday party with three incredibly talented young guitar-playing sons of a good friend. Each child could play a fleet of individual riffs with vastly more panache than I could, but the two younger brothers hadn't yet captured the part of music that is about playing together. Instead, each was in his own world, practising his own riff without regard to what the others were playing. Drawing on my growing understanding of music theory, I was able to act as conductor and managed to get the boys to jam together in unison – something they had never really done before.

If my experience is any guide – and it fits pretty well with the meagre scientific literature – the comparison between children and adults isn't a simple matter of saying one is better than the other; rather, children and adults have their own strengths and liabilities. Children bring to the table enormous patience and fast fingers; adults have a vast reservoir of implicit knowledge, cultivated through years of listening, and far more facility with abstractions.

Ageing baseball pitchers sometimes manage, late in their careers, to shift from brute force – throwing nothing but 'heat', or fast balls – to cunning, keeping batters off balance by throwing a wide variety of slower pitches. I never had the heat, but maybe at thirty-nine I could use my experience (and knowledge of the science of aesthetics) to bring at least a little something to the musical table.

TRUE TALENT

Hard Work Isn't Everything

As I sat at camp trying to master the bass, the importance of practice was certainly not lost on me. But is practice the only factor that matters? Nine out of ten recent pop-psychology bestsellers seem to suggest that talent doesn't exist or at least that (to borrow the title of one) talent is overrated. The psychologist Anders Ericsson went so far as to write, 'New research shows that outstanding performance is the product of years of deliberate practice and coaching, not of any innate talent or skill.'

How I wish it were true. The notorious behaviourist John Watson said something similar back in the 1920s when he famously wrote:

> Give me a dozen healthy infants, well-formed, and my own specified world to bring them up in and I'll guarantee to take any one at random and train him to become any type of specialist I might select – doctor, lawyer, artist, merchant-chief and, yes, even beggar-man and thief, regardless of his talents, penchants, tendencies, [and] abilities.

Practice does indeed matter – a lot – and in surprising ways. But it would be a logical error to infer from the importance of practice that talent is somehow irrelevant, as if the two were in mutual opposition. To use an analogy, the trees that grow the tallest aren't just the ones that get the most water; they are also the ones with the best genes, the ones that can most efficiently build new structure by metabolizing sun and light. Great musicians, like the tallest plants, need optimal conditions: ideal genes and ideal environments.

♪

One night after camp ends, I take the camp's director, Tobias, out to dinner, and after some brief chitchat about the unbearable summer heat the conversation quickly turns to the central issue he, I, and all aspiring musicians want to understand: the relation between talent, practice, and success. We start with the easy part: Is practice essential? Hell, yes. So long as you practise efficiently and effectively, focusing on fixing your weaknesses and learning new things (not just rehearsing what you already know), the more practice, the better.

Tobias knows every significant musician in Baltimore and can instantly rattle off both their strengths and weaknesses as musicians (this drummer plays well and has a gift for knowing what sounds to add to complement any song, but sometimes he rushes, inadvertently accelerating the beat; that guitarist has a gift for transforming what he hears directly into actions with his fingers). Tobias also knows what each individual's practice regime is like: at what age each person started practising and how much time he invests in practice nowadays as an active professional musician. And he sees a strong – but not perfect – correlation between skill and practice. Indeed one of Tobias's big regrets is that he feels that as a working musician he has less time for practice than he likes because he needs to spend time on self-marketing. A good friend of his, he says, is less savvy about self-promotion – and as a result less wealthy, with fewer sponsorship deals – but also the better musician: less time marketing leaves more time for practising.

But when it comes to the notion that talent doesn't exist, practice *über alles,* Tobias won't bite. He goes on to say that in private lessons he's taught literally thousands of novices the chords to 'Wild Thing' (G, C, D); he shows them how to hold their hands for each one (this is your G), and plays the sequence in rhythm and tempo, and asks the students to do the same. Almost everyone struggles at first, even any number of students who have gone on to become great guitarists; yet a handful get it instantly, never having touched a guitar before. Some students, he says, you teach for an hour, and they learn 'this much,' extending his hands wide, and 'others much less', his hands nearly closed.

Tobias and I spend much of the rest of the evening discussing a teenager I'll call Richard, who in Tobias's opinion is far and away the best student he's ever had or seen. Better than the best kid I've seen at the camp? I ask. 'In a different league', says Tobias, without hesitation.

Richard, it turns out, is congenitally blind and also (I infer from Tobias's description) autistic. Because of his visual impairment, Richard plays with the guitar in his lap, and he knows the fretboard perfectly, by feel alone. The autism likely helped, by allowing for a level of concentration that many other children wouldn't be able to match; along with that concentration came an extraordinary sense of pitch and rhythm: as a sort of party trick, Richard had learned to identify different cars by the sounds their engines made, and he could keep such careful track of time that he could estimate a car's velocity over a certain wood bridge by the tempo of the tyres thumping against the slats.

Tobias recounted an incident in which he played for Richard a Steve Vai song called 'For the Love of God', a ridiculously complex seven-minute song that is filled with alternations between slow melodic lines and insanely fast shredding. It's by far Vai's most famous piece, and it took Tobias months to master. Richard? All he had to do was listen once. He slowed down a few of the faster bits, almost as if he were translating them into his own language, but otherwise reproduced the entire piece on his first listen, almost flawlessly. 'I will never be able to do that', said Tobias, one of the world's great shredders, 'no matter how much I practise.'

♪

'I'm a huge fan of Malcolm Gladwell,' one well-known music industry insider told me. 'I loved *Blink* and *The Tipping Point*. But I think *Outliers* [his book on talent, practice, and success] is just too glib a formulation. It's not that anybody with ten years [of practice] is going to be the Beatles.' Maybe anybody could learn to be a decent musician from practice alone, but to be truly great, a musician needs more than hard work. Musical skill is, for everybody, something that must be cultivated, but there are differences in how fast people learn, and perhaps in the levels they can ultimately attain. The Beatles themselves learned almost everything they knew on the job, but they put in more like two thousand hours, not ten thousand, even counting all the once- and twice-a-day shows at the Cavern Club and in Hamburg. Meanwhile, thousands of musicians have put in their ten thousand hours without becoming stars or producing any music of lasting note; to focus solely on practice is to unfairly dismiss talent. Consider, for example, Jimi Hendrix and Jimmy Page; neither started until he was an adolescent (relatively late in life by musicians' standards), but both were playing professionally within a year or so of when they started. They clearly learned faster than most of their peers and (it goes without saying) eventually attained heights that almost nobody else ever did.

As popular as the 'it's all practice' meme is, there are many reasons why we should be sceptical. To begin with, consider the strikingly large number of top musicians who come from musically inclined families. Paul McCartney's father was a professional bass player (leader of Jim Mac's Jazz Band), and Paul Simon's father played bass professionally, too, often appearing on television. Folks like Ziggy and Damian Marley, Dweezil Zappa, Jakob Dylan, Rosanne Cash, and Sean and Julian Lennon all carry on their family traditions, as do Jason Bonham, son of the late Led Zeppelin drummer, John Bonham; Bebel Gilberto, daughter of João Gilberto; and the star saxophonist Joshua Redman, son of Dewey. Fela Kuti (deceased) has his sons Femi and Seun. And then there is the onetime R& B player Joseph Walter Jackson, who had nine children: Randy, Marlon, Tito, Jermaine, Jackie, Rebbie, Janet, La Toya, and the late Michael – eight of whom earned gold records. There are the Wainwrights – Loudon III, his sister Sloan, and his late wife, Kate McGarrigle, and Loudon and Kate's two children, Rufus and Martha – along with the Roche family (Maggie, Terre, and Suzzy, of the Roches, and their brother, David), who joined forces when Loudon III got together with Suzzy Roche, giving rise to the ascending singer-songwriter Lucy Wainwright Roche. I could also mention the absurdly talented Marsalis brothers, Wynton, Branford, Delfeayo, and Jason, all offspring of the professional pianist Ellis Marsalis Jr. Fans of classical music will know about the Strauss family (Josef, Eduard, and Johann I and Johann II), the Mozarts, and the Bach family (Johann Sebastian, Carl Philipp Emanuel, Johann Christian), not to mention the contemporary chart-topping Ahn sisters, Maria, Lucia, and Angella. And although some second- or third-generation musicians play in much the same style as their parents, others, like the singer Norah Jones, daughter of the sitarist Ravi Shankar, sound nothing at all like their parents. And then there's the late singer Jeff Buckley, who sounds eerily like his biological father, Tim Buckley, even though the two met only once. Even before modern genetic techniques were available, the heritable component of music was already clear.

Of course there's nothing special about music in this regard. When I was growing up, my favourite baseball player was Cal Ripken Jr. His father was a professional baseball player who eventually became the manager of the Baltimore Orioles, and his brother Billy was also good enough to play infield for several years in the major leagues. Kobe Bryant's father was a professional basketball player; National Football League quarterbacks Peyton and Eli Manning, two of the best American football players in recent years, were sons of Archie Manning, himself an NFL quarterback. Ditto for Chelsea midfielder Frank Lampard Jr, who began his career at West Ham United, where his father, Frank Sr, played leftback for many years.

I have no doubt that Cal Ripken Jr learned a lot about baseball at his father's knee – and probably had opportunities that most children do not. But it is also unlikely that all these family clusters are a simple product of the environment. Instead, careful studies of identical twins show time and again that – on virtually any indicator of human behaviour that anyone has tried to measure – genetics is a better predictor than living in the same family. There is good scientific reason to think that talent matters in a wide variety of domains, from sport to chess to writing to music. Cognitive activities are a product of the mind, and the mind is a product of genes working together with the environment. To dismiss talent is to ignore all evidence from biology.

♪

Still, that doesn't mean the human genome contains genes specifically tailored to music (or, for that matter, professional sport). Individual genes build proteins, not behaviours. The chain of causality from gene to protein to neuron to behaviour is vast and immensely complicated; we are not likely to find a gene specifically dedicated to remembering major scales or playing trills. But there doesn't need to be: genes need not be so specific to have a dramatic impact. The gene FOXP2, for example, is a prerequisite of human language, but it does not exist solely for that purpose; it also underwrites some function in the lungs and in fact can be found in all vertebrates, from fish to monkeys to people. New functions are often cobbled together out of old genes.

Our capacity to acquire music comes not from a set of genes that are specific to music but from a host of genes that have differing effects on broader aspects of personality, cognition, and perception. There is ample evidence, for example, that individual variation in genes affects memory efficiency (vital, obviously, in learning songs). Variation in other genes can modulate curiosity (which can mediate how much effort people put into learning music), and still a third modulates sensitivity to absolute pitch. Another recent study shows that variation in another particular gene correlates with people's scores on tests of musical composition and improvisation. This gene isn't uniquely dedicated to music – it plays an important role in social interaction in humans as well as other species – but the fact that a gene has far-reaching consequences doesn't mean it isn't essential for music, too. In keeping with the idea that music is a skill that builds on a multiplicity of brain circuits, it is also a skill that draws on many different genes – each of which may contribute in some way or another to an individual's talents for music.

Practice – even deliberate practice, working hard at one's weaknesses and not just noodling around having fun – can't by itself fully predict musical achievement. Other factors, including general intelligence, auditory aptitude, and working memory capacity, are also demonstrably critical, even after the effects of practice are statistically controlled for. Not surprisingly, the highest-level performers are likely to be people who combine the greatest talent with the most practice. (And, if you want to be technical about it, practice itself isn't entirely independent of biology. How we respond to experience, and even what type of experience we seek, are themselves in part functions of the genes we are born with. It's not nature versus nurture; it's nature working together with nurture.)

In hindsight, the writing was already on the wall: as important as practice is, the 'talent is overrated' craze never really made sense. An earlier study with identical twins had suggested that some genetic factors must play a role. And if you look at the original study by Ericsson and others that so many people have recently written books about, you'll find that there was a substantial amount of individual variation that couldn't be predicted by how many hours a person put in. Plenty of serious violinists, for example, had practised for twenty years without becoming as good as others who had played for only eight. When one looks carefully at the science literature on practice and success, all it shows is that *on average* the more people practise, the better they perform. In no way do such studies show that practice is the *only* important factor. Meanwhile, everyone seems to have overlooked an incredibly comprehensive study of musical aptitude, conducted in the 1960s and to this day by far the most comprehensive of its kind: a three-year longitudinal study with virtually every ten- and eleven-year-old in four schools. The team's leader, Edwin Gordon, discovered that nearly half of the variation in how well schoolchildren played musical instruments could be predicted three years in advance, on the basis of talent alone (as measured by musical aptitude tests that examined factors such as tonal and rhythmic imagery). Talent matters, and practice matters; neither can be ignored. If I put in my ten thousand hours, I might become a good guitarist, maybe even a very good one, but that doesn't mean I'd be anywhere near as good as Hendrix was after half as much practice.

The flip side to talent, of course, is the lack of talent. Eighteen months or so into my guitar-playing adventures, I figured out one of the reasons why music had always been such a struggle for me: rhythm turns out to be deeply tied to the balance-tracking vestibular system. Since I was a child, my vestibular system has been lousy. I could never bear to ride on a swing, despised being bounced up and down, routinely became nauseated when sitting in the back of the car, and opted out of roller coasters altogether. A new study showed that electrical stimulation of the vestibular system can directly affect rhythmic perception, and in retrospect it is easy to see why rhythm has always posed a challenge for me. It's a pretty safe bet that Jimi Hendrix enjoyed being bounced as a baby a lot more than I did.

♪

That same summer I sat in on a Q&A session with Pat Metheny, one of the world's leading jazz guitarists. Metheny, obviously a brilliant man, was clear, lucid, and frequently funny; he also left no doubt that he is one of the hardest-working musicians in the business. He performs over 150 times a year, and when he is not performing, he is almost constantly working on composition, trying to develop new material for new shows and new albums. (Curiously, he does most of his composing on piano; Metheny plays guitar in concert because that's what he's known for, but like several other guitarists I met, he finds composition easier on the piano.)

At one point, a member of the audience got up and declared that Metheny was a perfect example of the practice-makes-perfect thesis. But it was almost as if the questioner had missed half of what Metheny had just told us. Metheny didn't just practise hard; he came from an incredibly musical family. His brother, father, and grandfather all played trumpet, and did so extremely well. His grandfather played with John Philip Sousa (the most famous composer of military marches), and his brother was playing with the Kansas City Orchestra by the time he was ten. Pat was, for a little while, the slacker in the family, jealous of the attention his brother was getting. It was only at age twelve (in part as a rebellion against his brass-playing family) that Pat picked up the guitar. But – and here's the key point – it didn't take him anywhere near ten thousand hours to get good at it; within three years, young Pat was already good enough to get gigs at the best jazz clubs in Kansas City.

Later, I got a chance to talk with Pat in great depth, and he explained that he saw musical talent as a sort of grid. Some musicians, he said, moving his fingers as if on an invisible fretboard, are blessed with physical dexterity, others with exceptionally sensitive ears. (Hendrix probably had both.) Metheny saw his own physical dexterity as limited, developed more by brute practice than natural instinct, but he also knew that he himself had been an adept listener since his earliest days. As a child, he'd gotten a perfect score on a musical aptitude test, and in the time since, he'd honed his ears in ways that few other musicians could ever hope to match. Metheny has an astonishing sensitivity to the details of other musicians' styles, not just at the coarse level of who was good or bad, but exactly which elements of music they were most proficient at, and exactly how any given musician fit into the pantheon of predecessors. Metheny could decompose every note he heard into a mini history lesson. A question about Wynton Marsalis, for instance, led to a disquisition on how Wynton's breathing techniques drew on both Miles Davis and a lesser-known trumpeter who had once played with Marsalis's father. Talking to Metheny was like talking to a sport scout who knew the exact mechanics of every young phenom's pitching motion, which minor leaguer lifted his shoulder in a funny way, and which ones released a pitch to the batter a moment too soon. Metheny, it was clear, was born with golden ears.

♪

Of course, playing guitar is only one element of becoming a musician; writing songs another. One of the most amazing illustrations of the rapid eruption of sheer musical talent that I can think of is the story of Bob Dylan's emergence as a songwriter. In the folk tradition, in which Dylan was trained, writing original tunes simply wasn't done; and it wasn't until he was about twenty that he started seriously writing songs. Dylan's first album consisted mainly of covers; out of thirteen songs, only two were his own compositions. But the minute Dylan started writing songs in earnest, a torrent was unleashed. Within three years, he'd written 'Blowin' in the Wind' (which became an immediate hit in the hands of Peter, Paul, and Mary), 'Maggie's Farm', 'Subterranean Homesick Blues', and 'The Times They Are A-Changin''. Within another two he'd written 'Positively 4th Street', 'It's Alright, Ma (I'm Only Bleeding)', 'It's All Over Now, Baby Blue', and 'Like a Rolling Stone'. Only a handful of songwriters, no matter how many decades they've put in, have ever matched what Dylan did in those first few years.

INTO THE GROOVE

How Music Really Evolved

Wednesday and Thursday at the camp pass by in a blur: endless rehearsals, many mistakes, much anxiety. But little by little, things get better. On Friday, the final morning of DayJams, we get a last chance to rehearse.

Our first run-through – after what seems like hours of sound checks – is quite shaky. Fortunately, our band's instructor, Michael, quickly deduces the source of our problems. It's not that the band has forgotten everything we've learned; it's that our drummer, who sits behind a giant Plexiglas screen (to spare us from deafness), can't hear the rest of the band. In principle, a drummer is supposed to get feedback from a 'stage monitor' – a speaker positioned so that it sends a bit of the sound from the rest of the band back behind the Plexiglas screen. But the drummer's monitor was switched off, and Riley, who's only been onstage once before, doesn't even realize he's supposed to be able to hear us; he just soldiers on without a monitor, happily playing his part without realizing that the rest of us are out of sync. After Michael sorts that out, we play through a second time, and now the band sounds like a real band. We do a third take, and the camp staff gets it down on MP3. Our first live recording!

Afterwards, Michael decides to do something different, to try to keep us loose – and the minute he does, something clicks. Rather than forcing us to rehearse our song yet again, he moves over to the keyboard (we've only ever seen him play guitar, and didn't even realize he knew how to play keyboard) and tells us all to start jamming in the key of G. Riley lays down a beat he's been working on, and the rest of us play whatever we like, as long as it's in time and in that key. And together we produce real music. Michael then moves over to drums and asks us to jam in F and G, alternating between the two chords. Freed from the challenges of counting sevens, and freed from the responsibility of having to achieve perfection, I feel liberated, and it's obvious that the whole band feels the same way. As a listener, I never especially liked 'jam' bands like the Grateful Dead and Phish, but for a performer, a well-coordinated jam, in which each person makes up a part that fits together into a spontaneously generated whole, is nothing less than euphoric.

But what really clicks is not the music; it's my understanding of the origins of music. In a single moment, I suddenly understand the origins of music in a whole new way.

♪

The dominant theory of music evolution – introduced by Darwin, developed by Geoffrey Miller, and endorsed by Daniel Levitin – is that music is all about sexual selection: guys play music because girls like music, and guys like girls. Playing music was good for Jimi Hendrix's genes, and, so the story goes, our love of music evolved as a way of getting primeval men laid. Hendrix, Miller tells us, had

> sexual liaisons with hundreds of groupies, maintained parallel long-term relationships with at least two women, and fathered at least three children in the United States, Germany, and Sweden. Under ancestral conditions before birth control, he would have fathered many more.

Mick Jagger has had seven children, Jimmy Page five. Were 'musical notes and rhythm . . . first acquired . . . for the sake of charming the opposite sex', as Darwin wrote? Miller piles on the evidence, reporting, for example, that in a sample of six thousand recent jazz, rock, and classical albums, 90 percent were produced by men.

But I'm not convinced, and not just because Beethoven appears to have been childless. Although the sexual selection theory sounds very clever, it has a slew of serious flaws.

First, in most aspects of physiology that are shaped by sexual selection, we generally see a significant dimorphism, which is to say noticeable variation between males and females. Peacocks have plumage, their female counterparts don't; male songbirds sing, females generally don't. At one point in human history, one might have conceived of human music in the same way – as the product of males alone, and Miller's data on recordings initially seem consistent with that. But in hindsight, that apparent dimorphism is most likely more about opportunity and sociology than a necessary fact about human biology. We now know with certainty that women can be just as capable musicians as men. Consider, for example, what has happened in the classical world in recent decades. Before the advent of blind auditions (in which aspiring musicians play behind a screen), men drastically outnumbered women in most orchestras; now most symphonies are near parity. My hometown orchestra recently became one of the first major symphonies to hire a female conductor (Marin Alsop), and many more are sure to follow. The Songwriters Hall of Fame is filled with women, like Carole King ('You've Got a Friend'), Marilyn Bergman ('The Way We Were'), Betty Comden ('Singin' in the Rain'), Dolly Parton ('I Will Always Love You'), and Joni Mitchell ('Both Sides Now'). In the contemporary rock world, performers like Tori Amos, Sinead O'Connor, and Alicia Keys are every bit as talented and original as their male counterparts; Mariah Carey has had more No. 1 hits than Elvis. Meanwhile, women like Alison Krauss, Mary J. Blige, Linda Perry, and Missy Elliott helped finally break the glass ceiling in the world of music production. There's no reason to believe that in humans there is a bona fide sexual dimorphism in either the listening to or the creation of music.

Second, the Jimi Hendrix theory conflates the powerful image of a single exceptionally talented guitarist with the realities of most musicians. Some musicians probably do indeed do it to get girls, but only about half of university-degreed musicians, for instance, are even able to make a living in a musical career; a handful make a living soloing with symphonies, but most make a living giving music lessons or leave the field altogether. Even after Juilliard, one out of four graduates can't make ends meet as a musician. Most musicians pursue music because they are passionate about music, not because it makes them rich or popular. 'I sing lead vocals in a death metal band' may be a come-on, but 'I teach trombone to nine-year-olds' probably isn't. Even in the time of Mozart and Haydn, as one historian of music put it to me, musicians were not particularly well regarded, typically dressing in livery, like servants, not living like modern-day rock royalty. The Hendrix theory only works if it turns out that *on average* people who invest the many hours required for musical expertise have more offspring than people who spend that time in other ways, and I know of no data to support that conjecture.

Third, the Hendrix theory is premised on a view of the present that hardly resembles the past in which we evolved. Hendrix lived in a time in which it was possible for musicians to make millions of dollars and become internationally famous, but whatever genes contribute to music evolved long before there were radio stations or record deals. Court jesters made music, too, but their status was hardly that of contemporary rock stars. Before Mozart in the 1760s and Paganini's rise in the early nineteenth century, few performers became internationally renowned, and the big money arrived only in the age of recording (and is disappearing again, now, in the download era).

Fourth, the Hendrix theory makes it sound as if there were a specific music module in the brain that was somehow targeted by evolution, but as we saw earlier, there is no distinct 'music centre' in the brain, but rather a coalition of neural tissue, virtually all of which predates music – suggesting that the Hendrix theory is after the wrong quarry.

Finally, the Hendrix theory – as well as just about every other theory of music evolution I have ever encountered – is musically naive, because it makes it sound as if all music were equal. Play any old song, get mate, end of story. Would that it were so easy! As anyone who has ever produced a record realizes, we humans are a fickle lot. No one genre pleases everybody, and no one song pleases everybody. Making good music is hard work, and often unpredictable. The Hendrix theory makes it sound as if our love for music were undiscriminating, as if we listeners were helpless creatures in a snake charmer's bucket. In reality, our love for music is far more individual and idiosyncratic. Some arrangements of notes move us; others don't.

Another common claim is that music evolved because it leads to social bonding. No one would argue that music can't bring people together, but such theories miss the point in at least two different ways: they don't say why patterns of sound organized over time should play any special role in bonding, and they miss the fact that many other things that weren't part of our adaptive heritage – like the relatively modern invention of drinking beer – also induce social cohesion.

♪

Precisely parallel issues arise in all the arts. Why do we love poetry? Sculpture? Painting? Forty-eight-minute crime dramas? For every art, there's an evolutionary theory. But none of them is particularly persuasive. The standard explanation for just about everything in evolution is that we engage in a certain behaviour because it's in the interest of our genes. But most art, whether we are spectators or participants, isn't in the interest of our selfish genes.

For a Picasso or a Dalí, the maths may work out. The genes that underwrote their creative work made them legends, and with fame came considerable access to sexual partners; hence, as judged by the yardstick of evolution – reproductive fitness – they were winners. But for every Picasso or Hendrix there are hundreds or thousands of unsung heroes, poets, and painters who toil in obscurity, perhaps becoming famous after death (like van Gogh), when it is too late to spread their genes, or never getting any recognition at all. For the vast majority of people, investments in the arts are, from a strictly genetic perspective, weak bets. Time spent on art – especially as a spectator, but even as a participant – is time away from gathering food, building shelter, developing new skills, or making babies. People don't indulge in the arts because it's good for their genes; they do it despite their genes.

♪

To paraphrase the great philosopher Waylon Jennings, scientists have been looking for explanations of creativity in all the wrong places. The brain has not evolved a special-purpose music instinct or art instinct, any more than it evolved a special instinct for craving small portable electronic gadgets. Just because we like something doesn't mean we evolved a specific taste for it.

Instead, scientists who have considered the evolution of music and art have often made what I think of as 'the error of the historical present': people tend to automatically assume that what's true now was always true; we see a mountain and think it's been there forever. Contemporary music and modern arts are incredibly compelling to contemporary brains, but the first question is whether the artistic productions of our ancestors would be equally compelling. We may get a kick out of seeing cave paintings, but that doesn't mean your average cave painting would capture a human brain's attention to the same extent as the 3-D computer-generated renderings in *Avatar*. The artistic media that capture our imagination now far exceed anything available to our ancestors.

And that's because over the years, artists, especially commercial artists, have gotten savvier and savvier at understanding what makes human beings tick. Take, for instance, the image of Mickey Mouse. As the late Stephen Jay Gould once pointed out, over the decades Disney has slowly but surely retooled Mickey's image every few years, in ways that might initially escape the eye. Yet the direction of change has always been the same, toward cuter and cuter: less adult, less threatening, more juvenile, more adorable.

My contention is that music is like Mickey: not the direct product of evolution at all, but the product of artists evolving their craft in order to tickle the brain in particular ways. Music, art, and iPhones spread not because we have innate circuitry for funky dance beats or electronic toys but because musicians, artists, and inventors are often uncommonly talented at reverse-engineering the human psyche.

♪

What clicked the morning I was jamming with my bandmates was exactly the thing that so many of those musicians have been striving for: not sexual selection or anything quite so linear, but a state of joyous immersion, wherein one loses all sense of time passing – the wondrous state that the psychologist Mihály Csíkszentmihályi (pronounced 'chick-SENT-me-high-ee') has called 'flow'.

Flow, according to Csíkszentmihályi, is a state of being fully engaged in a challenging activity requiring skill, a merging of action and awareness. It is characterized by a sense of concentration on the task at hand and a sense of control, a loss of self-consciousness, and an altered sense of time.

This defines jamming almost perfectly, and it also, I believe, gives a big clue into the true prehistory of music. Music isn't a special inborn modular mental mechanism; it's a *technology,* refined and developed over the last fifty thousand years, in no small part to maximize flow.

Each new generation of artists craves new ways to broaden the palette, and hence better ways of keeping both listeners and performers entranced, in a state of flow. The technological underpinnings of music are most immediately obvious in the evolution of physical instruments. The piano, for instance, represented a huge advance over its immediate predecessor, the harpsichord. Both instruments used keyboards to span a vast pitch range, but the harpsichord had no dynamics, which is to say that each note could be played either loudly or not at all. The piano, invented by Bartolomeo Cristofori in about 1700, basically added a volume control for each individual note, replacing a set of picks or plectra, often made of bird quills, with a system of padded hammers that could strike a given note loudly, softly, or somewhere in between. Once Cristofori's technology became refined, the piano (short for *pianoforte,* from the Italian terms for 'quiet' and 'loud') almost entirely replaced the harpsichord, much like a new species displacing an old one, because the more variable dynamics of the piano offered the musician a whole new world of expression. New playing techniques developed as well, as musicians learned to exploit the possibilities in varying the loudness of notes and later discovered ways of adding complexity to the parts they played with their left hand; as the psychologists Andreas Lehmann and Anders Ericsson have argued, the level of sophistication of piano players has steadily increased over historical time as new techniques have been developed and disseminated.

Synthesizers and electric guitars (especially in combination with pedals that add complexity to the guitar's intrinsic sound) similarly multiplied the range of options available to musicians, and the microphone opened equally compelling new worlds for vocalists, allowing whispers to be as audible as screams. It is no wonder that all these innovations spread rapidly once developed; they are the musical equivalent of new species, which open new niches and are in some ways better adapted to the environment than many of their predecessors. Ditto for the advent of multitrack recording: once the cat was out of the bag, every musician wanted to experiment with the new possibilities that techniques like layering and overdubs opened up.

♪

Something that is less obvious – but no less important – is that some of the most innovative technologies of music have been intellectual rather than physical. Until roughly A.D. 900, virtually all music was mono-phonic, which is to say it consisted of only a single melody, perhaps sung in unison by multiple singers, as in Gregorian chant; ideas like coun-terpoint (with multiple voices singing distinct lines) had not yet been invented: no barbershop quartets, and no delicate Simon and Garfun-kel harmonies. Around A.D. 900, or perhaps a bit earlier, some musician or set of musicians came to realize that two singers didn't have to always sing the same note at the same time to sound good together. One musi-cian could sing the note C, another could sing G (forming the interval known as the perfect fifth), and the two would sound good together. This observation gave rise to a form of music known as organum, in which two different musicians sing separate (but related) melodic lines. Even then, though, composers tended to stick to only a small subset of possible musical intervals (the perfect fifth and the perfect fourth); such harmonies often sound stilted to modern ears. The notion of a major or minor chord had not yet been invented – that wasn't until around the twelfth century, when composers began to toy with including three distinct voices, including major thirds and minor thirds, the intervals that help define major and minor chords, respectively. Then, and only then, was something we might recognize as modern Western harmony invented.

Eventually, what these composers initially worked out for singers was mapped onto keyboards and other musical instruments. Composers and keyboard players figured out strict rules for which sets of notes (chords) sounded good together and which sounded dissonant, and they figured out rules for which sets of chords sounded good in sequential combination and which ones didn't, giving rise to techniques like three-part harmony and barbershop quartets; virtually all modern music depends on this discovery of how harmony and its attendant units, chord progressions, function. Once that knowledge, a kind of technological innovation, was developed, it spread rapidly throughout the world.

The favour was returned when the notion of a steady percussive beat was imported from Africa into the West. Virtually every song you hear on the radio nowadays combines these two musical techniques – harmony and steady percussion – both of which in essence had to be invented.

To take another example of a technology that is more intellectual than physical, consider the musical form known as the twelve-bar blues, a particular set of chords played in a particular order, which literally couldn't have been invented before the idea of harmony was developed. The twelve-bar structure is found in countless blues songs and more broadly throughout modern music, ranging from the Clash's 'Should I Stay or Should I Go?' to the Beatles' 'Why Don't We Do It in the Road?' and dozens of tunes by Chuck Berry and Eric Clapton.

Part of its popularity is merely historical accident: any convention that is widely known can be useful for musicians, because convention gives immediate common ground for groups of musicians who may not have previously played together. But a considerable part of the popularity of the twelve-bar blues has to do with the way in which the form itself fits in with human psychology. The twelve-bar blues – an invention of the early twentieth century – seems almost perfectly designed to maximize the combination of two psychological rewards: familiarity and novelty (which I will discuss further later).*

None of these modern innovations are strictly necessary; a simple unadorned melody can still be compelling. But on the whole, earlier forms of music that lack harmony – like Gregorian chants – often feel flat to modern observers, like paintings from before the discovery of perspective: worth a look, but not central to most modern people's aesthetic experience. Chants, for instance, rarely get heavy playlist rotation, in part because they don't exploit the flow-inducing properties of harmony. As a result we habituate faster, enjoying them briefly because of their novelty but soon growing tired of them. (The last pop tune to feature Gregorian chant – Enigma's 1990 anthem 'Mea Culpa' – didn't rest on chant unadorned, offering its listeners nothing but voices in unison. Instead, it enhanced the underlying monophonic chant with all sorts of modern production techniques, ranging from close-miked, sexy French-language overdubs to drum machines, sound effects, and electric guitar solos.)

Music may not be improving over the ages in an artistic sense – that's up for debate and a matter of taste. But the craft and the reservoir of techniques constantly improves, in music as in any other technology, and that gives musicians more and more options, which means it is easier to keep listeners in a state of flow.

Inevitably, some new musical inventions turn out to be fads, techniques that remain on the scene for but a brief period of time. But others – like Western harmony, percussive beats, the microphone, the piano,

---

* One might make similar remarks about common song structures like the *aaba* form (Gershwin's 'I Got Rhythm', Jerry Lee Lewis's 'Great Balls of Fire', the Beach Boys' 'Surfer Girl', and, in modified form, the Beatles' 'I Want to Hold Your Hand') or an older form, typically *abaca*, known as the rondo, in which a main theme keeps returning. (The end of the first act of Mozart's *The Marriage of Figaro* is one example.) No one structural form has a lock on all music, in part because we like variation itself, from one song to the next. But alternations of verse and chorus, unfamiliar and familiar, keep listeners in the game and keep dopamine – likely a key player in the neural basis of flow – coursing through our brains.

and the electric guitar – spread rapidly and stick around when invented, and for good reason: they fit well with the psychology of the human mind. What advocates of music as an evolved instinct often forget is that the music we see now – and that seems so compelling to us – is at least as much a production of *cultural* selection as it is of natural selection. New tools and ideas lead to new musical techniques, and the ones that are better (or at least more effective in holding listeners' attention) stick around.

With all of the techniques at the disposal of the modern producer – ranging from the intellectual (like harmony and regular percussion) to the technical (like equalizers, limiters, and compressors, which help clarify and amplify the distinctive sounds of each instrument) to the logistical (like click tracks, which keep musicians tightly and pleasurably in time) to the sonic (like synthesized sounds, distortion pedals, and techniques like echo, delay, and reverb) – we can't help but get into the groove.

ONSTAGE

Face-to-Face with My Fears

Before we know it, it's time for Final Assembly, wherein the camp's director, Tobias, teaches us some rules of live performance. People with Fender guitars should set their pickups to notch two or four so there won't be lots of buzz; don't use your whammy bars, or you might go out of tune. You're welcome to jump around onstage, but only if it won't mess up your playing. (I planned to stand rock still, lest I lose my timing.)*

When Ryan tells me 'The longer I wait, the nervouser I get', I know exactly what he means.

♪

For some musicians, stage fright can come to define an entire career. Steely Dan's Donald Fagen suffered from it famously (as did his mother,

---

* In hindsight, keeping still may have been a mistake. Many musicians are better off tapping a foot in rhythm with the music, rather than standing still. But tapping itself requires practice, especially for those who are congenitally rhythmically impaired, as I am, and at the time, tapping just seemed like one more thing to have to keep track of, another demand on an already overloaded brain.

suggesting a possible genetic connection), and Barbra Streisand, Carly Simon, and XTC's Andy Partridge have all battled stage fright as well. Whole books, such as *The Inner Game of Music*, have been written about how to cope with it, so that musicians can play as well onstage as they can offstage in practice. I knew from my teenage years, when I was a relatively serious amateur juggler, that I could never do my best tricks in front of a crowd; even a tiny audience of a few friends can be nerve-racking.

The youngest children often feel no fear. One friend of mine had her first recital when she was three and a half and smiled the whole time, even as she bungled the piece. When she sat down, her mother asked why she was smiling, when it was pretty obvious to both that the performance was not as good as it could have been. My friend's response? 'My teacher told me, "If you just smile, no one will know."' It's only later, towards adolescence, that the sense of fear and mortification sets in.

Stage fright (or performance anxiety) stems from a mix of different factors, physiological and psychological. On the one hand, getting ready for a performance tends to elevate heart rate; on the other hand, different people interpret that heart rate in different ways. Performers who are less prone to stage fright seem to use that elevated heart rate as a spur to better performance. In performers who are more prone to stage fright, the physiological state of arousal sometimes gets interpreted as fear ('If I blow this recital, my career is ruined').

Nowadays, it's not uncommon for professional musicians to take cardiac medications known as beta-blockers, which were originally designed to combat high blood pressure. These drugs reduce the physiological symptoms, and the psychological symptoms may diminish along with the decreased arousal. The best long-term solution is likely practice: the more often one is onstage, the more predictable everything is, and the less one's fears seem realistic.

Concretely, stage fright is a problem not just because it is unpleasant but because it can inhibit performance. As the body tenses, it becomes more difficult to maintain fluid rhythms and harder to recall memorized sections of music. In my own case, nothing was really at stake – no chance that I was about to ruin a lifetime as a professional musician – but twenty minutes of waiting in the wings was certainly enough to give me a taste of what professionals are up against.

♪

At long last, the audience was seated, sound checks were complete, and Tobias took the stage, introducing himself as camp director and making some mercifully brief remarks about the camp itself.

Next he announced our band, Rush Hour, and the curtains opened.

As the only person in our band with experience speaking in front of crowds, I earned the right and responsibility of introducing the band. 'Ladies and gentlemen,' I shouted, in my best P. T. Barnum voice, 'if you check your watches, you will see that it is 5:00 p.m., and that means it's time for . . . RUSH HOUR!'

And that was Greer's cue. We're off! He plays a few measures of his elegant classical piece, and then (all according to plan) Riley bursts in with eight loud beats on his drums. Beat nine comes, Riley's cymbal is right on time, and the rest of us join in. Twice through the verses, and then everybody else drops out, and it's my turn to play my little bass fill. Two more verses, and then it's on to our menacing chorus. Greer's piano solo (accompanied only by Riley on softly hit cymbals) is next; then Ryan joins in for a verse. At the start of the next verse Sarah and I return together. Twice more through the verse, twice more through the chorus, and a drum solo for Riley, who winds up and holds his sticks high to signal our big finish: everyone hits a loud G chord, and we're done!

Everything has gone according to plan, and we get a thundering round of applause. We're a real rock band now!

When the concert ends, I hunt out my bandmates, and we pose for

♪

band pictures. On the way out I feel a particular mixture of elation and sadness that I haven't felt since graduating from university. I'm often among the first people to leave social events, but today I'm the last. I keep my own parents waiting as I say good-bye to the greatest bunch of eleven-year-olds I've ever known.

THE WORST SONG
IN THE WORLD

What Makes a Good Song?

Having survived the week at camp and the creation, practice, and performance of our own original piece, I was starting to think about the nature of songs. I wasn't ready to write a piece entirely on my own, but I began to study some of the best examples – and some of the worst.

What goes into making a song? And why do some work better than others? I'd always been a kind of passive listener, knowing what I liked without knowing why; a year into my journey I wanted to go deeper in my understanding. I had started asking my music teachers questions and started reading articles on the psychology of pleasure and aesthetics.

At around the same time, Microsoft introduced a new computer program, Songsmith, that would allegedly help anyone write his or her own songs. The idea behind Songsmith was simple: user sings, program creates backing track. Presto, voilà. Pop tunes are made.

Or at least that's how the program was supposed to work.

In reality, Songsmith turned out to be a total flop, ripped to shreds by everyone from *Entertainment Weekly* magazine to the *New York Times*. YouTube is crawling with Songsmith-created disasters: 'Roxanne' remade with Sting's vocals, steel drums, and an insipid, vaguely Hawaiian-sounding backbeat (over 571,000 views and counting); Ozzy Osbourne's 'Crazy Train' redone as a truly unlistenable polka (over 150,000 views).

From a technical standpoint, Songsmith's songs make perfect sense. A sophisticated algorithm derives the pitch contour of a user's vocals and layers on top a set of chords and rhythms that are musically consistent with the user's inputs. Chords and bass lines are chosen to be harmonious with the melody, according to principles that any first-year music theory student would recognize. By rights, Songsmith's songs ought to sound good. But they frequently don't, and I soon began to wonder why. What makes a good song, and what was Songsmith missing?

♪

In fairness, Songsmith's compositions don't sound truly awful, just regrettably bad.

The title of this chapter (The Worst Song in the World) comes not from Songsmith but from an allusion to an art project of a slightly different title by the conceptual artists Vitaly Komar and Alexander Melamid and the violinist and composer Dave Soldier (who happens to spend his days as a neuroscientist at Columbia University). Komar and Melamid had received a ton of attention in the mid-1990s when they used survey data to create what they described, tongue lodged firmly in cheek, as the 'most wanted' and 'least wanted' paintings. America's 'most wanted' painting, for instance, consisted of an autumnal landscape dotted with wild animals, a family enjoying the outdoors, President George Washington, and the colour blue (a recurrent theme in virtually every country surveyed).

Following a similar survey method, Soldier set out to find 'the most unwanted music', determining based on a series of questionnaires that it would be a composition that is over 25 minutes long, veers wildly between loud and quiet sections, between fast and slow tempos, and features timbres of extremely high and low pitch, with each dichotomy presented in abrupt transition. The most unwanted orchestra was determined to be large, and features the accordion and bagpipe (which tie at 13% as the most unwanted instrument), banjo, flute, tuba, harp, organ, synthesizer (the only instrument that appears in both the most wanted and most unwanted ensembles). An operatic soprano raps and sings atonal music, advertising jingles, political slogans, and 'elevator' music, and a children's choir sings jingles and holiday songs. The most unwanted subjects for lyrics are cowboys and holidays, and the most unwanted listening circumstances are involuntary exposure to commercials and elevator music.

He then proceeded to recruit a crack team of professional musicians with whom he composed an excruciating – yet strangely bearable – piece along exactly these lines (which you can hear on his Web site and which aired on America's National Public Radio).

The 'most wanted' properties, meanwhile, consisted of 'music of moderate duration (approximately 5 minutes), moderate pitch range, moderate tempo, and moderate to loud volume' – everything we have come to expect from pop music. Soldier's tongue may have been lodged firmly in cheek, but his results – and their curious resemblance to the hallmarks of pop music – do raise a question about whether our aesthetic experience can be captured with scientific laws.

♪

In the field of screenwriting, perhaps no book is more notorious than Robert McKee's *Story,* which suggests that a surprisingly large part of the art of screenwriting can be reduced to a simple set of principles. Writers I know either love it or hate it: one playwright friend of mine adores *Story,* another despises it with all her heart. The filmmaker and screenwriter Charlie Kaufman (*Being John Malkovich, Eternal Sunshine of the Spotless Mind*) found the whole notion so ridiculous he made McKee and his principles the butt of a 114-minute joke (otherwise known as the film *Adaptation*).

According to McKee, plots should be divided into devices known as 'beats', reversals of fortune, fake endings, inciting incidents, and so forth. In his books and well-attended seminars, McKee discusses a dozen or so such techniques, each designed to carefully maintain the viewer's interest.

Perhaps none of his techniques are necessary (*Koyaanisqatsi*, for example, violates them all), and they certainly aren't sufficient (only one of McKee's own screenplays was ever made into a film, and that one was for TV, not the big screen). And they aren't going to tell anybody how to come up with the sorts of clever plot twists that make films like *The Sixth Sense, Memento*, and *The Usual Suspects* so memorable. And as McKee himself would point out, his strategies are geared more towards commerce than art. Yet his remarks have an element of truth.

Can music be similarly deconstructed? Are there really principles that can explain what music we like and don't like?

♪

The first thing to say about this question is that what we like starts with inherent properties of a given song (such as its melodies, its rhythms, and its lyrics), but many other factors matter, too.

One of the biggest factors is mere exposure. Simply listening to a song has a tendency, other things being equal, to make us like it more, an illustration of a broader phenomenon known as 'liking for familiarity'. One of the first studies to document this phenomenon had subjects look very briefly at a set of faux Chinese characters – just two seconds each – and later asked the subjects to judge the beauty of a larger set of ideographs, some of which they'd seen briefly, others of which were new. Brief encounters proved potent; characters that subjects had seen before systematically got higher ratings. Since then, hundreds of experiments have replicated and extended these original results, with virtually every kind of stimulus you could imagine, including music. In the 1950s, guys with paper bags full of cash used to pay off DJs to play their songs; it might have been illegal, but it was almost certainly money well spent. Songs can become hits only if people hear them, and the more they hear them, the more they tend to like them.

Another important factor may be when we first hear a song. Many of us tend to like the music we hear as teenagers more than anything else. As Robert Sapolsky put it, 'Not a whole lot of seventeen-year-olds are tuning in to the Andrews Sisters, not a lot of Rage Against the Machine is being played in retirement communities, and the biggest fans of sixty non-stop minutes of James Taylor are starting to wear relaxed jeans.'

Is rebellion a key factor? The economist Tyler Cowen once quipped, 'The problem with old music is simple. Somebody else already liked it.' But in the course of writing this book, I have seen any number of twelve-year-olds rocking out to tunes by Led Zeppelin, and nowadays it's not uncommon to see whole families at the shows of megastars like Bruce Springsteen and U2. Music by Bach and Beethoven stayed in vogue for hundreds of years (and remains popular in some parts of the world, especially where rock and roll is less accessible as an alternative and where music education is still robust). The fact that today's children so often listen to different music than their parents do may stem more from a blossoming of alternatives – more music is available now than ever before – and the simple fact that children typically have a lot more time than adults to listen to new music. Today's kids (especially the kind I met at rock-and-roll camp) frequently soak up both the best songs from their parents' era *and* whatever is hot at the moment. It's not that kids are rebellious; it's that they are sponges: it's U2 and the Flavour of the Month, not either-or.

On a broader scale, context plays a critical role. A given song may fit perfectly into a film yet sound overly sweet when heard on its own. Someone with no background in classical music may have trouble grasping what makes one sonata better than the next, and some albums, like Lou Reed's *Metal Machine Music,* are despised at their release and only decades later hailed as enormously influential. The author Jason Hartley has riffed about how some artists are too 'advanced' for their listeners; his 'central premise is that artists like Bob Dylan and Lou Reed didn't suddenly start to stink in the 1980s but had, instead, advanced beyond most people's comprehension. If an artist like Reed was ahead of his time in the 1960s, the theory goes, it is plausible that he was still ahead of his time in the 1980s, when most people mistakenly thought he "lost it".' Whatever one makes of mid-80s Dylan and Reed, there's little doubt that a song's potential for commercial success relates in part to the musical background of potential listeners.

♪

To make things even more complicated, no one song can satisfy every listener, because different types of people listen to music for different reasons. One recent study found that a considerable amount of the differences between individuals' musical taste could be predicted by their personalities, with each of the 'Big Five' personality traits (extroversion, agreeableness, conscientiousness, emotional stability, and openness) playing an important role. People who score high on openness, for example, tend to like music that is reflective and complex, while extroverts have a greater tendency than introverts to like music that is energetic and rhythmic. In this way, the value of a song derives partly from the temperament of the listener. Novices, meanwhile, may be driven more by the emotional content of a song, whereas experts may listen more analytically. Are we listening for a simple groove to dance along with or the rarefied pleasure of understanding an abstract conceptual innovation? How a song strikes us is in part a function of what we are listening *for*.

It's also a function of what our *friends* listen to. A couple years ago the sociologist Duncan Watts contrived to give participants on the Web the opportunity to listen to and download original music, in an experimental design that manipulated what the participants knew about what other people were listening to. The coolest part of the study faked out one group of Web site visitors by flipping a control group's rankings for how often particular songs were heard. Song No. 1, 'She Said', by the Parker Theory, actually listened to a total of 128 times, was portrayed as song No. 48, with 9 listens so far, while song No. 48, 'Florence', by Post Break Tragedy, actually listened to 9 times, became listed as the No. 1 song, with an alleged 128 listens. Instead of trusting their own ears, listeners flocked to the songs with artificially inflated popularity scores.

That's the bad news. The good news is that over time, at least one song – 'She Said', the song judged No. 1 by the independent group – started to recover. Social pressure is powerful, but not absolute. If a song is really truly exceptional, it just might make it to the top no matter what.

♪

Thinking about that study, I can't help but think of 'Stairway to Heaven.' As the lead guitarist, Jimmy Page, has observed, audiences were giving 'Stairway to Heaven' a standing ovation in concert long before they had ever heard a recording of it – there was no liking for familiarity, no social pressure because fans knew their friends liked it. The song just worked. At the opposite extreme of the spectrum is the brute fact that most songs – even those released by major labels – flop. Marketing and social factors aside, a turkey will always remain a turkey. The way in which a song falls upon our ears and brains is something that money just can't buy. At the end of the day, after personality, marketing, and cultural context are all factored out, there is still something about the music itself that remains. Why do we like music so much? And what makes one song work better than the next?

♪

Some of the pleasure we get from music can derive from a single note, like the long reverberations of a single bang on a metallic gong; in the right circumstance, that resonance can bring a sublime, almost unearthly sense of connectedness to the universe. Conversely, even a single note played on a cheap synthesizer may sound unpleasant, unpolished, or even downright abrasive. We generally prefer lush notes filled with resonance to simple sine waves produced by old-fashioned synthesizers, possibly because notes on musical instruments sound more like the sounds of nature. The psychologist, music writer, and former rock producer Dan Levitin told me that he once spent an entire summer working on nothing but playing whole notes on his saxophone, because as he, and many other musicians, realized, the beauty of a work as a whole must begin with the beauty of its elements.

As Levitin has noted, in contemporary music, the focus of production is often as much on timbre (of individual notes and of collections of instruments, often synthetic) as on classical elements such as the main melody and its accompanying harmony. Why? Perhaps because nowadays it is easier to create sounds that truly sound new than to create melodies or harmonies that break genuinely new ground, and the songs that stand out are the ones most likely to be remembered (and purchased). If you can find a new sound, you've already taken a giant step towards a hit record. Just think of the crashing chord at the beginning of the Beatles' 'Hard Day's Night', the forty-second E major chord at the end of their 'Day in the Life', the creaky-coffin sound that opens Michael Jackson's song 'Thriller', or the subway-like screeches that open Moby's song 'Extreme Ways' (theme to the Jason Bourne films).

Single notes and chords can only get an artist so far, though. A resonant gong may thrill for a moment or two, but no one note could ever sustain anyone's attention indefinitely. No matter how captivating any individual note or chord might be, sooner or later the listener yearns for more. Ultimately, music is not so much about single notes as about *streams* of notes, organized into larger wholes.

The minute we move from one note to two – whether they are played at the same time (harmonically) or in sequence (melodically) – the listener searches for a relation between the two. Even untrained listeners, for example, begin to try to figure out (unconsciously) what key a piece is in.

An analysis of a database of hundreds of song melodies taken from ten different cultures shows that melodies aren't random, with any one just as plausible as any other; instead, certain tendencies seem widespread, from one culture to the next. Most melodic steps in most songs most of the time, for example, are small. Small jumps – those of just a note or two on the piano keyboard – vastly outnumber larger leaps. There are exceptions, to be sure – like Swiss yodelling and the vertiginous jumps up and down in the Queen of the Night's solo 'Der Hölle Rache' in Mozart's *Magic Flute* – but such exceptions are relatively rare.

Likewise, most notes in most melodies most of the time tend to be 'in key'; a song in C major will consist mainly of the white notes on a piano keyboard, with stops on black notes relatively infrequent and typically only for brief periods.

If I were to whack randomly on the piano, eliciting considerable dissonance, you might get a kind of rarefied intellectual pleasure from hearing me break the rules, but at the end of the day you probably wouldn't be all that into it. There are subgenres of music like 'noisecore' and what I jokingly refer to as 'vacuum cleaner music', made most prominent by the band Merzbow, but it is relatively unlikely that

Merzbow will ever outsell the more melodic if arguably less original Kenny G.

Still, a little bit of dissonance is fine (like blue notes in the midst of a blues song), and appetites for dissonance have increased over historical time. Familiarity breeds affection not just for particular songs, but for styles and musical conventions. Composers in the Middle Ages, for example, strenuously avoided the dissonant-sounding interval known as the tritone, but nowadays millions hear tritones every day, as the opening credits to *The Simpsons* leap from A to D-sharp from 'the' to the first syllable of 'Simpsons'. The first two syllables in 'Maria', in the musical *West Side Story,* represent another example, as do the *oo-ee* of a European police siren and the start-up sound on the old Macintosh II. (There's also differing sensitivity to dissonance between individuals, with the differences sharper for musicians than for nonmusicians.)

♪

Why does the untutored human mind prefer consonance to dissonance? The original and most common theory goes back to Pythagoras, who noticed that the ratio between the frequencies of any given pair of notes was more elegant in consonant intervals such as perfect fifths than in dissonant pairs of notes. As a rough matter, one can order the intervals from most consonant (perfect fourths and fifths, for example) to least consonant (minor seconds and tritones), and the correlation with the simplicity of the ratios seems strong.

But Pythagoras was a better mathematician than he was a psychologist, and he didn't realize a perfect fifth can still sound pretty good even when it is slightly out of tune, in which case the ratio starts to become rather hairy. What does this tell us?

Pythagoras was on the right track, but for the wrong reasons. He imagined a kind of mystical beauty inherent in perfect ratios, but what actually makes harmonic notes sound good together is not some physical property of vibrations per se. Instead, listeners tend to assimilate slightly out-of-tune notes into the categories they know best. But that calculation itself depends on the vocabulary of musical elements that a listener has developed, which is presumably part of why experienced musicians are more sensitive to consonance than nonmusicians.

As the music scholar David Huron put it, an out-of-tune note, or a dissonant chord, is like an out-of-focus picture: the brain struggles to make sense of the underlying scene. One can learn to love dissonance, much as one can learn to love the fuzziness of Impressionist paintings, but other things being equal, the brain's natural preference is for that which it can most easily make sense of.

In the 1920s, the composer Arnold Schoenberg tried to challenge that, creating deliberately dissonant music consisting of 'tone rows', which were sequences of twelve notes in which every note, black and white, was used equally often, with the intention of breaking the listener's reliance on tonal centre. In my view, Schoenberg's experiments were noble but unsuccessful, and, as such, instructive about just how flexible (or not) the mind's ear can be. Many academics see Schoenberg as the pivotal composer of the twentieth century, but in truth few ordinary people enjoy his work. On a recent trip to the Haus der Musik museum in Vienna, I saw room after room devoted to some of Vienna's most famous composers – Haydn, Mozart, Strauss, Beethoven, and Mahler – each one proudly playing the music of the city's native sons. Poor Schoenberg got only shared quarters, a third of a tiny room. And his room, unlike the others, was silent, presumably because the museum's curators thought that tone rows would scare away the tourists.

This is not to say that dissonant music, such as that composed by Schoenberg and his contemporaries, is without value, but it is perhaps better considered an acquired taste than something that comes naturally to the human ear. One of the twentieth-century composers who followed Schoenberg, the late Milton Babbitt, notoriously wrote a manifesto called 'Who Cares If You Listen?' (allegedly titled by his editor) in which he lobbied for a kind of specialist music that might be appreciated only by a tiny community of experts, presumably on the basis of a set of skills that could be learned only through hard work. Nothing is wrong with Babbitt's notion – in any art, certain works are better understood by insiders, and specialists are entitled to their fun – but any efforts at a psychology of music have to start with an understanding of that which is most naturally appreciated.

♪

Consonance and dissonance are only colours in a palette, where the real concern is the shape of the artwork as a whole. The French composer Edgard Varèse once defined music as 'organized sound', a definition that may be both too broad (does the repeated tapping of a sewing machine count?) and too narrow (how about the random notes of a John Cage composition?). Cage also challenged our definitions by creating pieces like *4'33"*, which consisted of four minutes and thirty-three seconds of silence. Whether or not *4'33"* or Cage's random pieces should really count as music (or just conceptual art) may depend on your own personal definition; few people would find either to be especially pleasing. They might both be technically considered to be music, if your defi-⊠ nitions are liberal enough, but neither *4'33"* nor Cage's random pieces contain the essence of what makes music compelling: the juxtaposition of two ostensibly contradictory forces, novelty and familiarity.

Cage's randomly generated pieces, for example, have a certain kind of novelty; by definition, each new note is independent from the last, hence there is no way to predict what comes next. But they altogether lack repetition, a technique that is startlingly common in almost all other music. In song after song, in both popular music and classical pieces, small elements and larger ones get repeated over and over, so much so that music notation is itself filled with a whole slew of symbols like vertical bars (which indicate when sections should be repeated) and the notation DC (which means repeat from the beginning, derived from the phrase *da capo,* Italian for 'from the head'). One of the most important figures in the history of music theory, Heinrich Schenker, once wrote, 'Our understanding of musical technique would have advanced much further if only someone had asked: Where, when, and how did music first develop its most striking and distinct characteristic – repetition?'

It is in fact startling the extent to which music, relative to other arts, overflows with repetition. To be sure, poets sometimes include repeated phrases, but it is rare to see repetition in prose, and films repeat scenes sparingly if at all. A nonfiction author who repeats a sentence is likely to be scolded by his editor; a playwright who repeats his dialogue is either David Mamet (forging a distinctive style) or a fool. Few people pay to hear actors say the same line twice, much less if it's literally repeated word for word.* But when is the last time you heard a pop song that didn't repeat its chorus?

A rare example that violates that rule, in which the lyrics never repeat – no chorus, no refrain, no nothing – might be Dylan's 'Boots of Spanish Leather', but even there the melody and chord progression (sequence of chords) do repeat; the same can be said for Billie Holiday's powerful version of 'Strange Fruit'. Rock and pop songs typically have chord progressions that repeat every eight or twelve measures, often with considerable repetition within those measures. Songs and chord progressions in which there isn't some immediate repetition are called through-composed – the Beatles' 'Happiness Is a Warm Gun' is a rare example – but one hardly needs a list for songs *with* repetition. Repetition, both in song structure and in listening, is a central part of music.

Still, repetition on its own would be dull and has to be balanced by

---

* Repetition sometimes works in poetry, but rarely in prose. The musical provocateur John Cage once wrote a lecture in which a single page was repeated fourteen times, with the refrain 'If anybody is sleepy let him go to sleep' (Cage, 1961). Midway through, the artist Jean Reynal stood up and screamed, 'John, I dearly love you, but I can't bear another minute.'

♪

some other element. Listen to the music to the Ramones' 'I Wanna Be Sedated' without the vocals and you might be tempted to commit hari-kari. With the added texture and variation of the lyrics, the song becomes engaging, even for folks like me who don't particularly want to like it. I recently had the pleasure of seeing Joey Ramone's younger brother – Mickey Leigh – in concert, in a tiny venue, with not more than thirty or forty people present. Most of the songs were covers, in tribute to Leigh's late brother. Try as I did to hate the lyrics ('I wanna be sedated/I wanna be sedated'), I couldn't help but be carried along. Likewise, 'Blitzkrieg Bop' delivers what it promises, driving the listener headlong into an almost overwhelming compulsion to dance. There's no point in listening to the song while sitting down and no ability to resist when you're standing up. The primary tool of 'Blitzkrieg Bop' is overwhelming repetition – simple guitar riffs delivered at mind-numbing speed, the rhythm part a steady diet of eighth notes, entirely downstrokes, forming a repetitive upstroke-free pattern that no folk guitarist would be caught dead playing, elegance traded for insistence. Yet it works. The lyrics – three verses and three repetitions of the 'Hey ho, let's go' refrain – are hardly compelling ('They're piling in the back seat/They're generating steam heat') but manage to convey just enough counterpoint to make the whole thing work.

Symphonies begin with themes that modulate through keys and movements, pop songs pepper verses with choruses and refrains. Sometimes guitar riffs get repeated over and over ('vamping', in the lingo of musicians), but generally there is a soloist providing variation that runs above that background, lest the song sound monotonous. Philip Glass's minimalist compositions (such as the soundtrack to *Koyaanisqatsi*) deviate from much of the classical music that preceded them, with much less obvious movement than, say, the Romantic-era compositions that his work seems to rebel against, yet his works, too, consist not only of extensive repetition but also of constant (though subtle) variation. Virtually every song you've ever heard consists of exactly that: themes that recur over and over, overlaid with variations.

Vocal music tends to be more popular than instrumental music (in both the pop and the classical worlds) in part because of the immediacy of lyrics and in part because of the expressiveness of the human voice – but also in part because vocals (even when in a foreign language) add a new dimension of repetition and variation, a new way of keeping one thing constant (melody) while overlaying variation (lyrics) – and novelty conveys its own separate reward. Synthesizers and drum samplers may have become widespread for a similar reason. By enriching the sonic palette, new technologies expand the ways in which an intrinsically repetitive theme can be layered with colour and novelty, allowing the brain to collect two rewards – novelty and familiarity – at the very same time. If I had to sum up human music for intergalactic travellers in a single concise phrase, it might be this: 'Repetition, with variation.'

♪

All that repetition (feathered with variation or otherwise) would likely be considerably more annoying if our memories were better. If listeners could commit every detail of a song to memory the first time through, they might not want to hear it repeated eight times. But most of us can't remember the exact details of a melody on a first hearing, just the outlines, and one recent study found that many listeners don't recognize repetitions, even when asked to listen for them explicitly. The first time we hear a song, it's as if we've formed a fuzzy picture in our heads; the second time, the picture becomes a little less fuzzy; the third or fourth time through, we might actually remember the melody but still revel in textures and intricacies we didn't notice the first few times through. Experimental research suggests that (depending on the song) it can take dozens of listens before we become truly bored.

Although people often believe that music is easier to remember than other things, there are no real data to support that assertion, at least for nonmusicians. Under careful laboratory conditions, strings of musical notes are harder for nonmusicians to remember than carefully matched lists of letters (R, C, J, E, L, and so on), and arbitrary letters themselves are pretty hard to remember, relative to, say, coherent sentences. Moreover, recent studies suggest that auditory memory in general is significantly less powerful than visual memory. As one researcher put it, 'The "special" power of music as a mnemonic device may be that it fosters excessive rehearsal' – and not that we are intrinsically good at it. In other words, naive listeners tend to remember songs well only because they listen to them a lot. And, ironically, one of the reasons that we listen to songs a lot is because they are hard to remember.

♪

Oddly, one musical ingredient that doesn't matter much, most of the time, is overall order and cohesion. Classical analyses of music are replete with laudatory discussions of how this or that composer has beautifully organized the global structure of this or that sonata symphony. Beethoven, for example, is often praised for his realization that the weight in a sonata could be placed in the final movement rather than in the initial movement, so as to define a narrative structure that culminates at the end of the piece. 'If the movements of a great sonata are switched around', enthused the *Britannica Book of Music,* 'the results will be musically inferior.'

That thought may initially seem convincing, or even majestic, but on close inspection it turns out to have little to do with empirical reality. Many listeners – even trained listeners – are often remarkably indifferent to the overall structure of a piece. Even some of the most revered musical arrangements are not immune to this indifference. One psychologist took a series of piano sonatas and string quartets and rear-ranged the order of the movements of each of the series; listeners didn't care. The subjects liked both the scrambled versions and the originals – with no difference between the two. A later study randomized the order of Bach's *Goldberg Variations* (often associated with Glenn Gould) and found similar results. Yet another study tried carving musical com-positions by Bach, Mozart, and Schoenberg into finer slices – about six seconds each – and found, yet again, that nonmusician listeners didn't really care if the pieces were randomly permuted (although they could tell the difference between more and less expressive performances). Yet another study went a step further and made new (classical) pieces by hybridizing sections of three different piano solos from Shostakovich's *Fantastic Dance 3;* after just a few listenings, subjects (including some who were university students with ten years of musical training) actu-ally preferred the bastardized combinations to the original, more cohe-sive pieces. Our sense of a composition largely inheres in how we feel about the individual parts; narrative arcs are almost always essential in drama but (unless there are lyrics involved) often less essential in music.

♪

All of this is, I suspect, again symptomatic of human memory limita-tions. We live, to a remarkable degree, in the present; what happened thirty seconds ago is already rapidly fading from our memory (or at least rapidly becomes harder for us to retrieve). Nicholas Cook tested this fairly explicitly by having people listen to passages from composers such as Beethoven and Liszt that had been doctored so that they ended in keys that were inconsistent with their beginnings. If the key changes happened within a short window, people noticed them, but if a piece gradually shifted from its moorings over a span of a couple of minutes, hardly anyone noticed. (Perhaps this is why nobody seems to mind when a pop song switches from a verse to a bridge that is musically distinct.)

As long as the last few seconds seem coherent, that's all that matters. In this respect, I am reminded of optical illusions such as the Escher-like devil's fork, a picture that at first glance appears perfectly ordinary.

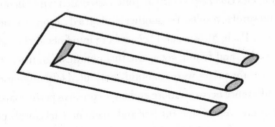

Only with focused concentration does the viewer realize that something is amiss, with figure and ground hopelessly confused. As long as the local bits look okay, we fail to realize the incoherence of the whole. (The same thing can happen in language, as when we initially fail to notice the oddness in a sentence like 'More people have been to Russia than I have.' Each pair of words makes sense taken individually, but the whole does not.)

Our tastes in music, as in every other aspect of life, come from the organization of our brains: how our brains interpret the auditory world, how our reward systems work, and what we can remember.

From the outset, the automatic song-generating program Microsoft Songsmith was probably destined to fail. As a social matter, the only thing that might be more likely to provoke an us-versus-them reaction than music generated by a machine would be music generated by a corporate machine. If the songs the program produced were repackaged as the fruits of a teen band, people might have rather more tolerance (or at least sympathy). And the Songsmith parodies themselves are easy for a clever critic to make. Virtually every cover that anyone makes is an uphill battle, because the original version of a well-known song always has a built-in advantage of incumbency, born from our inherent liking for familiarity; interlopers proceed at great peril. A few covers succeed, but most don't.

On the technical side, what the program has going for it is a sophisticated analysis of how melodies relate to chord progressions and a detailed database of what is statistically common in Western music. But the programmers who created it were focused too much on the statistics of music and not enough on the underlying psychology. Larger structural questions about repetition, novelty, and variation simply weren't on the agenda. Disaster may have been inevitable.

Despite all this, I actually think Songsmith is a good idea, if poorly executed. The truth is that modern musicians use computerized tools all the time, from drum machines to complex software. Programs like the sheet music editor Finale can automatically generate four-part harmonies. Pop music producers routinely use programs like Logic Pro, which includes among its vast array of musical tools a so-called humanizing function that can add variation and random noise to drum sequences in just the right proportion to keep the listener engaged. Another program, called Band-in-a-Box, has been used for years to create quick and dirty orchestrations (which are often hand-tweaked afterwards).

The problem with Songsmith is not in using machines as tools, nor in its noble intention of bringing rank amateurs into the fold, but rather in the particular way in which the machine was built. Although there are no absolute rules in music, a song that disobeys most conventions (flouting predictability) is likely to fail, but so too is a song that adds nothing original to the existing canon; by sticking slavishly to the statistics of its database, Songsmith ignored novelty and hence missed half of what drives our love of music.

♪

In the history of scientific and philosophical discourse on the arts, music has often gotten the short end of the stick. For example, the great German philosopher Immanuel Kant, arguably the most significant philosopher since Plato and Aristotle, talked about a hierarchy of arts and placed music near the bottom, since it 'plays merely with sensations'. And the psychologist Steven Pinker famously (and controversially) likened music to 'auditory cheesecake'. The philosopher of music Peter Kivy has described music as 'sonic wallpaper'.

Kant's argument was that music (particularly instrumental music) had no intrinsic content, whereas a novel or a fable might supply vivid ways of encoding vicarious lessons ('Be careful what you wish for'). Music without lyrics isn't (in any obvious way) about anything in particular. For Kant, this left music as a sterile exercise, decoration for decoration's sake, and nothing more.

In the revised edition of his book *How the Mind Works,* Pinker writes that hardly anything he has ever written has gotten more flak than his suggestion that music might not be a direct product of natural selection.

Yet we have already seen at least two good reasons to believe that Pinker is right: there doesn't appear to be any specific neural module devoted to music (as you might expect if music had been specifically tuned by natural selection), and only a small part of the machinery that allows us to become musical seems to be innate in the first place. Virtually all humans can learn to appreciate video games, but that doesn't mean our ancestors evolved a specific taste for *Pong*. Why should music be any different?

I'm with Pinker on this one. But his characterization of music does raise a question: If music is dessert for the brain, why does it taste so good? Why is music virtually ubiquitous, when many other arts have a smaller presence in daily life?

♪

In some respects, music is quite similar to other arts. There is, for example, in all arts an affiliative component: other things being equal, if you like the paintings I do, we're more likely to be friends, and ditto for sculpture, film, and music. The human mind longs to divide between us and them, and each art gives us a fresh dimension in which to distinguish friends from foes.

In other ways, music might be seen as a step ahead of other arts. As the record producer Roger Greenawalt put it, 'Many musicians don't realize that they are floating in an ocean of math [but] music is the most mathematical of all arts', a calculus of repeatable motifs and patterns that can be embroidered into a fabric of novelty.

As Greenawalt points out, there can be music without melody or harmony, but there is almost no music without rhythm – one of the most overtly mathematical elements of any art, as beats are divided into halves and quarters, eighths and sixteenths. Beyond this lattice of fractions lies an even more complex algebra of transposition and harmony.

Music also unfolds over time. Paintings and photographs may be compelling for an instant, but few static arts sustain interest over time. People are willing to pay so much for views of lakes or oceans in part because they are always changing; any static view eventually loses its hold. Moving scenery keeps us engaged, and music is always moving.

Meanwhile, as one recent study has confirmed, at least two distinct neural systems contribute to the dopamine that is released when we listen to music. As I have been suggesting, music allows us to get rewards for both novelty *and* prediction simultaneously, in a single package. Repeat a melody and the brain pats itself on the back: I've predicted something correctly. Now vary the lyrics at the same time: a reward for novelty. Composers have an almost infinite supply of tools for tapping into two of the most important yet complementary systems that drive human reward simultaneously: the one that rewards us for making successful predictions, and the one that rewards us for discovering something new. In any given song, you will see repeated elements, be they melodies or harmonies or lyrics, and you will see those elements juxtaposed against variations occurring over the same expanse of time. As a temporal art, music, like film, is in good position to deliver both rewards.

At the same time, the intrinsic difficulty we have in remembering music in full detail helps keep music perpetually new. Especially since the Middle Ages, Western music has been filled with rich harmonies and complex orchestrations that cannot be apprehended in one glance, and the same has become increasingly true of rock and roll, especially in studio work, which is often filled with overdubs. As the music writer Rikky Rooksby pointed out, in his insightful *How to Write Songs on Guitar*:

> One of the most powerful devices for making a song commercial is counter-melody. A counter-melody is sung by a second voice (or backing vocalists), sometimes using different words. A good counter-melody can not only liven up the repetition of a verse but introduce devastating strength to the chorus.

If there is just a single melodic line, it is easy for a musically adept listener to replay the song in his or her own mind; add a second hook and the listener wants to go out and buy the record, to re-create what is too hard to reconstruct on his own. (Simon and Garfunkel used the technique frequently, perhaps most effectively in 'Scarborough Fair'; so-called thug-love duets, like the Method Man/Mary J. Blige collaboration 'I'll Be There for You/You're All I Need to Get By', also elicit compelling contrapuntal effects.)

Finally, there is a connection between music and motion: music, unlike painting or photography, draws in listeners, making them want to dance or tap along, perhaps because of the automatic tendency to bridge between senses, and because the perception of rhythm appears to be directly tied to neural machinery involved in sequencing motor (muscle) actions. That physicality makes music especially immersive. Watching a sport can have a similar quality, but few other arts do, and none (save dance, with its obvious relation to music) so consistently combine music's physicality with its rich formal structure and extended temporal dynamism.

♪

One of the most important modern theorists of aesthetics, the go-to academic source after Kant, is the Prague-born philosopher and critic of music Eduard Hanslick, who wrote in 1854:

> Music is a kind of kaleidoscope, although it manifests itself on an incomparably higher level of ideality. Music produces beautiful forms and colors in ever more elaborate diversity, gently overflowing, sharply contrasted, always coherent and yet always new, self-contained and self-fulfilled.

I have yet to see a better definition. Music is a perfect storm for the human mind: beautiful in form, intricate, and eternally new.

KNOWING WITHOUT KNOWING

Pleasure in the Absence of Expertise

Two minutes and two seconds into the song '(Get Up, I Feel Like Being a) Sex Machine', the Godfather of Soul, Mr James Brown, famously asks his organ player and backup vocalist, Bobby Byrd, 'Shall I take 'em to the bridge?'

According to my iTunes library, I've listened to the song over two dozen times, but until recently I had no idea what Brown meant. Music, like virtually all crafts, has its share of vocabulary and specialized knowledge, and I was able to enjoy the song even when I knew vanishingly little about the mechanics of music.

Brown's bridge, as I now realize, was musical, not physical; he was telling his bandmates to bring on the next part of the song. A bridge is a kind of transition; it's a new bit of music that differs from what came before but helps move the song forward; the *b*, for example, in a song that has an *aaba* structure. It relieves the listener of the agony that comes from too much repetition, yet, done skilfully, it also sets the stage for the finale.

The funny thing is, listeners don't need to know what a bridge is in order to appreciate the music, any more than patrons of a magic show need to know the trick that allows a magician to pull a rabbit out of his hat. One can enjoy a film or a novel without knowing anything about tension, resolution, or climax, just as one can enjoy a photograph without knowing anything about film speed, contrast ratios, or the rule of thirds. Most of us are just consumers, not producers, and generally that's okay: we understand and appreciate much of what we see and hear, even if we can't produce it ourselves.

Another great example of how we can appreciate artful composition without recognizing what is going on comes from the Beatles' 'Yesterday'. Before I began immersing myself in music theory, I had listened to the song hundreds of times without once realizing that its statements of yearning for the past ('all my troubles seemed so far away', 'I'm not half the man I used to be') follow ascending melody lines, while statements that return to the present ('Now it looks as though they're here to stay') follow descending melodies. That neat bit of musical architecture undoubtedly enriches the song, yet many listeners never recognize it explicitly.

Film viewers don't need to know anything about acts or narrative arcs to appreciate film, and many music listeners don't even know the names of the musical notes, let alone, say, that classical sonatas tend to repeat their second theme in the so-called tonic key, or that popular songs can be divided into components like bridges and turnarounds. How can we so thoroughly appreciate what we can barely articulate?

♪

It's not just audiences, though. Sometimes even performers can't explicitly articulate the tools that they are using. Terre Roche told me about the first time she and her older sister, Maggie, went to record their own music. Terre was just eighteen, and although she was already an accomplished musician who had been touring for several years, and had even sung some harmonies for Paul Simon's album *There Goes Rhymin' Simon,* aside from that one studio session with Simon she'd almost never performed with anyone other than her sister. Suddenly Terre and Maggie found themselves in a studio in Muscle Shoals, Alabama, with the legendary Muscle Shoals Rhythm Section, a team of top-notch studio musicians who recorded hits with everyone from Percy Sledge and Rod Stewart to the Rolling Stones and Lynyrd Skynyrd. At one point, while they were working on Maggie's song 'Burden of Proof', the piano player Barry Beckett turned to Terre and asked her, using a common convention known as the Roman numeral or Nashville numbering system, if the song went to 'the IV chord' in the second half of the first measure of the verse. Terre froze; she had no idea what a IV chord was. As she recalls:

> All I knew was that I was playing an F chord. Suddenly I felt as if I was the stupidest person in the room. I was the youngest person in the room (just twenty-one) and . . . Maggie [and I] had never played with anyone else but each other. Listening back to those tracks, I am amazed at the music that we put together without anyone ever telling us what a IV chord was.

The point of the Nashville numbering system is that it allows you to describe a song independently of its key. But the vocabulary itself is not nearly as integral as the musicianship it seeks to describe.

Perhaps a year or two later, Terre, who had learned mainly by watching other people play, saw a girl play a song in which she suddenly jumped up to the seventh or eighth fret on the guitar in the middle of the song. Terre decided she'd write one like that, which ultimately became 'Mr Sellack', featured on the first Roches record (the one the *New York Times* judged 1979 Album of the Year). As Terre recalls, 'I was in the key of D, playing all of the chords I knew, then just jumped up to the higher frets and tried different shapes. Years later I learned that I had gone to a B major chord, taking me out of the key of D, but playing a secondary dominant leading to E minor. The whole thing took a little journey out of the key of D and found its way back in by the end of the bridge. At the time I didn't even know what the term "bridge" meant.'

Some years later, the tables were turned. Terre eventually became deeply interested – and deeply fluent – in music theory; she began teaching music theory and started taking courses in complex jazz harmonies. At around the same time, she found herself working with a good friend who was a talented yet totally unschooled musician, capable of reproducing entire Beach Boys and Beatles records in his home studio entirely by ear. One day he and Terre were working on one of his songs, and he wanted Terre to sing a harmony in a particular way, but Terre wasn't sure that her friend had really meant for her to do what he was asking. 'Yesterday you told me to sing [my note at a] third [above yours]', she said, attempting to clarify, 'and now you want me on the ninth', which in C major would be nine keys apart rather than three. Her friend's response? 'Why don't you just shove all that book learning you've been doing and just sing the friggin' song!'

As the composer and mathematician Dmitri Tymoczko has put it:

When composing, I make various choices about chords, scales, rhythm, and instrumentation to create feelings of tension, relaxation, terror, and ecstasy, to recall earlier moments in the piece or anticipate later events. But I do *not* in general expect listeners to be consciously tracking these choices. Listeners who do ('ooh, a dissonant #9 chord in the trombones, in polyrhythm against the flutes and inverting the opening notes of the piece!') are like professional magicians watching each other's routines – at best, engaged in a different sort of appreciation, and, at worst too intellectually engaged to enjoy the music as deeply as they might.

In short, the formal elements of music theory have their uses, but one can certainly appreciate – and even play – music without them. In the early 1990s, a French cognitive psychologist named Emmanuel

♪

Bigand set out to find the differences between experts and novices in how they listened to music. There was at that point already a sizeable literature on the basic sensitivity of novices and experts to pitch and rhythm. Simply put, experts' ears are more sensitive to fine-grained details; they are more prone to noticing when something is slightly out of key and (as mentioned earlier) better able to recognize precisely how far apart two notes are. Experts are also quicker to detect deviations in a rhythm, and they can often identify the individual notes in a chord, something that novices can rarely, if ever, do.

But a lot of what Bigand found was surprising. He went in expecting to find huge differences between musicians and nonmusicians but instead in many cases discovered that nonmusicians knew far more than anyone could ever have anticipated. The usual terminology in this literature distinguishes between experts and novices, but Bigand eventually started to realize that all of his adult subjects, trained or otherwise, were experts of a sort: they were all expert *listeners*.

Even without musical training, Bigand began to realize, the average listener comes to know implicitly many aspects of the formal structure of music. Untrained listeners won't necessarily be able to articulate that knowledge; professional musicians can often describe what's going on in a song with far more precision than mere listeners can. And professional musicians are obviously (by definition) much more capable of producing music than nonmusicians are. To paraphrase the great baseball manager Yogi Berra, 'You can hear an awful lot, just by listening.'

For instance, one of Bigand's first studies focused on a theory that had been introduced by Ray Jackendoff and his collaborator Fred Lerdahl, aimed at understanding how sophisticated listeners interpreted complex pieces. The idea was that in any given piece, some notes figure more centrally than others; if you were a jazz saxophonist improvising changes to the melody in 'Over the Rainbow', some notes might be safely changed, whereas modifications to others might leave the listeners scratching their heads. Bigand set up an experimental test of Lerdahl and Jackendoff's theory about which notes were critical and found that expert musicians more or less behaved as Lerdahl and Jackendoff had predicted. But so did the *non*-experts; ordinary listeners seemed to have much the same intuitions, if in less precise form, as the experts. After that, Bigand conducted dozens of other studies – looking at aspects of music such as resolution (whether a composition returns to the root of a key) – and found much the same pattern: experts were invariably better than non-experts, but non-experts always did a lot better than mere chance. A novice might not be able to say which particular key a musical piece was in, but experienced listeners who lacked formal training could still tell when a musical composition broke the rules. Other studies showed that nonmusicians were often nearly as good as trained musicians in their capacity to recognize the emotion of a piece from a brief excerpt, and that untrained listeners could often do a fairly credible job of learning to recognize new pieces.

Looking at the same question from a neural perspective, Bigand found still further evidence that untrained listeners were able to extract a great deal of the structure that underlies music. As he put it, although there are surely differences between musically trained listeners and untrained listeners, 'the human brain is already intensively trained to music through everyday life experience: adding supplementary training in music schools makes it possible to acquire specific skills [like reading sheet music or naming musical intervals] indispensable to be professional musicians, but [formal training] is not what determines the musical ability of human beings.'

Listening is what first gets us into the game.

♪

In the late 1970s, two cognitive psychologists, Richard Nisbett and Timothy Wilson, wrote a groundbreaking paper – still worth reading thirty years later – called 'Telling More Than We Can Know', which reviewed dozens of studies showing that human beings often have no idea why they do the things they do. It is possible, occasionally, for a human being to articulate exactly what he or she is doing and exactly why, but it's also eminently possible for average people to act without any particularly clear awareness of why they do what they do, justifying their actions after the fact, rather than thinking them through beforehand. In one famous study, hundreds of shoppers were asked to look at an array of nylon tights and decide which they liked the best. Subjects tended to browse the array from left to right and, far more often than chance would allow, chose the pair of stockings farthest to the right. None of the subjects mentioned position as a reason for making their choice, and when position was offered as an explanation, everyone denied it played any role; in reality, people often tend to take the last choice simply because whatever comes last is easiest to remember.

Our lack of awareness of our brain's internal operations similarly extends to many athletic endeavours. The act of catching a fly ball in a baseball outfield, for example, can be calculated in terms of a complex stew of calculus and tangent lines, but there are thousands of primary school kids who have yet to take calculus and still manage to catch these high-flying balls just fine. Just because the actions of a musician can be described in the abstract mathematical terms of music theory doesn't mean the musician needs to be explicitly aware of those abstractions.

♪

Philosophers sometimes distinguish between 'knowing how' and 'knowing that'. There's a difference between knowing how to do something, sometimes referred to as muscle memory (really a kind of memory in the brain), and being able to explain what you are doing.

The brain uses distinct systems for encoding facts and for encoding actions. Facts, stored in declarative memory, have been associated with a section of the brain known as the medial temporal lobe (centred on the seahorse-shaped hippocampus) and (after they have firmed up) with the temporal and frontal cortices. Action programmes (the not always consciously accessible product of what I referred to earlier as 'automatization') are largely associated with procedural memory, encoded in a loop that centres on structures such as the cerebellum and the basal ganglia. One reason for the decoupling of formal musical knowledge and practical musical skill is that the two are treated by the brain in fundamentally different ways. Declarative knowledge has been optimized for conscious knowledge; procedural knowledge has been optimized for rapid reflexes that aren't necessarily accessible to consciousness.

If we sometimes find it hard to consciously articulate what our muscles are doing, it's because the memories that feed our conscious thoughts are largely separate from those that control our muscles. It is only with considerable conscious effort and reflection that one can really learn to traffic back and forth fluidly between the two.

Bill Evans, one of the most influential pianists of the twentieth century, most famous perhaps for his piano solo on Miles Davis's 'So What', first made his mark largely by changing the composition of the chords he played, altering what are known as the voicings of a chord. Drawing partly on impressionist composers like Debussy and Ravel, Evans began to experiment with looser interpretations of chords, omitting notes, extending them over time, interspersing others while still retaining the overall flavour. At the time, nobody else could figure out what Evans was doing, and Evans himself might have been hard-pressed to fully articulate his techniques. Even Evans's own brother Harry, who was a well-known pianist, was initially puzzled.

Although Bill must have had some idea of what he was doing, the bulk of what he was doing was procedural; his muscles and basal ganglia knew how to create these novel chord voicings, but in the early stages of his experimentation that knowledge had yet to be translated into declarative facts. Eventually, though, someone did figure out what Evans was doing, and it wasn't so complicated that nobody else could understand it; instead, once the translation was made, 'Bill Evans's Chord Voicings' became a standard part of the jazz curriculum and a tool in every jazz pianist's kit. What happened in that particular case is not uncommon; improvisers work out innovations by feel alone, and only later do those innovations get codified into theory that can be explicitly encoded into declarative knowledge. The real virtue of music theory in a case like that is not to forge new ground but to provide a language for sharing discoveries with other musicians.

A lot of jazz, in fact, is about blending the declarative with the procedural. The jazz pianist Marilyn Crispell, often compared to the great Cecil Taylor, and longtime member of Anthony Braxton's group, explained to me that in her improvisations she often blends conscious, explicit knowledge of the overall frame or direction of a piece with a kind of unconscious playing in the immediate moment. I've overheard Pat Metheny express much the same. To some degree, classical compositions can be played fairly well by sheer rote (drawing entirely on procedural knowledge), and a lot of rock can, too, but satisfying jazz almost always requires a kind of mixture. On the one hand, the jazz player must depend heavily on highly practised habits that allow the musician to rapidly ascend scales or otherwise play lightning-fast riffs. On the other hand, to be truly compelling, jazz musicians must also integrate declarative knowledge in the form of plans, ideas, and concepts – schemas that help shape a piece and yield music that, as Crispell put it, feels 'composed, and not merely improvised'.

Classical used to be this way, too. Bach, for example, was a legendary improviser, capable of creating four-part fugues on the fly. And until the nineteenth century, when the spirit of improvisation began to fade in favour of orthodox interpretations of canonized great composers, performers in the classical tradition improvised frequently, especially in the sections known as cadenzas – forerunners to modern guitar solos, filled with fast, virtuosic passages. The idea of an entire piece being written out note for note, fully annotated with markings, is a relatively recent tradition. In global and historical perspective, the improvisational impulse behind jazz is the norm rather than the exception. And the best players have probably always been those who could mix the declarative and conscious with the automatic and unconscious.

♪

In the real world of guitar, sometimes musicians don't even know the names of the chords they are playing.

Perhaps the easiest song ever to play on guitar is America's 'A Horse with No Name'. There are only two chords in the song, and both are easy to play, requiring just two fingers each on the fretting hand.

One of the two chords is the common E minor chord, in which the middle and index fingers hold down the second frets of the fourth and fifth strings. The other is obscure but equally easy to play; instead of holding down the second frets of the fourth and fifth strings, the guitarist switches to holding down the second frets of the third and sixth string – still two fingers, and hardly any motion involved (and as any guitarist realizes, the less motion required, the better).

But what is the second chord called? You won't find it in any list of the top forty most common chords. As the guitarist and bass player David Hodge points out, the other chord could go by about five different names, not one of which would be familiar to the average guitarist. You could call the second chord in 'A Horse with No Name' a Dadd6add9, an F#dim7 (add 6), or an F#m7 (no 5)(add 4)(add 6); you could also think of it as E11 or Bm11. But the guy who wrote the song – Dewey Bunnell – quite likely didn't think of the chord in any of those terms; more likely, he was just fooling around on the fretboard, and once he stumbled onto the Dadd6add9 (or whatever you prefer to call it), he had the good sense to trust his ears, even if he couldn't explain in exact technical terms what he had created.

♪

In the mid-1990s, the journalist Daniel Goleman wrote his influential book called *Emotional Intelligence,* which argued that there was more to intelligence than the sort of puzzle solving you'd see in an IQ test; Goleman argued that people's social and emotional savvy was as important to professional success as their raw analytical intelligence. There can be little doubt that social and emotional insight matters for music, too.

Goleman illustrates emotional intelligence with a story he borrowed from a friend who happened to be one of the first Americans to journey to Japan to study martial arts. On one particular afternoon Goleman's friend found himself on a subway in Tokyo when a drunk and hostile passenger got on. The drunk started screaming – and eventually taking swings – at the other passengers. Finally, Goleman's friend had had enough; he stood up and steeled himself for battle. But before he could enter the fray, an old man dressed in a kimono cheerily shouted 'Hey!' as if he had spotted an old friend. By startling the drunk, the old man postponed the imminent violence.

'Why the hell should I talk to you?' the drunk asked.

The old man replied not with an answer but with a question, 'What'cha been drinking?' When the drunk said 'Sake, and it's none of your business', the old man began to turn things around. 'Oh, that's wonderful, absolutely wonderful', he said. 'You see, I love sake, too. Every night, me and my wife (she's seventy-six, you know), we warm up a little bottle of sake and take it out into the garden, and we sit on an old wooden bench.' Painting a picture of the persimmon tree in his garden and pondering the nature of sake, the old man added, 'Yes, and I'm sure you have a wonderful wife, too' – at which point all the drunk's remaining aggression melted away.

'No', wailed the drunk, 'my wife died. . . .' Soon the drunk was sobbing, explaining how he had lost his wife, his job, and his home; by the end, the drunk had cradled his head in the old man's lap.

In defusing the situation, the old man displayed a spectacular command of emotional intelligence – or what cognitive scientists often call 'intuitive psychology' or 'theory of mind', the art of reading (and anticipating) the beliefs and desires and needs of others. And it is that intuitive psychology, more than the formal apparatus of music theory, that really matters most: the ability of a performer (or songwriter or composer or artist) to anticipate the pull that a work will have on its audience, and to figure out how to get that audience to share in some mood or feeling. Perhaps Bruce Springsteen, said it best:

> I always write with an audience in mind. If I feel that [connection] coming back at me then I feel like I'm doing my job. That's why people come to my music – for some emotional experience or a perspective, either on their own lives, or on the world that they're living in.

♪

Some of the best, most in-depth discussions on the art of songwriting I have ever encountered have been interviews conducted by the author and songwriter Paul Zollo. In one, Zollo interviews James Taylor and after some easy questions starts delving deeply into advanced topics in music theory, asking Taylor questions about technicalities such as diminished chords and twelve-tone scales, elements that might lie outside the average pop star's range.

Taylor, however, is unfazed and has no trouble keeping up. He explains, for example, that he learned from Paul Simon how to use diminished chords as a way of 'escaping from a melody, or from [one] harmonic sort of context and jumping into another one'.

From there Taylor moves on to his former mentor Paul McCartney, and a discussion of an unusual chord McCartney played in 'Michelle':

> Paul said that was the only jazz chord [he and John] knew. They used to go down to a record store in Liverpool and there was somebody there who played guitar and he showed Paul and John this [unusual] chord. So the second chord in 'Michelle,' under 'ma belle,' that second chord is a very unlikely chord. . . . And you wouldn't expect to see it.
>
> . . . But, boy, the way he [Paul] bounces one onto another. It's really very much like cubism . . . it represents so much [emotion] in just a simple line.

And that's what music is all about. What really matters is not how many chords you know, but how you use the ones you do know.

TAKE IT TO THE LIMIT

What Experts Know That Novices Don't

The thing about guitar, Lenny Kaye, longtime guitarist for Patti Smith, said to me, is that you 'have to make it your friend'. What did he mean by that? Did making it your friend mean spending thousands upon thousands of hours with it? Did it mean knowing and celebrating its capabilities and how they complement your own? Or did it mean being yourself in its presence? What do expert musicians know that novices don't?

As I sought to carve out my own tiny corner in the musical world, I soon realized that there are as many answers to this question as there are musicians. While just about every expert I met knew some things that I clearly didn't, like how to hold a steady beat, there was enormous variation between the experts, and in their expertise. Some could read music, many couldn't. Some could play blisteringly fast, others not. Some had an encyclopaedic knowledge of the history of the music that preceded them, others only an intuitive notion of the music they themselves wanted to create.

♪

Expertise begins with a fine appreciation for detail. More than once I've seen a roomful of musicians argue about the duration or loudness of a single note. Expertise of this precision and kind lies not just with musicians but with sound engineers and producers, who help musicians transform raw recordings into finished products. In our perceptions of sound, as in our perceptions of the visual world, the brain has no absolute rules; instead, it often relies on context and sometimes gets fooled. Musicians, engineers, and producers, of course, know this all too well.

In one session I sat in on, Rebecca Cherry (a fantastic violinist who has played with Kanye West), Dave Soldier (who, aside from his work on the 'most wanted' and 'least wanted' songs, has composed string sections for David Byrne), and Rory Young (a Grammy Award–winning producer and engineer) worked together on an album that was to be called *The Complete Victrola Sessions*. The conceit of the project was that the whole album was recently unearthed, a piece of virtuoso piano music originally recorded in 1914. The project would serve as a score for a short Winsome Brown film, starring Ms Cherry, who plays a Russian violinist who becomes an opium addict while touring in New York City.

Each song, four or five or six minutes long – the sad slow song 'Mata Hari, Ballerina de Java', a bouncy tribute to the boogie-woogie pioneer Meade Lux Lewis, and so forth – was played over and over and scrutinized intensely. To the musicians' refined ears, absolutely nothing was perfect; passages that sounded absolutely fine to me – even incredible – drew scowls. Was there too much breathing there? Violinists, it turns out, breathe (perish the thought), and microphones (curse their stupidity) have trouble discriminating between the exhalation of a violinist and the exaltations of a gently modulating bow. Was there enough space between the phrases? Or should a rest from another part of the song be inserted? 'I could make it dark', Rory offered at one point, or 'we could find some other silence we like'.

Another conversation concerned a barely audible thud, as the bow bounced against the violin. Dave, who at this point was sitting quietly, reading a book about the bluegrass inventor Bill Monroe, seemed unperturbed, but Rebecca (whose bow was doing the bouncing) wasn't so sure. Rory said, 'I could fix that – but it might sound too perfect.' Ultimately, Rory's argument held the day, and the subtle bounce remained. The goal, everyone agreed, was to make not a perfect recording but a human one. A moment later, on another point, Rebecca, by then convinced, declared, 'I like this bit dirtier.' With modern technology, the choice was theirs.

At another juncture, Rebecca wondered aloud, 'Hmm – I like the sound of the first passage a lot, but I like the sound of this [second section] less.' Rory, who is as expert at production as many are at performance, immediately piped up: 'One thing is, the context is very different. Since it [the violin] is by itself [here], that obviously makes a big difference. You've got to fill it out more and make it more self-sufficient. Whereas the other thing somehow has to fit in with the piano. Plus . . . everything is relative, so if the piano plays a bass-y note, that makes [the violin] note seem *less* bass-y. So you use that piano note to benchmark it somehow. I don't think in context it's ever going to sound the same.' In short, our ears were fooled, because all perception is relative.

Rory's point is actually the auditory equivalent of the old illusion in which two identical lines seemingly have different spans, based on the arrowheads that surround them.

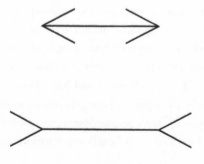

A good producer (or sound engineer) must know as much about how we hear things as about the music itself – and also, as another Grammy Award–winning producer, Russ Titelman, put it to me, serve as therapist, motivator, and casting director, figuring out which musicians will fit together well on a particular project and trying to get every single member to produce his or her very best work. Or sometimes must just sit back and let the artists play: one of Titelman's most successful albums as producer, Eric Clapton's *Unplugged,* was recorded in just two takes, with a single edit splicing between the two. In the presence of true genius, all bets are off.

♪

Probably the least important skill among popular musicians is the ability to read sheet music; what matters is the music itself, not how (or even whether) it is written. None of the Beatles could read or write music, and neither can Eric Clapton, nor for that matter could the great Tin Pan Alley composer Irving Berlin. Indeed, Berlin, who wrote standards such as 'There's No Business Like Show Business', 'White Christmas', 'God Bless America', and 'Anything You Can Do (I Can Do Better)', was such a limited piano player that he could only play in the key of F-sharp, but that didn't stop him from making music. Eventually, he got a special custom piano with a shift lever on the right that would allow him to transpose his work into other keys.

Classical musicians, of course, are expected to read music, and it is a handy skill to have for any musician, but in the broader musical world sight-reading is hardly essential. Many of the world's musical traditions exist entirely without musical notation, and there are scores of brilliant blind musicians like Stevie Wonder and Ray Charles who never read a note. Those who can sight-read can get certain gigs (like Doug Derryberry's studio work with *Sesame Street*) that nonreaders can't, but there's plenty of work for skilled studio musicians who can't sight-read, like my new acquaintance Smokey Hormel, a grandson of Jay C. Hormel, the man who invented Spam.

When I first met Smokey, by chance, at a divey Mexican restaurant around the corner from my apartment, I noticed his guitar and asked him whether he played for fun or for a living. He was a bit reticent to tell me at first, but over time, I discovered that he'd played with Beck, Neil Diamond, Tom Waits, and Justin Timberlake. He'd also played with Sia on 'Breathe Me' (the haunting song that accompanies the final scene of the final episode of *Six Feet Under*), and, even more amazingly, he'd played on Johnny Cash's last recording, a cover of the Nine Inch Nails song 'Hurt', one of the most moving covers ever. Not long after I met him, Smokey got a regular gig in Norah Jones's band, chosen by Norah herself, who didn't seem to care at all that he couldn't read music; she'd hired him by reputation for a single session and liked him so much she made him a regular member of the band. Smokey is practically the Zelig of studio musicians, able to blend in with anybody, in any style; with ears like his, notation is not required.

As Paul McCartney said in a television interview, 'As long as the two of us [John and Paul] know what we're doing, we know what chords we are playing, and we remember the melody, we don't actually have the need to write it down or to read it.' Who could argue with Sir Paul?

♪

McCartney and I aren't drinking buddies, but I was able to ask Smokey how he managed without being able to read sheet music. He explained to me that for him it's all geometric: he remembers shapes and patterns, and how they relate to the ear. The so-called first position of the B minor pentatonic scale, for example, is fingered in the same way as the first position of the A minor pentatonic scale, except that the entire pattern is shifted down by exactly two frets towards the base of the neck. In musical notation, the two scales would look rather different: the A minor consists only of 'natural notes' (A, C, D, E, and G), while the B minor pentatonic contains four natural notes (B, D, E, and A) but also one sharp (F#). On the guitar it's completely natural to move from one to another because the fingering remains exactly the same. What matters is the geometry, not the names of the notes (or how they would appear on the page).

The undisputed master in the geometry of the guitar is the jazz genius Pat Martino, who sees the fretboard as a kind of clock with different groups of chords represented by superimposed geometrical figures like squares and triangles. As Martino explained to me, he takes the physical layout of each musical instrument to be a distinct window into the landscape of music, with the physical layout of the guitar leading to a different set of natural movements (both geometrical and musical) from that of other instruments, such as the piano. Martino himself happens to be fluent in music notation, but he views notation as merely a tool for recording (and sharing with his bandmates) the geometry that is at the true core of all that he plays.

♪

If reading music is optional, hearing music, and being able to connect what you hear with what you play, are not. Nearly every musician I spoke to mentioned improving that connection as a key goal. As David Bromberg, one of the leading studio guitarists in the 1960s, put it, at his peak in his early twenties he felt as if there were 'a direct connection between [his] ears and [his] fingers'. Music came in, and he automatically knew what to play, how to ornament a vocal melody, or how to compose a solo that would follow a given chord progression. Tom Morello said much the same, explaining that part of his intensive daily practice during university was aimed at being able to 'translate any idea in [his] head directly to [his] fingers'.

That translation between ear and fingers actually takes several steps and is something a cognitive scientist might refer to as the alignment of (or calibration between) representations. Think, for example, of the prism adaptation studies: the owls in those studies needed to learn not just what the visual world looks like or what the auditory world sounds like but the *relation* – the alignment – between the two, so that when they heard a sound fifteen degrees to the right, at an elevation of fifteen degrees, they knew where to look, and not just where to listen.

Becoming an expert musician requires the alignment or calibration of at least four distinct sets of representations (five if one happens to read sheet music): the notes the musician hears, the notes the musician wants to play, the location of those notes on the instrument, and the physical actions that the fingers must undergo in order to play the right notes at the right time (and, if applicable, the notes to be read). The musician must draw direct mappings between a mental representation of the instrument and a physical location of where those elements (say, the frets on a guitar or the keys on a piano) are instantiated on the instrument being played at a given moment. The player must have both 'egocentric' representations (of where his own body is) and 'allocentric' representations (of where things lie on the guitar, independent of how the guitarist is holding the guitar) – and, most important of all, fluent mappings between the two, which must be updated in real time as he and the instrument shift position. (All this is bumped up an extra level of difficulty for a guitarist who plays different guitars, since different guitars often differ in their precise physical layout; the strings on a classical guitar, for example, are farther apart than the strings on an electric guitar.)

One of the most important yet seemingly moronic pieces of advice that an aspiring rock guitarist may hear is 'Make sure your strap is adjusted so that the guitar is in the same relation to your upper body when you stand up (onstage) as when you are sitting down.' Guitarists who don't heed it are often skewered by the discrepancy between the allocentric and the egocentric coordinate frames. Alignment is all.

♪

That particular piece of advice is so important because the brain's ability to map between representations is generally crude: more trial and error than sophisticated three-dimensional trigonometry. Consider, for instance, what happens when you try to help someone else put on a tie and face him: the usual relation between hands and eyes becomes reversed. Effectively, all you've done is invert directions, the equivalent of simply multiplying an equation by −1, but most people feel entirely flummoxed.

In principle, you could imagine memorizing the fretboard in the abstract and then using some sort of formula to calculate exactly where your fingers should go, factoring in your own posture and the three-dimensional angle and position in space of the guitar at a given moment. A robot might do exactly that, but the human brain doesn't work that way. Instead, our brains solve these sorts of problems not so much by running equations as by tapping large databases of experience, retrieving similar episodes from memory. (The data for this come from experiments in which researchers performed prism adaptation experiments on human beings: participants relearn mappings between visual and motor space bit by bit, rather than by formula.)

The upshot is twofold. First, the fact that our maps between visual space and motor space are piecemeal means we need an enormous amount of practice. Second, our knowledge of the relation between the fretboard and the dynamics of one's fingers is fragile; tiny alterations from what we are accustomed to can slow us down or lead to error.

This is one reason why even expert musicians should do warm-ups before going onstage. Warm-ups have a physical role to play – increasing the flow of blood to the fingers, wrists, and forearms – but they probably also have a mental role to play: a warm-up refreshes the brain's memories about the calibration between the abstract (egocentric) representation of notes and the precise (allocentric) physical movements needed to play them.

♪

When representations aren't aligned, the results are quite different. Most 'poor-pitch singers' (believe it or not, a technical term in the literature), for example, can recognize melodies just fine; they are not literally tone-deaf, even if they've long been told they are. In reality, poor singing is generally an alignment problem, an often correctable issue of properly aligning the pitch they hear on the inside with the precise motor movements they need to adjust their larynx into proper position for a given note.

A great deal of singing training is thus (explicitly or implicitly) about helping novices learn to coordinate the motor control of their vocal tracts with their internal models of the sounds they want to produce. Especially important is the complex mapping between so-called chest voice (rich and resonant, but lower in pitch) and head voice (thin, and higher pitched). Amateurs 'flip' crudely between head and chest voices, with noticeable breaks as they shift between registers. The first step towards effective singing is to coordinate those two 'voices' (which, literally speaking, consist of two different techniques for controlling the vocal apparatus) into a single smooth mix. Expert singers are able to perform such shifts effortlessly, and without conscious thought, precisely because they've learned to put all their representational ducks in a row.

Incidentally, in skilled technical performance, it's not enough to simply guess and then adjust according to trial-and-error feedback. If you've ever sung into a microphone in a game like *Rock Band* or *Guitar Hero,* you've seen the little arrow that tracks your pitch over time, along with a set of lines at different heights that indicate the pitch you are supposed to sing. If you try something, and if it doesn't work, you can tinker with it. If you come in too low, you can raise your pitch by shortening your vocal cords; if you come in too high, you can lower your pitch by doing the opposite. Such feedback can be extremely useful in learning to sing, but in actual performance one can't always rely on it. In traditional Italian bel-canto-style singing (like you would hear at the opera), for instance, the singer must hit the note squarely from the outset. In rock or blues, you might get away with a bit of gliding into place, but in bel canto, the musical equivalent of upper class diction, one must *start* at the right place; anything else just isn't cricket. In singing bel canto, the brain has to *anticipate* what needs to be done – calibrating the vocal folds properly with the internal desired pitch – and do so without stopping to wait for feedback. None of which can happen unless (or until) all one's internal representations are perfectly aligned.

In a professional, those representations are so well aligned that a musician can know what sound his or her instrument would produce even if he or she can't actually hear the instrument being played. In the whole scientific literature on music, my favourite study may be one in which a dozen skilled pianists were asked to play a variety of pieces, mostly unfamiliar, on digital pianos that had been electronically muted – which meant that the pianists couldn't actually hear what they were playing. The catch was that afterwards they were asked to listen to auditory playbacks of those songs, some reconstructed from the digital records of their own playing, others from the digital records of other musicians who had played the same pieces. To make things even harder, the experiments controlled for tempo and overall loudness. Even so, the pianists were way above chance at being able to identify their own playbacks. By imagination alone, by exploiting the exquisite alignment between their fingers, their brains, and what their ears would have heard, the pianists managed to relate what their fingers had done with the sounds they would have created.

In the late 1920s, in my hometown of Baltimore, Maryland, a classically

♪

trained composer named Otto Ortmann set up a laboratory at the Peabody Conservatory, with the idea of using then-innovative technologies such as high-speed photography to look at the motion of skilled pianists' fingers. Measuring everything from arm weight to wrist flexion and finger length, Ortmann discovered an astonishingly complex choreography. Skilled pianists didn't just hit the right notes at the right time with the correct fingers; they planned (unconsciously) in advance: a pianist's index finger might start moving toward the third note in a phrase even before the middle finger had struck a key corresponding to the second note. (The articulators in our vocal tract do something similar; even before you pronounce a given consonant, your lips might already be pursing to form the following vowel.) In technical terms, this process is known as co-articulation – in which the nature of one motor movement influences the next. Such results show a high degree of anticipation, which is the only way our relatively slow muscles can cope with the speed-intensive demands of producing speech and making music, which are among the fastest-paced things humans can do. The pianist must solve a complex problem, since there are multiple fingers that might strike any key and multiple ways of getting there; so, too, with a guitarist. Ortmann's studies, and many that have followed, show that one hallmark of expert musicians is remarkable efficiency.

Another hallmark of experts lies, ironically, in the kinds of errors they make. Whereas the errors of novices may be all over the map, the errors of experts tend to be of three main types. The least interesting, perhaps, are the kinds of simple mistakes that chess masters might call *Fingerfehlers* – German for 'slips of the finger'. Beginners, it goes without saying, make these all the time; experts far less often.

The second type of mistake, known as the anticipation error, goes hand in glove with advance planning: in a memorized work of classical music, the better you know a piece, and the more your fingers are preparing in advance, the more likely you are to inadvertently skip ahead, playing a note ahead of schedule – sort of like saying 'I took the shop' when you meant to say 'I took the car to the shop'. Novices, who must painfully plan out each note, one by one, without doing much planning for the future, actually make fewer of these particular errors than experts do.

A third common kind of mistake is analogous to what linguists would call a semantic substitution error, like calling a grapefruit an orange. When beginners make errors, they may play, say, an adjacent note that happens to be entirely out of key, unrelated to the melody that was to be played. When experts play from memory, to the extent that they make errors, they typically substitute other notes from the same key, frequently from the very chord that is currently serving as the accompaniment.

On the practical side, this tendency towards replacing notes with related notes is a good thing, since within-chord errors tend to blend in, and studies show that listeners rarely even notice such mistakes. On the scientific side, substitution errors help to illuminate what's going on inside the brain: the novice's brain represents individual notes as arbitrary, almost meaningless letters in an alphabet in a language he may not understand. In the brain of the expert, each note is part of a larger meaning, precisely because the song is understood more abstractly, in terms of things like scales and harmonic motion, rather than just random notes that some composer happened to have written. To the novice, the first measures of Bob Marley's 'Redemption Song', the notes G, A, B, G, might as well be some mysterious incantation; to the expert, they are simply a ride up and down the G major pentatonic scale.

The expert's knowledge of music also comes through in studies of 'transfer', in which a musician is taught one piece and then asked to play a second piece that is related yet different, for example, the same rhythm with different fingering, or the same fingering with different rhythm. Novices tend to be tightly tied to the specific details of what they learned, such that (for instance) translating a rhythm from the left hand to the right can pose a serious challenge, whereas experts make such transfers almost effortlessly, and with little error, presumably because their overall system of musical representation is at a much deeper level.

♪

Efficiency, abstractness, and fluid mappings all come easy for computers. Feed a MIDI score (essentially sheet music in machine-readable form) into your computer, in a program such as GarageBand, and it will be able to play back that score at any tempo, in any key, without ever breaking a sweat or making a mistake. What is it that distinguishes a true artist from a machine or from a music school graduate who can sight-read perfectly yet plays with little soul?

One of the biggest secrets lies with timing. If it takes a machine to play exactly like a metronome, it takes a person to deviate from a metronome in interesting ways.

It's always been obvious that timing is important in music; rhythm is about the spacing of notes in time, and if two musicians play together and don't coordinate their sense of time, they sound out of sync. If a funk band – drums, bass, brass, and guitar – plays exactly in time, we drop our jaws in admiration. To make sure players perform in sync, studio performances are now often played to a 'click track' that allows all the musicians to play in time together, even if in reality (as is often the case these days) each musician records his or her tracks at a separate time – perhaps even in a separate location, as with the debut album of the band the Postal Service (best known for the song 'Such Great Heights').

But sheer synchrony isn't the only thing important about timing; expert musicality is also often about subtle *variations* relative to an otherwise seemingly steady pulse. Some of the first scientific documentation of this fact came in 1932 when an Iowa PhD student named Leroy Ninde Vernon began to examine piano rolls that had been prepared by professional musicians to be played back on player pianos. Even before Vernon's research, it had become obvious that piano rolls prepared directly from sheet music didn't really sound good; although they could be technically perfect, they often sounded flat. Manufacturers of player pianos, like the company Duo-Art, didn't want their expensive gadgets to sound mechanical or sterile, so they contracted real musicians to play, recording their performances onto the rolls of paper that would then be fed into the machines. Vernon analysed those rolls to see why they sounded better than straight conversions of sheet music.

What Vernon discovered was that even if the relative sequence of notes was the same in a piece of sheet music and an actual performance, the exact moments at which notes were struck – and the durations for which they were held – differed.

Some of the variation might have just been random; machines can follow perfect metronomic time, never deviating, but a human musician may find it difficult to play exactly on the beat, even if he or she tries. Because of 'noise' (essentially random variation) in the firing of individual neurons, a human – even a trained musician – who tries to tap in perfect time with a metronome will at some point make an error. In a moderately fast-paced song, 120 beats per minute, such as 'Billie Jean' by Michael Jackson or 'Borderline' by Madonna, most people's taps would come within a few percent of the target time on most beats, but few people would nail it on every beat. For novices, some errors could be as big as 3 to 6 percent, and even experts aren't perfect.

♪

If some of the timing variation is apparently random, or accidental, or at least beyond voluntary human control, some of it – the part that separates experts from amateurs – is far more systematic. Any fool can miss the beat by a few milliseconds here or there by accident; what separates the professional from the novice is the deliberate manipulation of time.

Vernon discovered, for instance, that human pianists often did things like play the lead melody of a song (typically with the right hand) just a few milliseconds ahead of the accompaniment. This tiny difference – slightly less than a hundredth of a second and notated nowhere in the score – is enough to highlight the lead, or melodic instrument, and separate it from the accompaniment, and it's one of the many ways in which musicians use microscopic changes in timing to make music meaningful.

To begin with, playing a section (or a phrase, or even a note) slowly tends, other things being equal, to make that passage sound sad; playing it quickly makes it sound happy or energetic. Insofar as anyone can tell, this general tendency is true around the globe. Slow down a Sami *yoik* – a traditional, yodel-like Scandinavian folk song, often sung a cappella – and you get a sad, even mournful *yoik;* speed up, and your *yoik* will likely sound happier and even bouncy; the fact that you won't understand the lyrics makes remarkably little difference to your subjective impressions.

The power of subtle timing cues transcends not just cultural background but also expertise; novices who listen regularly to particular genres can appreciate them nearly as well as experts. The only real differences are that experts can often report tempo changes that novices might not explicitly recognize and that experts have much better control over tempo variations, such that they can produce them at will; a novice has enough trouble keeping a steady beat and much less facility with the deliberate micro-changes in tempo that characterize expert playing.

♪

How do expert classical musicians memorize complex pieces? The best way to understand learning is to study errors that people make along the way, and the psychologist Roger Chaffin has done just that. In one study, he followed a cellist, Tânia Lisboa, over a period of three years as she prepared for – and ultimately performed – a demanding prelude, from J. S. Bach's Suite No. 6 for Solo Cello.

What Chaffin found was that not all notes are created equally. Looked at on a page of sheet music, any musical piece could ostensibly be thought of as a long stream of notes and rests, no one note or rest any more important or harder to remember than the next. To a machine such as a player piano, the 117th note in a sonata has exactly the same status as the 118th note; each one has a pitch and a duration, and that's all there is to it.

To a human musician, the situation is rather different. Studies of musicians' errors have shown that pieces are memorized not simply as long streams of arbitrary notes but instead as structured hierarchies. A concerto as a whole, for instance, typically consists of three movements, and each movement could be divided into subsections, which consist of sets of phrases, and individual phrases can typically be conceptualized in terms of how they relate to entities such as melodies, chords, and musical scales. And, strikingly, the errors musicians tend to make lie at the fault lines between phrases and sections. In their practice sessions, skilled pianists rarely stumble over the first or last note of a piece. The errors they make tend to be at the junctures between larger units, probably because the brain stores longer pieces of music in terms of smaller chunks; what's inside a chunk is fully mastered, but sometimes the musician fails to make the right switch from one chunk to the next.

The really good pianists know this (intuitively, if not explicitly) and therefore often devote the greatest portion of their practice to the transitions between larger units. As Chaffin puts it, experts place 'performance cues at key points to provide a safety net in case a performance is disrupted by a memory failure or lapse in attention'. Such cues sometimes begin as physical annotations on the score but ultimately must become transformed into mental notes that must be remembered. Performers use cues like these both to indicate formal boundaries between sections of a piece and to indicate 'expressive boundaries' (which represent changes in musical feeling), as well as places where there are changes in tempo or technique (such as, for a cellist, a shift in the direction of bowing). In essence, these transitional moments are the moments at which the musician can least afford to be on autopilot: when something changes, the player needs to be alert. The classical guitar teacher Meliset Abreu asks her students to think about their pieces when they are away from their instruments (for example, on the train on the way to work), telling them that the place where they space out or forget what they are doing is precisely the place they need to focus on when they return to their instruments. A good part of expertise comes from diagnosing one's own likely mistakes.

♪

When one is playing live in front of an audience, yet another set of skills can come in, known in the technical trade as primary movements, or, more colloquially, as showmanship: voluntary actions and facial expressions that aren't strictly required for the music but that convey emotion and keep the audience involved. Singers have the most physical freedom (think Michael Jackson and the moonwalk), but Jimmy Page and Pete Townshend would windmill their arms during rests between phrases; Jimi Hendrix became famous in part for his music but also in part for his habit of smashing guitars (as well as playing behind his back, with his teeth, and with his guitar on fire). Chuck Berry hopped across the stage on one leg. Nils Lofgren sometimes plays on a trampoline, and at a Bruce Springsteen show I once saw him do a flip right in the middle of a guitar solo.

Even without jumping up and down, guitarists can make an impression by exploiting the redundancy of the fretboard. Because of the nature of the guitar, it is often possible to play a single melody at multiple places on the fretboard, and many guitarists will slide their hands up and down the fretboard not because they have to (musically speaking) but just because the sudden dramatic motions keep the audience engaged (and seem more difficult than they really are). Violins, too, have a certain degree of redundancy (meaning that some notes can be played in multiple places on different strings), and long before rock and roll was invented, the early-nineteenth-century violinist Niccolò Paganini developed one of the slickest moves of all, a trick of continuing to play even if a string or two on his violin broke. His shining moment, according to legend, was a solo finished on a single string.

♪

Playing in a group with other musicians requires still another set of skills, starting with a strongly developed capacity for hearing and, especially, anticipating what one's bandmates will play. As Richard Barone, lead singer for the 1980s rock band the Bongos, put it, 'The first thing I learned onstage is the importance of listening.' According to the versatile scientist, composer, and trombonist Peter Keller, at least three skills are involved in musical coordination between individuals. First, and most fundamentally, one must adapt to changes in tempo made by other musicians, whether those deviations are accidental or intentional (perhaps to express a mood or to delineate structure). A second skill – extremely hard for beginners – is learning to divide one's attention between one's own playing and the playing of the other people in the ensemble. Third, recent work suggests that expert musicians frequently use the auditory equivalent of mental imagery to anticipate the upcoming sounds of both themselves and other performers.

Outside the carefully controlled confines of the studio, all this can be even more difficult, as in a situation that some friends of mine recently faced. Their band – Jessie Murphy in the Woods – specializes in delicate harmonies, but on this particular occasion they found themselves playing in a smallish room that was literally inside a larger nightclub, in which every amplifier was apparently turned up past eleven. As a result, Jessie and company didn't merely have to attend to one another, as they would have to do on any ordinary night; they also had to simultaneously filter out the loud four-on-the-floor thumping that leaked through from next door (usually at different tempos from their own). It was the musician's equivalent of calmly brushing one's teeth while standing on the front lines of a war zone.

As Lenny Kaye explained to me, in the final analysis, empathy between musicians can outweigh virtually all else. Kaye himself doesn't read sheet music, and he confessed that he still could barely distinguish between a dominant seventh chord and a major seventh chord, relying more on geometry and well-rehearsed patterns than on explicit formal knowledge. Yet Patti Smith has stuck with him for nearly forty years. Why? Because of Kaye's ability to anticipate Patti's moves and moods, to know where she is headed and to be there waiting for her when she arrives. Smith is well enough known to have her choice of guitarist and could certainly afford someone who plays faster or has more technical skill, but nobody knows her better than Kaye, and that's why she sticks with him. Or, as Terre Roche put it, 'There's no substitute for the amount of time a band spends in the same room with one another. And that includes the van.'

♪

When I first met Doug Derryberry (the guitarist who works with Bruce Hornsby), he mentioned that he was 'a super stickler for tuning', but it was only later, when I visited him in his studio, that I truly understood the scope of what he meant by this. As a conscientious beginner, I already knew how important it is to tune one's guitar before each practice session. Unlike a computer keyboard, a guitar is a physical instrument whose exact sounds depend on factors such as temperature and humidity. In order to have the strings sound good in combination with one another, one has to make subtle adjustments to the tension of the strings each time one plays. Some musicians can do this by ear, comparing the strings with one another or with some external reference note (say an E played on a piano). Others (like me) use electronic gadgets that monitor vibrations to detect what note a particular guitar is playing at a particular moment, supplying feedback as to whether that note is spot-on, too sharp (high), or too flat (low).

The way I, and most other beginners, do this is invariably by tuning the 'open strings' on the guitar, which is to say I make sure each string matches a particular reference pitch when I strum it without holding down a fret; the bass string is tuned to E, the next string to an A, and so on.

When I talked with Derryberry, I realized that there was a whole different world. Western music uses something called an even-tempered scale, in which the frequency of each note is multiplied by a constant value (one plus the twelfth root of two) to yield the next. Unfortunately, the even-tempered system isn't quite perfect (and for complex mathematical reasons, no single system can be). Intervals of a fifth, for example, sound slightly flatter than the ideal ratio of 3:2. To a beginner, the difference would be scarcely noticeable, but Derryberry is a guy who used to tune pianos for fun.

Instead of taking the one-size-fits-all approach that I (and virtually every other amateur) might take, Derryberry tunes his guitar differently for *each individual song,* taking into account what particular chords and melody notes might play a prominent role in that song. If most of the song hovers around the middle of the neck, he optimizes the tuning to get that part perfect; if the song consists mainly of open chords played at the top of the neck, he might instead tune around the second fret. Compromises that I was blithely unaware of were of the utmost importance to Derryberry. (I later learned that professionals doing studio work will sometimes retune a guitar for the purpose of dubbing in a single chord.)

Beyond this, there is an entire realm of alternate tuning (or what classical players refer to as scordatura), which consists not of tweaking the pitching of individual notes but rather in changing the set of notes available on the fretboard and where they are located. Beginners almost always stick to something called Spanish or standard tuning. But guitarists like Joni Mitchell, Ry Cooder, and Keith Richards (who learned in part from Cooder) are famous for retuning their guitars to different reference notes, changing the palette of notes that are readily available. There is a cost to this – alternative tunings tax the memory of a guitarist even further, since many of the fingerings of many painfully learned chord shapes change accordingly – but some guitarists happily pay the price because alternate tunings often open new musical frontiers. Open-D tuning, for example, allows the guitar to sing, as it were, one note deeper than it ordinarily could.

A guy like Derryberry knows not only the songs and melodies and gear that his fellow guitarists use, but what tunings they use, and for which songs. At one point, for example, he said to me, 'I play slide [guitar] in standard tuning or open E, like Duane Allman or Elmore James. I haven't done much open-G tuning on guitar. I know a lot of guys do.' (Richards's guitar work on 'Honky Tonk Women' grew directly out of a lesson he got from Cooder in open G.) Other alternate tunings are designed to make certain chords easier or to extend the pitch range of the guitar (as in Robert Fripp's 'New Standard Tuning'). Each alternate tuning in some way subtly alter the musician's options, changing the dynamics of which chords are easily played and which chords transition easily to the next.

♪

Experts must also come to master the idioms of the genres in which they play. A heavy metal guitarist, for example, strikes each note in a sharper way than a folk guitarist might. Genres are defined not just by melodies and rhythms but also by the harmonies they favour and even by details about how individual notes are sounded and held. As one musician put it, 'Itzhak Perlman is a great violinist, but that doesn't mean he can play klezmer' [a Yiddish folk-jazz hybrid]. Even once one has mastered all the basics, each new genre demands a different kind of nuance. The capacity to recognize expressive timing differences, for instance, is tuned to particular genres; people who know jazz notice micro-variations in jazz compositions but sometimes miss equivalent micro-variations in classical compositions, and vice versa. I have no doubt that Perlman could learn to be a great klezmer player if he wanted to, but the list of things a musician can learn – and bring to bear on new music – is endless.

♪

'I can play every note that Jimi Hendrix ever played', the guitar deity Steve Vai once said. 'And I can play each note exactly the way he played it, but I can't imagine how he thought of it in the first place.'

Many thousands of musicians have mastered all the minutiae I was struggling with – like a rock-solid sense of time and fast and fluent knowledge of where to find all the notes and chords – without making any sort of mark musically whatsoever. A few – like Vai, Yngwie Malmsteen, and Joe Satriani – are known primarily for their technical proficiency, but musicians like Lenny Kaye make it clear that technical prowess is just one route among many. Musicians can make their mark with the originality of their compositions (as Bob Dylan did, despite lacking a classically melodic singing voice), with their modulation of dynamics (part of Led Zeppelin's magic), or with their sheer stage presence (think KISS or Ozzy Osbourne). Many punk rockers could barely play their instruments but developed a new kind of energy – aggressive and biting – that drew legions of fans. As a 1996 article in NY Rock put it, somewhat sarcastically:

When the Ramones first hit the rock circuit roughly 20 years ago, all members had at least a fundamental grasp of their respective instruments. Tommy Ramone, for instance, spent the better part of two weeks mastering the drums before the band played its first gig at CBGB.

As Danny Goldberg, former president of Atlantic Records, put it to me, 'There's a separate category between being able to replicate something and being able to create something. The first requires enormous technical skill and musicality. But the ability to improvise and create new music as a writer is a separate skill. Some people possess both, and some, such as classic studio musicians, are people great at playing, not great at writing or creating something new. Those are two different talents. Sometimes they are embedded in the same person, like Hendrix had both talents.'

♪

Whereas the amateur simply takes his or her instrument as a found, unalterable object, the true artist often tries to press the limits. Les Paul pretty much invented the solid-body electric guitar, and less dramatically but still with considerable impact Keith Richards removed the entire low bass string from some of his guitars. (You can hear this on songs like 'Honky Tonk Women' and 'Brown Sugar'.) In his words, 'I found I was getting sort of jaded on the whole six string, the regular tuning stuff, [so] that I really needed something to perk me up and start again.' Jimmy Page brought a violin bow to his guitar. Stevie Wonder was among the first piano players to experiment with synthesizers, and the Beatles were among the earliest adopters of the Mellotron, an unholy hybrid between a piano keyboard and a tape deck that is featured prominently in 'Strawberry Fields Forever', and among the first to use the studio itself as an instrument, creating new sounds with backwards tapes and overdubs.

Jimi Hendrix manipulated not just the tuning of his guitars but the very nature of the guitars themselves, overseeing virtually every detail of their construction. As the biographer Dave Henderson tells it, Hendrix preferred Fender Stratocasters in part because they were easy to modify. He would begin by bending the tremolo (whammy bar) 'by hand for several hours to get it to go down [in pitch] three steps, instead of the customary one, also get it near enough to the body so he could tap individual strings and raise and lower their pitch'. This also allowed Hendrix to play with the whammy bar at the same time as he manipulated the tone controls. Sometimes Hendrix would even remove the back panel of the guitar so that he could reach the string from behind, in service of creating yet a new kind of sound. He also re-coiled the electromagnetic pickups on his guitar, experimented with unusual combinations of strings (extra heavy on the bass side, super-light on the treble), fiddled with the tuning of his guitar while he was playing, and used a special neck plate anchored with tempered steel so that he could safely bend his guitar's neck. Hendrix was also a pioneer in the use of sound-altering pedals, like fuzz pedals, the wah pedal (subsequently identified with 1970s funk), and the pitch-shifting Octavia (which could raise the pitch of what he was playing by an entire octave). The net result was a conjunction of guitar and pedals that could produce a vast array of then-original sounds and an entrée into new parts of sonic space.

The exploratory tradition continues. Pat Metheny attributes an important part of his skill on the guitar to experience he had on his first instrument, the trumpet, and to a conscious effort to bring what he had learned on trumpet – especially about how to articulate phrases (sequences of notes) – to the guitar. Likewise, Tom Morello said that in his formative university years he spent roughly a quarter of his daily practice regimen experimenting with 'eccentricities' and weird noises, some created by rapidly toggling the pickup switch that determines how the guitar's sounds get amplified. Even then, he said, he was still more of a studio musician. It was only in the early 1990s, when he started listening carefully to DJs like Dr Dre and Jam Master Jay – and, crucially, thinking about how to import their scratchy warblings and synthesized textures into guitar – that he truly became a genuine artist, not just re-creating other people's sounds, but composing and playing his own.

♪

One of the most intriguing leaps forward in the history of music, both within an individual and in the field of music as a whole, was the afore-mentioned dramatic step Bob Dylan took after the release of his first album.

Even before Dylan had recorded his first album, he had a certain charisma; he'd developed a following in Greenwich Village and at age twenty was discovered by the legendary John Hammond (who had earlier discovered Benny Goodman, Billie Holiday, and Aretha Frank-lin, among many others). But at the time, many people still couldn't understand why Hammond had signed him. Dylan had a gruff voice and was endowed with a set of pipes far less elegant than Sinatra's or Elvis's; the delicate three-part harmonies that made Peter, Paul, and Mary so popular were wildly out of Dylan's reach. To top it off, Dylan's first album, for Columbia Records, flopped, selling only five thousand copies its first year. Many thought Columbia had goofed, and the whole episode soon became known as 'Hammond's Folly'.

The rest is history. Dylan soon started writing original songs in earnest and made a huge impact almost immediately. What happened between November 1961, when Dylan recorded his first album, and the summer of 1962, when he recorded his second, far more impressive album? Was it ten thousand hours of intense drafting and redrafting of songs? Vocal lessons? Yodelling practice?

By Dylan's own account, none of the above. There was practice aplenty, to be sure, and maybe even a singing lesson or two (though Dylan didn't let on, and who could tell?). But the real key, in Dylan's case, was not so much practice as a conscious, deliberate effort to find his own musical path. Dylan describes 'cramming [his brain] with poems' and listening endlessly to the songs of other musicians, seeking to understand their melodies and structure. Two incidents stand out in his memory – seeing a particular musical production and hearing a particular musician who at that point was unknown. Until then, Dylan had largely been (by his own account) a Woody Guthrie wannabe, wedded to Guthrie's style without adding much that was original to it. And he sat in on a theatrical production of songs written by Bertolt Brecht and Kurt Weill.

> My perspective ... was about to change. The air would soon shoot up in intensity and become more potent. My little shack in the universe was about to expand into some glorious cathedral ... [I] was aroused straight away by the raw intensity of the songs ... songs with tough language ... erratic, unrhythmical and herky-jerky. ... Every song ... seemed to have a pistol in its hip pocket, a club or a brickbat. ... They were like folk songs ... but unlike folk songs, too, because they were sophisticated.

Dylan was especially struck by a song known as 'Pirate Jenny' and how it used a 'ghost chorus' about a black freighter ship; he swirled the song over and over in his head to try to determine what made it tick. 'Each phrase comes at you from a ten-foot drop, scuttles across the road and then another one comes like a punch on the chin. ... It's a nasty song, sung by an evil fiend, and when she's done singing, ... it leaves you breathless. ... [T]he structure and disregard for the known certainty of melodic patterns ... [gave] it its cutting edge.' Dylan was inspired.

Not long after, John Hammond brought Dylan an album few people at the time (including Dylan) had ever heard of: *King of the Delta Blues* – by a singer named Robert Johnson. In Dylan's words:

> When Johnson started singing, he seemed like a guy who could have sprung from the head of Zeus. . . . I immediately differentiated between him and anyone else I had ever heard. . . . I copied Johnson's words . . . so I could more closely examine the lyrics and patterns . . . the free association . . . the sparkling allegories, big-ass truths wrapped in the hard shell of nonsensical abstraction. . . . I didn't have any of these dreams or thoughts but I was going to acquire them.

In combining what he'd already learned from Guthrie with his new discoveries from Brecht, Weill, and Johnson, Dylan invented a new art form; his enormous, searing labours and painstaking investigations were indispensable, but his insight and synthesis were what brought him to a new level.

The Beatles may have undergone a similar revolution when Paul realized that he could write songs about fictional characters outside of his own immediate experience. Out went love songs, in came Eleanor Rigby, died in a church, buried along with her name, and soon thereafter there were benefits for Mr Kite.

Radical innovations like these aren't about practice per se, but as the pioneering French biologist Louis Pasteur said, 'Chance favors the prepared mind.' McCartney and Dylan had both accumulated enough technical chops that they could put their new insights to immediate work without delay.

♪

'One thing I've noticed about some of the artists that I've admired and worked with', the record industry executive Danny Goldberg explained, 'is that there are certain artists who became very successful – Dylan is certainly one of these, Steve Earle is one, Springsteen is one, Elton John is one – who study the art form exhaustively. Not only are they artists, but they have this tremendous encyclopedic knowledge about the history, what came before. And then every once in a while you might meet somebody who is totally inner directed.'

Goldberg went on to name two immediately recognizable acts (off the record) and added, 'They know some music, but it's just clear the music is coming from something inside them, and not from enormous study. The most compelling music comes from inside, not outside, although you can learn some of the grammar and tools outside. [S]ome of the great masters balance what they can absorb from outside with an inner voice. To me that's what Dylan and Springsteen do.'

♪

At one point, I asked Doug Derryberry about his working relationship with other musicians: Did they talk technicalities? Not much; he had a lot of such conversations in his early twenties, but now that he was an accomplished musician, such conversations were rare. He could recall just one recent serious conversation about music with a fellow musician – a bass player – about the music of Antonio Carlos Jobim. Did they chat with instruments in hand, I asked, or were they more like chess masters, knowing the moves so well they could speak without a board in front of them? 'No', Doug said, chuckling, 'we didn't have our instruments in our hands, we had drinks in our hands.'

Later, Derryberry related a conversation he'd had years ago with his boss Bruce Hornsby, not long after Derryberry had joined the band. He recalled asking Hornsby about 'harmonic parameters', like, 'Do you think of this [chord] as a substitute dominant for this other chord because then it goes to this chord?' And, as Derryberry tells it, Hornsby brushed him off, saying something like, 'Yeah, yeah, yeah, that's great, that's good' – without really digging into the question at all. I asked if that meant Hornsby doesn't know his theory. 'Oh, no', Doug drawled in his Tennessee lilt, '[Bruce] is deep, deep. He went to Berklee [College of Music, in Boston] and the University of Miami. He knows [his music theory], but he wants to stay on the other side. Meaning on the more visceral, emotional side of it. Like, that you've gone through the mechanics of the theory of the whys and wherefore of why Bill Evans would play what he does or why Keith Jarrett would play what he does, and then you grasp all that. And then you emerge at the other side and make your own art.'

HEAVY METAL

What Makes It All Worthwhile

By any reasonable standard, my personal quest had been a success. A year and a half in, I was finally comfortable with many of the basic chords and could change between them smoothly, and at least roughly in tempo. Fundamentals like forming chords had gone from being painful, slow bits of declarative knowledge that I could talk about only abstractly to procedures that my fingers could actually carry out, automatically and almost effortlessly. My ears had gotten better, too. I was starting to be able to distinguish different music intervals, and I'd finally learned to count the beats in a song. Although my repertoire of songs was still tiny (to put it charitably), I'd learned to improvise and to make up my own music. Not well enough to headline a band, perhaps, but well enough to jam with my friends, and well enough that I wanted to keep playing and studying music for the rest of my life.

I also understood the music I heard vastly better than when I'd begun the project. I could pick out bass lines, recognize different drumming patterns, and tell what techniques different guitarists used. I had developed a sense of arrangement and how different songs were put together. Listening to Miles Davis's *Kind of Blue,* long my favourite jazz recording, became a transcendent experience. I could understand what the musicians were trying to do – the way they were playing around with scales and the rhythms they were exploring.

My brain had changed, too. Not to the extent that it would in an expert, but the differences in what I could perceive – and what I could produce – were truly astonishing. If I wasn't yet a bona fide musician, I was certainly on my way. I had found no miraculous shortcuts, but practice – especially carefully targeted practice aimed at developing specific skills and remedying weaknesses – worked, even for someone as congenitally arrhythmic as me.

I might not be picking up an instrument as quickly as an adept child might, but as an adult I still had some advantages. I had a greater capacity to understand the abstractions of music theory and a better sense of music composition as a whole. If practice, determination, and a greater conceptual understanding hadn't entirely overcome the twin obstacles of age and lack of talent, they had at least made for an even match. And, as I had come to realize, nobody was literally born with an instinct for music. Instead, music was a skill that each person would need to construct anew, from a wide range of brain faculties that evolved even before music existed. Everyone, no matter how innately gifted, would have to face all the challenges in mastering rhythm, melody, and harmony, in building the seamless and automatic connections that allow ear, brain, and body to flow together in time and musical space. Talent could help some people get there quicker, and maybe take them further; youth might be helpful, too. But even at my age, and even in my case, where innate talent was notably lacking, with the help of a good teacher and a pile of books and ear-training software, progress was not just possible but eminently realizable – frightening at times, to be sure, but on the whole immensely satisfying.

I was not about to quit my day job, but I participated in a studio singing gig and then had a live gig, playing lead guitar and singing lead vocals to a Beatles cover – 'With a Little Help from My Friends' – in front of two hundred people, at the music producer Roger Greenawalt's nationally covered Beatles Complete on Ukulele festival, in Brooklyn.

After eighteen months, I had even started to come to terms with my nemesis, rhythm. Just before Christmas, Roger (who had been giving me lessons) dropped me a note to say, 'You had a breakthrough yesterday. That was really music you were playing. Good work. You've come a long, long way.' I really had, in every sense of the word, become musical.

♪

Yet becoming musical has been, without question, the hardest project I've ever taken on; nothing else, except maybe chess, has required as much study. The question remains: Why do I try so hard? Why would anyone, especially an amateur who had no hope of making music into a career, put in so much time and effort?

In some ways, that question has only become more acute in recent years, as technology has raced ahead. It's not just that most of us will never be able to play with the imagination and dexterity of Jimi Hendrix, or even that no single human being will ever be able to reproduce the sounds of, say, a symphony the way a CD player can: within a few decades, it may be that no human being will be able to play a guitar with the technical perfection that a machine might. The cognitive psychologist Phil Johnson-Laird has built software that improvises jazz in psychologically realistic ways, and not long ago Toyota created the first robot violinist. Pat Metheny recently toured with a band that consisted entirely of robots. Ever since the first player piano, circa 1842, there has been a kind of poignancy in training for a lifetime to do what a machine could do in an instant.

In the era of the iPhone orchestra, I couldn't help but wonder: Why was I investing so much time trying to play a traditional musical instrument when machines, with their infinite patience and perfect sense of timing and pitch, can do nearly everything I can do so much better?

♪

Technology is always changing music. Earlier I discussed how artists like Hendrix and the Beatles used technologies that emerged in the 1960s; in the 1980s, other artists blazed trails with synthesizers, drum machines, and samplers. Today, there are clever software tools like Tristan Jehan's Swinger, which takes in an audio file and modifies each beat so that it has rhythm that swings, the first half of each beat longer than the second. The program's jazzy rendition of 'Every Breath You Take' doesn't quite take your breath away, but it's still pretty amazing.

Already, a great number of the world's teenagers, and some adults, get their musical fix from *Guitar Hero*. As one of the game's co-founders, Eran Egozy (who has since co-founded the company Harmonix, producers of the competing product *Rock Band*), told me, some musicians have already begun to think about how their songs fit into the game, tinkering with bass lines and guitar solos to make them more fun in *Rock Band*. The rap star Snoop Dogg remixed an entire album's worth of songs to make them fit better into the game. Meanwhile, the latest versions of *Guitar Hero* and *Rock Band* are extending a tradition of computer-aided instruction that is helping the process of acquiring music become more democratic. In the future, computers might unlock musical possibilities that more traditional musical instruments can't match. (Jehan and I, for example, talked about a future analogue to Photoshop that might let you change the genre of a song in much the way that a Photoshop filter can make a photograph look like an Impressionist painting.)

The more I talked with cutting-edge music technologists like Jehan and Egozy, the more I began to wonder why it is that we prefer (or think we prefer) music generated by people to music generated by machines, and, most important, why it is that we humans persist in labours – like playing piano or solving Sudoku puzzles – that could so easily be replaced by machines.

If one can get 40 percent of the benefit with 1 percent of the effort, will future generations of young people bother with real instruments?

♪

One of the most obvious reasons to persist in learning about music is that it may actually be good for your brain. Over a dozen studies in the last decade have shown correlations between musical training and achievement in other domains. There is reason to think that people with musical training may be better at learning foreign languages, and they tend, on average, to have higher IQs. One careful analysis suggests that musicians are disproportionately represented among Nobel Prize winners.

But such facts should also trigger scepticism. Are these correlations causal? Or could it be, for example, that brighter people gravitate towards music and that the correlation with achievement is an accident of both being facilitated by general intelligence? Or might pure *Sitzfleisch* – Yiddish for the patience to sit on one's behind long enough to get something done – be a vital component in both music and other kinds of achievements? Maybe the people who have the most self-discipline do best both in music and in school not because music makes you smarter but simply because people who are willing to work the hardest in music tend to be the people who are willing to work the hardest in school, too.

Only a few studies have tried to crack the causal nut, mostly by comparing the relation between music and success in other kinds of training, such as drama lessons and painting classes, suggesting that music might have a larger correlation with academic success. The single best study, done by the Canadian musician and developmental psychologist Glenn Schellenberg, suggests that there may be modest but systematic effects. Music may indeed be more effective than, say, drama lessons in eliciting intellectual improvement, but the data aren't (for now) overwhelming, with just an extremely small number of carefully controlled studies in which students were randomly assigned to groups. Schellenberg himself takes a relatively dark view, suggesting more recently that 'almost all of the available data can be explained simply: Individuals with higher IQs are more likely to take music lessons than their lower-IQ peers, and they are also likely to perform better on virtually any test of cognitive abilities'.

Even if music genuinely instills self-discipline or other cognitive benefits, and even if music turns out to compare favourably with, say, drama lessons in this regard (some evidence suggests that students with drama lessons show social advantages), we would still have a lot of research left to do before we could safely decide that music is any kind of magic educational elixir. Learning to program computers, for example, might be more efficient, in terms of cognitive payoff per hour of hard work invested, than music lessons. The most optimistic but fair read of the current literature is that training in music does bring some intellectual rewards that extend beyond an instrument in itself, but that those rewards still may not be of great enough magnitude to justify the thousands of hours many people require in order to become truly skilled. Whatever educational benefits music has turn out to be a bonus, not the reason in itself for learning.

♪

If the benefits of music are modest, why not just play a video game instead? *Guitar Hero* is a lot easier than real guitar, and many people enjoy it tremendously; for someone who doesn't have ten thousand hours to burn, *Guitar Hero* offers a simulation (however imperfect) of what it is to be a real musician. It may not instil the same sense of discipline, and the groupies are only imaginary, but *Guitar Hero* and its competitor *Rock Band* have grossed over three billion dollars. Clearly, even if they are not real music, music simulation games still exert a huge pull on the human psyche.

In some ways, *Guitar Hero* and *Rock Band* seem so simple-minded as to be almost pointless; mashing coloured buttons in time with falling dots hardly seems like a sport. Since the sequence and timing are provided by the game software, one doesn't really even need to know the songs. There's no need to strategize ahead (as in chess), no need for agile footwork (as in football), and no need to bluff past one's opponent (as in poker). Few games demand less of the player; I suspect monkeys could be trained to play, and at least two different teams of researchers have built robots, one known as Slashbot, the other as Guitar Heronoid, that can cruise through *Guitar Hero* on Expert, without knowing one bit about music. Yet – and I speak from experience – the game can feel intensely rewarding.

Part of the appeal is obviously social: people have always enjoyed sharing music with one another, and games like *Rock Band* (and the newer version of *Guitar Hero,* in which several people can play differ- ent instruments simultaneously) bring that experience, in a far more active way than just sitting around listening to record albums ever could. And (as in a real band or in any team sport) there is an undeni- able joy in the sense of a collective job well done.

And part of the appeal is a sense of fantasy, much as in any video game or simulation of virtual reality. That fantasy, implemented excep- tionally well in *Guitar Hero* and *Rock Band,* is what psychologists call the illusion of control: the more we believe ourselves to be in control, the happier we are. In one famous set of studies, participants were asked to solve simple arithmetic problems while sitting in a room in which sud- den blasts of noise occurred at random intervals. One group of subjects had no choice but to listen, the others had a panic button they were allowed to press in case the noise became too much. Though few par- ticipants actually pressed the button, the mere feeling of control made the entire experience considerably more bearable. In another famous study, dogs were put in an environment in which nothing they did cor- related with their situation; so-called learned helplessness – essentially a form of depression – was the result.

It turns out, however, that although we humans are quite fond of being in control, we aren't always so good at telling whether we actually have it. *Guitar Hero* is designed to yield an illusion of control when you don't really have it. Inferring control is really an exercise in inferring causality; we want to know whether A causes B, but sometimes all we know is that when A happens, B happens too. In technical jargon, in such cases we mistakenly infer causality from temporal contingency. *Guitar Hero* and *Rock Band* exploit this fact to deliver one of the most potent illusions of control I've ever seen: if the player presses the button at the right time, the computer plays back a recording of a particular note (or set of notes) played by a professional musician. If not, the note doesn't play (and you might hear a beep or feel a buzz, by way of negative feedback); the plastic controller adds to the illusion. The net effect is that you feel as if it were you and not Keith Richards playing the guitar. Your conscious mind may know better – and realize that it's all just a ruse, that you're not really generating the music – but your unconscious mind is completely and happily fooled.

♪

For all that illusion of control, video games haven't yet replaced the playing of real instruments. For now, anyway, the games have limits that real instruments do not. In *Guitar Hero* or *Rock Band,* the player is largely restricted to re-creating other musicians' work; opportunities for improvisation and creativity are limited. One young *Guitar Hero* addict I met reached the point where he could reliably get nearly 100 percent on every song he played – and then, with nothing left to achieve, promptly quit. The game is finite, in a way that no real instrument is.

At the same time, for many people, games like *Guitar Hero* and *Rock Band* have served almost like gateway drugs. Granted, many people never progress past the games, but plenty of others do, inspired to try their hand at a real guitar. My own situation is a case in point. But it's hardly the only one. Music publishers like Hal Leonard now put out sheet music to match the songs in *Rock Band* and *Guitar Hero,* and many guitar teachers have noted a strong uptick in how many clients they've had since the games came out. In an informal study done by Fender Guitar and a New Jersey–based educational organization called Little Kids Rock, almost two-thirds of the music teachers thought that enrolment had risen as a result of *Rock Band* and *Guitar Hero* (and less than 3 percent thought that enrolment had decreased).

♪

Of course, making music is not just about control, or even about achieving flow; there's something deeper. Something that for me has made the whole quest – a massive investment of my scarcest commodity, time – worthwhile. Becoming musical has brought balance to my life. In recent years, a great deal has been written about the science of pleasure, and how poor we are at predicting how happy we will be in various circumstances (winning the lottery, for example, brings only brief pleasure, while losing a job or romantic partner often brings only brief pain, despite the initial shock), as well as fascinating tidbits about what gives us the most pleasure in the immediate moment: parents enjoy taking care of their children slightly more than hoovering, but less than watching television or having sex.

But is immediate pleasure all there is? Any parent will tell you that that is not what parenting is about. A new science, known as the study of eudaimonia, asks not 'What can I do that will make me happiest right now?' but 'How can I live a balanced life and make choices, such that I will be happy in the long run?' There is a difference between the pleasures of the moment (hedonia) and the satisfaction that comes from constantly developing and living one's life to the fullest (eudaimonia). The psychologist Abraham Maslow famously suggested that after we take care of our most basic needs, such as food, shelter, and sex, we eventually strive for 'self-actualization', or the realization of our full potential; in his words, '[Even if all our other] needs are satisfied, we may still often (if not always) expect that a new discontent and restlessness will soon develop, unless the individual is doing what he [or she] is fitted for. A musician must make music, an artist must paint, a poet must write. What a [person] can be, he [or she] must be'.

Empirical data are still scarce, but one line of recent research – an investigation into the physical and psychological adjustment of older women – reports that having a greater sense of purpose and personal growth correlates with lower cortisol levels, better immune function, and more efficient sleep. Another study interviewed adults in twenty-seven cultures and found that orientations towards engagement and meaning predicted life satisfaction more reliably than did an orientation towards pleasure. A third used diary checklists and found that people who engaged in eudaimonic activities (for example, volunteering time, listening carefully to the points of view of other people) reported greater overall well-being and life satisfaction than those who engaged in exclusively hedonic activities (for example, getting drunk, relaxing by watching television, or playing video games). In the end, hedonia and eudaimonia almost certainly both matter. In careful statistical analyses, both pursuits contributed independently to people's long-term well-being, and the happiest people are those who find room for both.

Music may be especially potent – particularly for performers – because of its potential for combining the hedonia of enjoying music in the moment with the eudaimonia of a constant sense of progress, as the musician continues to learn new techniques, create new songs, and make new discoveries. From the strict perspective of the 'selfish gene' – in which all that we do is driven by the interests of our individual genes – music may never make sense, especially for duffers like me: playing guitar won't increase how many babies I have, nor will it make them healthier. But maybe, just maybe, the art of reinvention and acquiring new skills can give us a sense of a life well lived.

♪

All of this became especially clear when my twin interests in music and technology eventually converged on something known as the Moog Guitar, which had only recently been released. Guitars are among the most versatile instruments ever invented; they can play chords, they can play melody, soft and loud, rhythm or lead. Unlike on a harpsichord, on a guitar you can vary the loudness of a note, and unlike on a piano, you can bend between notes. Saxophones offer more expressive range note for note, but they can't really play chords. Yet guitars have always had a weakness, too: the instant you play a note, it starts to die. You could play fast, or use various effects gadgets, but true sustain, like what happens when you hold down the pedal on a piano, had always been out of the question. The Moog Guitar solves this problem, by using a system of electromagnetic mechanisms – entirely analogue (no synthesizers involved) – to literally vibrate the guitar's strings and keep them in motion. I played one at the house of a friend of a friend and immediately became enraptured; I could take the set of skills I'd already learned and produce an entirely new set of sounds. It felt like the closest thing I could imagine to giving the guitar the expressive power of a violin. I stayed up half the night looking at YouTube videos about the guitar and found my way to Fareed Haque, the award-winning lead guitarist of the band Garaj Mahal and the single person who best knew what to do with this unusual guitar.

Almost two years to the day since I had brought my guitar to my in-laws' cottage in Quebec and begun to fumble with my first chords, I flew out to take lessons with Haque. Suddenly I found myself on the cutting edge, equipped with a tool (I'd bought a Moog Guitar for myself) and know-how (courtesy of Haque) that almost nobody else in the world yet had. I was able to create sounds and textures I had never heard before. I might never be Jimi Hendrix, but for a brief moment I could sense what it was like to explore a new musical landscape.

No musician, and no scientist, could ever dream of anything more.

EPILOGUE

Music has brought two windfalls that I never anticipated. The first is a huge new circle of friends, every one creative and inspiring in his or her own way. Among many others there's Roger Greenawalt, the ever-clever record producer and master ukulele player who has begun (now that I play a half-decent guitar) to give me lessons, and his sometime co-conspirator Dave Barratt, an equally talented record producer who wrote a song made famous by Robert Plant and Alison Krauss. There's Terre Roche, who generously shared stories with me of her life in music, both as a star and as a music educator; the hard-rocking, classically trained keyboard player Carla Capretto, who once played on Johnny Carson's *Tonight Show;* and Jessie Murphy and her talented trio, who played my living room the night after playing at the Living Room (an elite New York club). There's Mary Farbood, harpsichordist and music nerd extraordinaire, who has quickly become my closest collaborator; Tam Lin, perhaps the cleverest singer-songwriter of his generation; Kathena Bryant, a five-foot-three-inch spark-plug émigré from Garland, Texas, who is the latter-day incarnation of Janis Joplin; Tobias Hurwitz, the Shred-o-Meter-inventing camp director; and the composer, violinist, and visionary Dave Soldier, who splits his time between neuroscience and professional-level music; to say nothing of the electronic music pioneer Morton Subotnick and David Rothenberg, a philosopher, naturalist, clarinettist, and author with a legitimate claim on the title of modern Renaissance man. The list goes on. I have lived and breathed music for (as I write this) two years, and in friendship alone music has brought rewards far greater than I could have imagined.

The second unanticipated fringe benefit is a whole new form of expression, not necessarily as precise as the written word, but in some ways vastly more powerful. In the middle of my second year of efforts to play guitar, I began to have enough confidence to start writing songs and one week went to my weekly lesson with Roger ready to write my first. A week later, I knew, I'd be visiting my uncle David, perhaps, I feared, for the last time. David, who had recently retired as a professor of education in North Carolina, had always been an inspiration to me, and for the last several years he had been quite ill. I knew, instinctively, that the song I was to write had to be for him – and about him. Roger asked me to free-associate. Pen and paper in hand, I recalled how David had brought me maths books when I was just a few years old – the first person outside my immediate family to take me seriously as an intellectual – and how my mother, as a child, couldn't pronounce his name, leading to a nickname by which he is known to his family to this day. More than that, I tried to capture his life's work – as a moral teacher and as a person who never ceased to struggle to find a spiritual path. I played a few minor chords that I thought captured David's seriousness of purpose, and within an hour Roger had helped me to craft the song into a beautiful, coherent whole. The refrain ('Uncle David struggles, struggles with the meaning of what it is to be a Jew') was set to some rapid chord changes – A minor to D minor and back in the space of two measures, then on to E7 and back to A minor – that I wouldn't have dreamed of trying a few months earlier.

EPILOGUE

As I flew to North Carolina, I knew the song was good, but I didn't know if I'd be able to play it in public. I was nervous the whole time and didn't tell my mother, lest I dash her hopes if I chickened out. On the last night my mom and I spent in North Carolina, the whole family – David, his wife, Elaine, their daughter, her husband, and the grandchildren – gathered, and somehow, with the aid of an old Martin parlour guitar from 1934 borrowed from my cousin's husband, I performed the song, making not more than two or three mistakes. David gave me a hug – the biggest he'd ever given me – and, with just the right mixture of praise and irony, described me as 'a nascent Bob Dylan'.

Later that night, after everyone else had left the party, David and Elaine and I had the deepest conversation we'd ever had. In the morning, my mother and I flew back north. Five weeks later, David was gone.

I can't help but cry as I write these words, but I also know that writing that song for David connected me to him one last time in a way that nothing else I could have possibly done ever could. And for that I am grateful, in ways that words alone could never express.

ACKNOWLEDGEMENTS

Book writing can often be a lonely existence, a writer locked in a study with nothing other than a laptop and the Internet. *Guitar Zero* was anything but, the most pleasurable experience I have ever had as a writer.

As I tried to transition from being a mere listener to being someone who could play for himself, I chanced upon three of the nicest communities of people I've ever encountered: musicians, music teachers, and the scientists who study music. Virtually everyone I met along the way welcomed me warmly. Perhaps the first was my new friend and colleague Mary Farbood, who is both a world-class harpsichordist and a scholar of music, and now one of my closest collaborators.

Master guitarists like Pat Martino and Doug Derryberry invited me into their homes. Tom Morello and Lennie Kaye both gave no less generously of their time. Music teachers like Ruth Alperson, Jamie Andreas, Rebecca Cherry, Curt Gill, and Michele Horner all welcomed me into their classrooms, while pedagogical pioneers Marienne Uszler and Edwin Gordon supplied historical perspective. Even Grammy Award–winning producers and record label presidents, like Russ Titelman, Danny Goldberg, and Bob Hurwitz, took the time to talk to me. Most extraordinary of all was the incredible Pat Metheny, who took three hours out of a rare Saturday morning in which he wasn't on the road to visit me in my own home, answering every question I could imagine on the guitar, technology, and the history of jazz, in exchange for nothing more than a chance to help spread the gospel of music.

On the academic side, virtually everyone I spoke to was delighted to help. Peter Keller read every word of the manuscript and prepped me for a public conversation with Metheny at the World Science Festival. Laurel Trainor helped me better understand the likely origins of my troubles with rhythm. Robert Rowe helped me to get to know many of

ACKNOWLEDGEMENTS

the music scholars at New York University, and Fred Lehrdahl, Ray Jackendoff, and Gene Narmour all spent hours sharing their wisdom on a science of music that they helped create. David Rothenberg carefully critiqued an early draft and opened his Rolodex.

One of the greatest pleasures in writing this book was the interviews I did, with Ruth Alperson, Richard Barone, Dave Barratt, Perry Beekman, Tim Burke, Sterling Campbell, Carla Capretto, Marilyn Crispell, Eran Egozy, Mark Freundt, Michael Geezil, Cirt Gill, Danny Goldberg, Jason Gonsky, Edwin Gordon, Fareed Haque, Hank Heijink, Smokey Hormel, Michele Horner, Hot Lixx Houlihan, David Huron, Elise Jackendoff, Ray Jackendoff, Tristan Jehan, Phil Johnson-Laird, Lenny Kaye, Paul Lamere, Cyril Lance, Lisa Margulis, Pat Martino, Pat Metheny, Tom Morello, Dan Morris, Patrick O'Brien, Caroline Palmer, Ani Patel, Terre Roche, Morton Subotnick, Laurel Trainor, Björn Türoque, Marienne Uszler, Paul Vo, Duncan Watts, and Brian Whitman. Meliset Abreu, Alex Demos, Anders Ericsson, Susan Fast, Paul Hoffman, Panos Mavromatis, Paul O'Keefe, Caroline Palmer, Adena Schachner, and Glen Schellenberg answered e-mails on everything from how to use your imagination to practise guitar on the subway to the foibles of chess masters, while Zoran Josipovic and Michael Dorfman made sure I saw all the latest studies. Danny Goldberg and Brady Brock set up my interview with the inimitable Tom Morello. Joe LeDoux introduced me to Lenny Kaye. Fareed Haque introduced me to Pat Martino, and Charles Lindsay introduced me to the Moog guitar.

More than a dozen musicians and scientists were gracious enough to read drafts of the book, including Doug Bemis, Iris Berent, Carla Capretto, Alex Denker, Lila Gleitman, Aaron Kheifets, Dave Rothenberg, Dave Soldier, and Morton Subotnick. Elika Bergelson, Mary Farbood, Erin Hannon, Josh McDermott, Ezequiel Morsella, and Athena Vouloumanos all deserve special thanks for the detailed, incredibly perceptive comments they made on early versions of the book, each bringing something significant that would not have otherwise been there. Carla edited

ACKNOWLEDGEMENTS

with the sharp eyes of a professional copy editor, and Michael Dorfman made so many helpful suggestions I lost count. Ken Perlin, Ofter Tchernichovski, and Zach Woods lent a valuable hand with early chapters and would happily have laboured through more. Even among all these exceptional readers, Terre Roche stands out, supplying the kind of comments an author can only dream of, line-by-line responses that made me laugh, cry, and reach for the cut-and-paste; never have I had a more supportive reader, nor one who brought so much new to a manuscript.

Terre, Fareed Haque, David Soldier, Paul Frazier, and Marlon Cherry later convened in my apartment in the Village and allowed me to sit in on an amazing jam session. Soldier also brought me into the editing studio to watch the dynamic duo of the violinist Rebecca Cherry and the Grammy-winning Rory Young. Jessie Murphy, Amy Schildige, and Marcia Webb were no less welcoming and even gamely backed me onstage when I endeavoured to sing 'With a Little Help from My Friends'. (Kathena Bryant lent a hand, too; Roger G. played ukulele. Dave Barratt helped record a studio performance.)

Richard Barone brought me inside the world of Gibson guitars and even helped me peek in on Dave Brubeck recording a new version of 'Take Five'.

Jason Gonsky introduced me to Michele Horner and graciously allowed me to watch the amazing Shiloh's first steps as a guitarist.

Michael Raitzyk introduced me to Tobias Hurwitz and the wonderful world of Day Jams. Tobias Hurwitz let me sit in on Day Jams and got me my first gig as a musician.

Seth Austen, Kathena Bryant, Terry Gourley, Roger Greenawalt, Fareed Haque, Tobias Hurwitz, Jessie Murphy, Terre Roche, Tyler Volk, Paul Weinfeld, and another gentleman who prefers to remain anonymous gave me lessons, each one putting up patiently with an absolute beginner who had far more curiosity than talent. Roger helped me write my first real song.

Athena read and improved countless drafts, supplying her usual mixture of laser-sharp comments and emotional sustenance, while never once demanding that I choose between her and my guitar.

Mom, Dad, Linda, Julie, Peg, Vickie, Nick, and George supported me, as they always do, even though they knew better than anyone else how ridiculous the whole endeavour seemed at first. Ed and Steve were there from the beginning and helped with everything from choosing agents to choosing titles. Josie, Eric, Zach, Sandy, Tim, Christian, Ken, and Katie brought friendship. At the beginning of this journey, Michael Dorfman was just a friend of friends; by the end, he was one of my staunchest allies. David, Elaine, Nancy, Gabe, Joe, and Michael stood by me during my first solo performance. (Michael even loaned me his heirloom guitar.) Zoe and Clare helped keep me in shape.

Daniel Greenberg managed to turn an unfinished proposal in a very uncertain market into a book contract with one of the best publishers in the business; his partner Jim, too, was incredibly supportive. Ann Godoff was the first person in the publishing world to see the book's potential. Ginny Smith helped shape a mere book proposal into a real book, reading more drafts than I can count and showing more patience and enthusiasm than any editor I have ever met. Bruce, Ingrid, Mally, and Meighan all helped in creating the final product.

I thank all of these people, but most especially I thank Greer, Riley, Ryan, and Sarah for giving me a chance to play.

GLOSSARY

absolute pitch: The ability to hear a given pitch and identify the musical note it represents; for example, to be able to hear a string vibrate at 440 cycles per second and identify it as the A note above middle C.

A minor pentatonic, the: An example of the minor pentatonic scale that is in the key of A; that is, it begins with the note A and proceeds to C, D, E, and G before returning to A.

amygdala: An almond-shaped interior region of the brain, implicated in emotions.

ascending: Used to describe a sequence of notes, as in an ascending major second, in which each successive note is higher in pitch than the previous note.

audiation: Edwin Gordon's term for the process of imagining and comprehending music.

auditory cortex: The part of the brain's temporal lobe that is responsible for processing sound.

automaticity: The process by which a behaviour can become faster, less conscious, and less effortful.

barre chord: A chord in which one finger, usually the index finger, holds down multiple strings at the same time, typically by lying flat across the neck. Physically challenging for beginners.

basal ganglia: A structure in the base of the brain that has been linked to motor control and learning.

Broca's area: The part of the brain's left hemisphere that has often been tied to language but also participates in music.

cerebellum: A striated region of the brain tucked beneath the cerebral hemispheres; associated with movement, timing, and rhythm; may also play a role in language.

cerebral hemispheres: Left- and right-half regions of the outer, wrinkled part of the brain.

chord: A set of notes, generally three or more, played simultaneously. For example, the C major chord consists of the notes C, E, and G played simultaneously.

chord progression: A series of chords – for example, C major, F major, G major, which is found in the choruses of 'La Bamba' and 'Like a Rolling Stone'.

consonance: Combinations of notes that sound natural together, as in the notes C and G, which form a perfect fifth.

corpus callosum: The major connection between left and right hemispheres of the brain.

critical period: Crucial period in development in which (by hypothesis) a certain skill must be acquired in order for it to be properly acquired.

descending: Used to describe a sequence of notes, as in a descending major second, in which each successive note is lower in pitch than the previous note.

dissonance: Combinations of notes that clash or sound unnatural together, as in the notes C and F-sharp, which form a tritone.

dominant chord: A chord that is a perfect fifth above the tonic. For example, in the key of C major, the G major chord is said to be the dominant chord. This chord creates tension and tends to leave the listener expecting a return to the tonic chord (C in this example).

fifth: See perfect fifth.

fMRI: Functional magnetic resonance imaging, a technique based on local changes in magnetic properties for inspecting the activity of the brain.

fusiform gyrus: The part of the brain's temporal lobe that is associated with face recognition.

harmony: Combinations of notes, chords, or (over time) chord progressions that (generally) yield a pleasing effect. Also, the accompaniment that goes along with a melody.

Heschl's gyrus: A part of the brain's auditory cortex associated with pitch and language.

hippocampus: A part of the medial (interior) portion of the brain's temporal lobe, associated with memory.

holophrastic theory: The idea that in the origins of the human species, linguistic phrases emerged before individual words.

interval: The relationship between a pair of notes. For example, the step from C to G is known as a perfect fifth; the step from C to D is known as a major second.

key: The musical centre for a song or subsection of a song. The key determines which notes sound more and less harmonious together. For example, the key of C major consists of the notes C, D, E, F, G, A, and B (which happen to be the white keys on the piano); in that context, which is to say in a composition consisting primarily of those notes, the notes C-sharp,

D-sharp, F-sharp, G-sharp, and A-sharp (which correspond to the black notes on a piano) sound dissonant. Conversely, the key of F-sharp major consists of all the sharp notes (black keys) and just two white keys (B and F, which some classical musicians would refer to as E-sharp); in that context the black keys and B and F (both of which are white) sound consonant, while the remaining white notes (C, D, E, G, and A) sound dissonant.

major second: An interval of exactly two semitones, such as the gap between C and D (which skips over C-sharp) or the gap between F and G (skipping over F-sharp).

major third: An interval of exactly four semitones, such as the gap between C and E (which skips over C-sharp, D, and D-sharp) or the gap between F and A (skipping over F-sharp, G, and G-sharp).

melody: A sequence of individual notes.

middle C: The note that is approximately at the centre of the eighty-eight keys of a piano, corresponding to a frequency of 262 cycles per second.

minor pentatonic scale: A five-note subset of the minor scale that is commonly used in the blues and rock. The exact notes depend on the key. For example, in the key of A, the A minor pentatonic scale consists of the notes A, C, D, E, and G.

minor scale: A sad-sounding scale, also known as the Aeolian mode, that in the key of C consists of the notes C, D, E-flat, F, G, A-flat, and B-flat. (Two variations with their own distinct sound are the melodic minor and the harmonic minor scales.)

monophony: Music, such as in Gregorian chant, in which all voices or instruments create the same note, in unison; contrasts with polyphony.

motor cortex: The part of the brain involved in planning and controlling voluntary action.

musical key: See key.

octave: (1) An interval of exactly twelve semitones, such as the gap between middle C and the C above it. (2) A specification of a set of notes, such as 'the octave of middle C,' which consists of middle C and the eleven notes that ascend above it. Increasing a note by an octave is equivalent to doubling its frequency.

organum: A form of polyphony, typically with just two voices, that was common in the Middle Ages.

pentatonic scale: A musical scale consisting of exactly five notes, in Western music most typically either the minor pentatonic or the major pentatonic.

perfect fifth: A pleasant-sounding interval of exactly seven semitones, such as the gap between C and G (which skips over C-sharp, D, D-sharp, E, F, and F-sharp) or the gap between F and B-sharp (skipping over F-sharp, G, G-sharp, A, A-sharp, and B).

perfect fourth: A pleasant-sounding interval of exactly five semitones, such as the gap between C and F (which skips over C-sharp, D, D-sharp, and E) or the gap between G and C (skipping over G-sharp, A, A-sharp, and B).

pitch: Ordinarily, the fundamental frequency of a note. For example, when the second-thinnest (open B) string on a guitar is struck, representing the note known as B below middle C, the string will vibrate at 247 cycles per second (along with other resonant frequencies known as harmonics that are integer multiples of 247).

planum temporale: A triangular portion of the brain's Wernicke's area (defined below), associated with language and music.

plasticity: The capacity for the brain to physically change, as an organism learns.

polyphony: The sound of multiple voices or instruments creating more than one distinct note; uncommon before approximately A.D. 900.

polyrhythm: Two incommensurate rhythms juxtaposed, as when one instrument divides each measure into three parts and another divides each rhythm into four parts. Relatively easy to appreciate (in some instances), but very difficult for a beginner to play.

power chord: A simplified chord, consisting of a note and the fifth above it, that sounds neither minor nor major; common in rock and heavy metal.

prefrontal cortex: The front part of the frontal lobes of the brain, associated with reasoning, decision making, and many other reflective processes.

proprioception: An internal sense of where one's limbs are.

relative pitch: The ability to identify one note given a reference point; for example, the capacity to identify a G note after hearing a labelled C note.

rhythm: A regular repeated pattern of sound.

right prefrontal cortex: The portion of the prefrontal cortex that is in the brain's right hemisphere, implicated in memory, self-recognition, and many other cognitive processes.

root: (1) The musical centre or home of a piece. For example, in a song that proceeded from C major to F major to G major and back to C major, the root (or tonic) would be considered C major. (2) The starting point for a chord. In the chord C major, the note C is considered the root. (Major chords also include a note that is a major third above the root, hence E in the key of C major, and a note that is a perfect fifth above the root, hence G in the key of C major.)

scale: A set of notes, often practised in strict ascending or descending order, that sound good together, even when permuted to different orders. Common scales in the West include the major scale, the minor (Aeolian) scale, the major pentatonic, and the minor pentatonic. Many others exist in other cultures, and each has its own characteristic sound.

sixteenth note: A duration that is one-sixteenth of the length of a whole note. The exact duration depends on the overall tempo of the piece, so that a sixteenth note is briefer in a song that is 120 beats per minute than in a song that is 80 beats per minute.

subdominant: A chord that is a perfect fourth above the root chord (for example, F major in the key of C); often referred to by the Roman numeral IV.

superior temporal gyrus: The part of the brain's temporal lobe that is roughly behind the ear and contains Wernicke's area, associated with recognition of sound and speech.

temporal lobe: The lower lateral lobe of either hemisphere in the brain; includes regions such as the auditory cortex, the hippocampus, and the superior temporal gyrus.

timbre: The sonic properties differentiating one instrument from the next; for example, a violin versus a flute.

tonic: The musical centre or home of a piece. For example, in a song that proceeded from C major to F major to G major and back to C major, the root (or tonic) would be considered C major.

triplet: A set of three notes, often played quickly, in a slot that would ordinarily be occupied by two notes.

tritone: An unpleasant-sounding interval of exactly six semitones, such as the gap between C and F-sharp (which skips over C-sharp, D, D-sharp,

E, and F) or the gap between F and B (skipping over F-sharp, G, G-sharp, A, and A-sharp). Once considered unacceptable, now much more widely tolerated.

vestibular system: The system for keeping track of balance and spatial orientation, located in the inner ear.

Wernicke's area: A part of the brain's superior temporal gyrus associated with language and music.

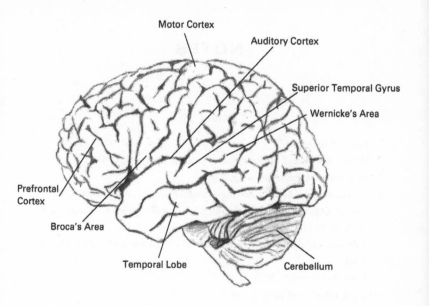

Basal Ganglia and Related Structures of the Brain

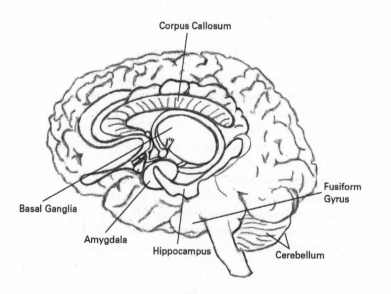

NOTES

Tuning Up

2 **Genie:** Curtiss, 1977.

2 **differences typically pertain more to accent:** Newport, 1990.

2 **near-native fluency:** Birdsong, 2009.

3 **literally keeping the blood flowing:** Mozolic, Hayasaka, and Laurienti, 2010.

3 **twenty-sixth-greatest guitarist:** http://www.rollingstone.com/music/lists/5945/32609/32772.

3 **didn't start until he was seventeen:** Morello, interview with author, May 20, 2010.

3 **Patti Smith:** Smith, 2010.

6 **must indeed start early:** Deutsch et al., 2006.

6 **don't control for total amount of practice:** Watanabe, Savion-Lemieux, and Penhune, 2007.

6 **the more you practise the better you get:** Ericsson, Krampe, and Tesch-Römer, 1993; Gladwell, 2008.

8 **Knudsen's original results:** Knudsen and Knudsen, 1990.

8 **adult owls can often get:** Linkenhoker and Knudsen, 2002.

Take Me to the River

11 **second languages in immersion programs:** Genesee, 1987.

11 **it takes the human brain a great deal of exposure . . . and we tend to forget:** Anderson and Schooler, 1991.

11 **Suzuki method:** Suzuki, 1969.

12 **'ten years' or 'ten thousand hours':** Ericsson, Krampe, and Tesch-Römer, 1993; Ericsson, Prietula, and Cokely, 2007.

12 **'deliberate practice':** Ericsson, 2008.

12 **most learners reach a plateau:** Ericsson et al., 2006.

12 **'zone of proximal development':** Vygotsky, 1978.

12 **neither too hard nor too easy:** Fisher et al., 1981.

13 **the level of challenge:** Salen and Zimmerman, 2004; Thompson, 2007.

NOTES

13 *Play Piano in a Flash!:* Houston, 2004.

13 *The Complete Guitar Player:* Shipton, 2001.

16 *Crash Course: Acoustic Guitar:* Mead, 2004.

17 surge of dopamine: Knutson and Cooper, 2006.

18 brain's representation of fingers: Elbert et al., 1995.

19 monkey that lost its middle finger: Merzenich et al., 1984.

19 taking some of the neural tissue: Bavelier and Neville, 2002.

19 the brains of musicians differ from those of nonmusicians: For a review of these studies, see Münte, Altenmüller, and Jäncke, 2002; Habib and Besson, 2009.

20 the planum temporale: Keenan et al., 2001.

20 the cerebellum: Schlaug et al., 1995.

20 slight deviations in . . . pitch, rhythm, and timbre: Kraus et al., 2009; Rüsseler et al., 2001.

20 musician's instrument of choice: Pantev et al., 2001.

20 Opera singers show specializations: Kleber et al., 2009.

20 tracked two groups of children: Hyde et al., 2009a; Schlaug et al., 2009.

21 brain changes correlated with the size of behavioural changes: Hyde et al., 2009b.

21 master at least three distinct sets of skills: Uszler, 2003.

22 eighteen hundred notes in a minute: Münte, Altenmüller, and Jäncke, 2002.

Learning to Crawl

23 by the end of the final trimester: Moon and Fifer, 2000.

24 'music instinct': To take four examples, the phrase 'the music instinct' served as the title of a recent PBS documentary, as a chapter title in Daniel Levitin's book *This Is Your Brain on Music,* as the title of a book by Philip Ball, and as the title of a recent journal article by Steven Mithen. Mannes, 2009; Levitin, 2006; Ball 2010; Mithen, 2009.

24 When infants heard large musical leaps amid a series of smaller leaps: Stefanics et al., 2009.

24 sudden absence of bass kick drum: Winkler et al., 2009.

24 recognize changes in timbre: Háden et al., 2009.

24 distinguish consonance . . . from dissonance: Perani et al., 2010.

24 *prefer* listening to consonance rather than dissonance: Trainor, Tsang, and Cheung, 2002.

24 infant chimpanzees: Sugimoto et al., 2010.

25 recognize a short melody even when it has been transposed: Plantinga and Trainor, 2005.

25 sometimes remember melodies for weeks: Saffran, Loman, and Robertson, 2001.

25 ten-month-olds are better able than adults: Hannon and Trehub, 2005.

25 young infants are sensitive to some linguistic distinctions: Werker and Tees, 1992.

25 babies are born with perfect or absolute pitch: Saffran and Griepentrog, 2001, but see also Plantinga and Trainor, 2005, for a different perspective.

26 only a few months to recognize some of the basic rhythms: Soley and Hannon, 2010.

26 discrete notes until they are at least two: Davidson, McKernon, and Gardner, 1981; Dowling, 1982.

26 rare phenomenon of perfect pitch: Deutsch, Henthorn, and Dolson, 2004.

26 miss many of the individual notes: Dowling, 1982.

26 recognizing that major chords: Kastner and Crowder, 1990; Dalla Bella et al., 2001.

26 detecting chords that are merely unexpected: Trainor and Trehub, 1994.

26 trouble paying attention to a background harmony: Ibid.; Moog, 1976.

26 Rhythm is no easier: Moog, 1976.

26 bop along to music: Phillips-Silver and Trainor, 2005.

26 can't bop *in time*: Rainbow, 1981; Frega, 1979; Eerola, Luck, and Toiviainen, 2006. One recent study does, however, suggest that children's capacity to keep time improves when their drumming is embedded in a social situation: Kirschner and Tomasello, 2009.

27 a precise sense of melody: Welch, Sergeant, and White, 1998.

27 Mastering the ability to stay in key: Davidson, 1985; Davidson, McKernon, and Gardner, 1981.

27 'children enter school': Welch, Sergeant, and White, 1998.

27 never learn to sing in key: Pfordresher and Brown, 2007; Dalla Bella, Giguère, and Peretz, 2007.

27 By the time a young zebra finch reaches the age of ninety days: Zann, 1996.

27 **without any obvious correction or feedback:** Kroodsma, 2005.

27 **Few humans can say the same:** Welch, 2008.

27 **better sense of pitch than most humans:** Friedrich, Zentall, and Weisman, 2007.

27 **Freud may have been [amusical]:** Roth, 1986.

28 **much more innate interest in music:** McDermott and Hauser, 2005.

28 **aspects of language that might be cross-culturally universal:** Two exceptionally accessible discussions of what universal grammar might consist of can be found in Pinker, 1994, and Baker, 2001.

29 **reading *draws on* a set of circuits that predate reading itself:** Dehaene and Cohen, 2007; Ramus, 2004.

29 **circuits in the temporal cortex:** Rauschecker, 2005; Rauschecker, Tian, and Hauser, 1995.

30 **far more precise than would be necessary for music alone:** Trehub, 2001.

30 **neural architecture, shared with other mammals:** Stein and Meredith, 1993.

30 **recognize when a vowel:** Kuhl and Meltzoff, 1982.

30 **true for rhythm:** Patel, 2003.

30 **and pitch:** Ross, Choi, and Purves, 2007; Curtis and Bharucha, 2010.

30 **infants prefer their mother's voice to instrumental music:** Standley and Madsen, 1990.

30 **only other study:** Marcus et al., 1999.

31 **infants couldn't grasp the patterns:** Marcus, Fernandes, and Johnson, 2007; Gervain, Berent, and Werker, 2009.

31 **paid more attention to rhythmical patterns:** Phillips-Silver and Trainor, 2005.

31 **information in any two senses goes together:** Lewkowicz, 2002.

31 **The coupling between music and motion:** Stein and Stanford, 2008.

32 **the fusiform gyrus responds more to faces:** Grill-Spector, Knouf, and Kanwisher, 2004.

32 **a vast mélange of brain regions:** On music and the prefrontal cortex, see Bengtsson, Csíkszentmihályi, and Ullén, 2007; Janata, 2009; Wilson et al., 2009; Leaver et al., 2009; Limb, 2006. On music and the superior temporal gyrus, see Chen, Penhune, and Zatorre, 2009.

32 **the superior temporal gyrus:** Hickok and Poeppel, 2004.

32 **Broca's area ... language:** Grodzinsky, 2001; Embick et al., 2000.

32 **Ditto for the planum temporale:** Hickok, Okada, and Serences, 2009.

32 **all kinds of auditory analyses:** Rauschecker, Tian, and Hauser, 1995; Howard et al., 2000.

32 **whether we are listening to speech:** Hickok and Poeppel, 2004.

32 **cerebellum is a key player in all kinds of movements:** Ito, 2008.

32 **the amygdala is implicated in everything:** On its role in fear, see Rogan, Stäubli, and LeDoux, 1997; Phelps and LeDoux, 2005. On its role in lust, see Baird et al., 2004. On its role in anxiety, see Wilson and Junor, 2008.

32 **Unexpected chords might trigger the amygdala:** Koelsch, Fritz, and Schlaug, 2008.

32 **so will electric shocks:** Phelps and LeDoux, 2005.

33 **evolvedlongbeforehumanbeingsdid:** Moreno and González, 2007; Poremba et al., 2004.

33 **increase as people learn to juggle:** Draganski et al., 2004.

It Don't Come Easy

38 **the most popular theory wasn't quite right:** Marcus et al., 1992.

40 **'A person who has not studied German':** Twain, 1880.

42 **we rely on 'cues':** Marcus, 2008; Anderson and Neely, 1996.

45 **Both children and untrained adults:** Trehub, Trainor, and Unyk, 1993.

45 **the general direction a melody is going:** Dowling, 1982.

45 **the difference between big leaps and smaller leaps:** Yust, 2010.

45 **too imprecise for music:** Cuddy and Cohen, 1976.

45 **recognize several intervals every second:** Burns and Ward, 1999.

46 **A more common trick:** Smith et al., 1994.

46 **considerable brain reorganization:** Fujioka et al., 2004.

47 **fingers don't naturally move independently:** Lang and Schieber, 2004.

49 **auditory illusions:** Repp and Bruttomesso, 2009.

49 **Art Blakey:** An amazing illustration of the accuracy of Blakey's timing can be found at http://musicmachinery.com/2010/02/08/revisiting-the-click-track/.

50 **devolves into one against one:** Summers, 2002.

50 **overflow errors:** Soska, Galeon, and Adolph, in press.

50 **illusion of independence:** Peters and Schwartz, 1989; Summers, 2002; Deutsch, 1983.

51 **speed-accuracy trade-off:** Fitts, 1954; Wickelgren, 1977.

51 **automatization or proceduralization:** Anderson, 1992; Moors and De Houwer, 2006.

51 **more efficient, larger units:** Rosenbloom and Newell, 1986.

52 **leave room for other tasks:** Expert soccer players, for example, become so accustomed to dribbling that they can dribble a ball through a slalom and still have enough mental resources left to identify shapes projected on a screen at the end of the slalom (Smith and Chamberlin, 1992).

52 **carefully coordinated processes:** On changes to gray matter during music learning, see Schneider et al., 2005. On changes in white matter during skill learning, see Scholz et al., 2009.

52 **made more efficient:** Harms et al., 2008.

52 **new dendritic spines:** Xu et al., 2009.

52 **proteins must be synthesized:** Luft and Buitrago, 2005.

52 **mental representations:** On the prefrontal cortex, see Grol et al., 2006; Poldrack et al., 2005. On the motor cortex, see Debaere et al., 2004. On the hippocampus and basal ganglia, see Rémy et al., 2008.

Talking Heads

54 **twin reflexes:** Katz and Pesetsky, 2009.

54 **creatures that can dance in time:** Patel et al., 2009; Schachner et al., 2009.

55 **still fail to acquire perfect pitch:** Deutsch et al., 2006.

55 **distinct 'modules':** Alossa and Castelli, 2009.

55 **impaired musical abilities:** Gall, 1825.

55 **musical impairments . . . alongside normal linguistic abilities:** Peretz et al., 1994.

55 **impaired language abilities . . . yet largely preserved musical abilities:** Tomaino, 2010.

55 **manage to recognize songs learned long ago:** Vanstone et al., 2009.

55 **orthopaedic surgeon who became obsessed:** Sacks, 2007.

56 **prefrontal cortex, which has been implicated in everything:** On sarcasm, see Shammi and Stuss, 1999; on pitch perception, see Zatorre and Gandour, 2008; on orgasm, see Tiihonen et al., 1994; on jazz improvisation, see Bengtsson, Csíkszentmihályi, and Ullén, 2007. The prefrontal cortex has also been tied to self-recognition (Keenan et al., 2000) and the perception

of fairness (Knoch et al., 2006).

56 **recent review by the neuroscientist:** Patel, 2008.

56 **the most systematic review:** Marin and Perry, 1999. The estimate of a third is likely an underestimate of the real proportion, since many patients who have impairments in both probably aren't deemed unusual enough to merit reporting in the literature.

56 **people who speak tonal languages:** Pfordresher and Brown, 2009.

56 **interfered with people's sentence comprehension:** Slevc, Rosenberg, and Patel, 2009.

56 **identify the emotions in speech:** Thompson, Schellenberg, and Husain, 2004.

57 **smaller units into larger units:** Fadiga, Craighero, and D'Ausilio, 2009.

57 **allow us to use tools:** Higuchi et al., 2009.

57 **so-called muscle memory:** Albouy et al., 2008.

57 **constellation of brain areas:** Marcus, 2006.

57 **draw heavily on our neural resources for memory:** Snyder, 2000.

58 **our memories lack the neat tabular form:** Marcus, 2008.

58 **Listeners get lost:** Ibid.

58 **musicians learning Philip Glass pieces:** Mary Farbood, personal communication.

58 **musical 'protolanguage':** Darwin, 1874.

58 *The Singing Neanderthals:* Mithen, 2005. The animal behaviourist Tecumseh Fitch has defended a similar view: Fitch, n.d.

59 **motherese may not be truly innate:** Ingram, 1995.

59 **infants pay more attention to it:** Fernald, 1985.

59 **intrinsically sound happy:** Singh, Morgan, and Best, 2002.

59 **developing skill at golf . . . tango:** Jäncke et al., 2009; Sacco et al., 2006.

60 **show almost no interest in music:** McDermott and Hauser, 2005.

60 **tone-deaf . . . can't reliably sing on pitch:** Pfordresher and Brown, 2007.

60 **extracting even simple musical intervals:** Trehub, Schellenberg, and Hill, 1997.

60 **seems deeply implausible:** Tallerman, 2007; Bickerton, 2009.

60 **ivory flute:** Conard, Malina, and Münzel, 2009.

60 **at least fifty thousand years ago:** Klein and Edgar, 2002.

60 **a few million years:** Bickerton, 2009.

60 **other kinds of tools far earlier:** Semaw et al., 2003. An unusual 2005 article

by Iegor Reznikoff argues that cave paintings (from roughly the same era) were placed in exceptionally resonant regions of caves, but none of the paintings Reznikoff points to depict anything that could reasonably be construed as musical imagery.

61 **lyrics are more easily remembered than melodies:** Peretz, Radeau, and Arguin, 2004.

61 **four-year-olds consider two songs:** Serafine et al., 1986.

61 **A more recent study has shown:** Lebedeva and Kuhl, 2010.

61 **enormously influential book:** Lerdahl and Jackendoff, 1983, and the papers in a 2009 special issue of *Music Perception,* celebrating the book's twenty-fifth anniversary.

61 **Jackendoff broke down the process of making a cup of coffee:** Jackendoff, 2007.

62 **both . . . draw from a wide range of important cognitive resources:** Jackendoff's view is further explained in Jackendoff, 2009.

62 **even mundane activities:** Zacks, Tversky, and Iyer, 2001.

63 **'Writing about music is like dancing about architecture':** http://www.paclink.com/ascott/they/tamildaa.htm and http://theonlinephotographer.typepad.com/the_online_photographer/2010/07/ot-we-hear-from-martin-mull.html.

63 **'the most popular':** Schiff, 1997.

63 **'begins with a languid trill':** Ross, 2007.

64 **interpretation and imagination of the clarinettist:** Schwartz, 1979.

64 **three physicists wrote an entire article:** Chen, Smith, and Wolfe, 2008.

64 **'Music expresses':** Copland, 1957.

Back to School

66 **'[Often, too much of a student's] attention':** Lehmann, Sloboda, and Woody, 2007.

70 **over 40 percent:** http://home3.americanexpress.com/corp/pc/2006/plat-lux_sur vey.asp.

70 **what makes music teaching effective:** Buttram, 1996.

71 **Suzuki method:** Suzuki, 1969.

72 **'growth' mind-set:** Dweck, 2007.

75 **Dalcroze method:** Mead, 1996.

76 **a class in music production:** http://www.cirtgill.com/Weaver.html.

79 **cult-classic book:** Andreas, 2005.

80 **memories solidify over time:** Luft and Buitrago, 2005; Wright and Sabin, 2007.

81 **parental support:** Creech, 2009.

81 **'all [Hendrix] really wanted to do in life was to play guitar':** Henderson, 1981.

82 *The Well-Tempered Keyboard Teacher:* Uszler, Gordon, and Mach, 1991.

83 **motivated by compositions that were fun to play:** McPherson, 2006.

83 **audiation:** Gordon, 1997.

84 **strict sequence of steps:** Ibid.

84 **Orff or Kodaly:** Buttram, 1996.

School of Rock

91 **gradually begins to decline:** Giedd et al., 1999.

92 **no firm break in the curve:** Hakuta, Bialystok, and Wiley, 2003.

92 **memory skills slowly decline:** Salthouse, 2009.

92 **interference and habits:** Iverson et al., 2003.

93 **'less is more':** Newport, 1988.

93 **Bulgarian children learning to play:** Rice, 1994, with thanks to Erin Hannon for the example.

93 **adults were systematically better:** Savion-Lemieux, Bailey, and Penhune, 2009.

93 **watch the same episode of a TV show:** Crawley et al., 1999.

94 **get there in the end:** Savion-Lemieux, Bailey, and Penhune, 2009.

94 **known as chunking:** Miller, 1956.

94 **known as attention:** Green and Bavelier, 2003; Memmert, 2006.

95 **familiar chunks:** Groot, 1965.

95 **grey matter tends to get denser:** Draganski et al., 2004.

True Talent

97 **'New research shows':** Ericsson, Prietula, and Cokely, 2007.

97 **'Give me a dozen healthy infants':** Watson, 1925.

97 **surprising ways:** Gladwell, 2008.

99 **The autism likely helped:** Richard is not alone in this regard. For a general discussion of the music ability of children with autism, see Miller, 1989.

100 **put in more like two thousand hours:** Weisberg, 1999.

101 **the two met only once:** Browne, 1993.

101 **Even before modern genetic techniques were available:** Scheinfeld and Schweitzer, 1939.

102 **genetics is a better predictor:** Bouchard et al., 1990.

102 **talent matters . . . from sports to chess to writing to music:** Vinkhuyzen et al., 2009.

102 **The chain of causality from gene to . . . behavior:** Marcus, 2004.

102 **FOXP2:** Fisher and Marcus, 2006.

102 **affects memory efficiency:** Cowansage, LeDoux, and Monfils, 2010.

103 **modulate curiosity:** Ackermann et al., 2010.

103 **sensitivity to absolute pitch:** Theusch, Basu, and Gitschier, 2009.

103 **Another recent study shows:** Ukkola et al., 2009.

103 **important role in social interaction:** Turner et al., 2010.

103 **statistically controlled for:** Ruthsatz et al., 2008; Meinz and Hambrick, 2010.

103 **nature working together with nurture:** Marcus, 2004.

103 **study with identical twins:** Coon and Carey, 1989.

103 **the original study by Ericsson and others:** Ericsson, Krampe, and Tesch-Römer, 1993; Sloboda, 1996; Jorgensen, 2002.

103 **without becoming as good as others who had played for only eight:** Ericsson, Krampe, and Tesch-Römer, 1993.

104 **study of musical aptitude:** Gordon, 1967.

104 **directly affect rhythmic perception:** Trainor et al., 2009.

Into the Groove

108 **'sexual liaisons':** Miller, 2000.

109 **break the glass ceiling:** http://www.usatoday.com/life/music/news/2006-04-11-female-producers-sidebar_x.htm.

110 **can't make ends meet:** Bennett, 2007.

111 **leads to social bonding:** Kirschner and Tomasello, 2010.

113 **retooled Mickey's image:** Gould, 1980.

113 **Flow:** Csíkszentmihályi, 1990; Nakamura and Csíkszentmihályi, 2009.

114 **The piano . . . represented a huge advance:** Ehrlich, 1990.

114 **sophistication of piano players:** Lehmann and Ericsson, 1998.

114 **the microphone opened:** Milner, 2009.

115 **the advent of multitrack recording:** Ibid.

115 **modern Western harmony:** Grout, Burkholder, and Palisca, 2006.

Onstage

120 *The Inner Game of Music:* Green and Gallwey, 1986.

120 **sense of fear and mortification sets in:** Kenny and Osborne, 2006.

120 **mix of different factors:** Craske and Craig, 1984.

120 **cardiac medications known as beta-blockers:** Tindall, 2004.

The Worst Song in the World

125 **hear on his Web site:** http://davesoldier.com/experimental.html.

125 **no book is more notorious:** McKee, 1997.

126 **to make us like it more:** Zajonc, 1968.

126 **'liking for familiarity':** Schellenberg, Peretz, and Vieillard, 2008; Szpunar, Schellenberg, and Pliner, 2004.

127 **hundreds of experiments have replicated:** Bornstein, 1989.

127 **paper bags full of cash:** Palmer, 1995.

127 **the music we hear as teenagers:** North and Hargreaves, 1995.

127 **'Not a whole lot':** Sapolsky, 2005.

127 **rebellion a key factor:** Cowen, 2007.

128 **too 'advanced' for their listeners:** http://papercuts.blogs.nytimes.com/2010/05/26/living-with-music-jason-hartley/?hp.

128 **personality traits:** Rentfrow and Gosling, 2003.

128 **experts may listen more analytically:** Muller et al., 2009.

129 **participants on the Web:** Salganik, Dodds, and Watts, 2006.

129 **flipping a control group's rankings:** Salganik and Watts, 2008.

129 **most songs . . . flop:** Vogel, 2004.

130 **the focus of production is . . . on timbre:** Levitin, 2006.

131 **what key a piece is in:** Bigand and Poulin-Charronnat, 2006.

131 **Small jumps:** Huron, 2006.

132 **differing sensitivity to dissonance:** McDermott, Lehr, and Oxenham, 2010.

132 **in which case the ratio:** Thomson, 1991.

133 **categories they know best:** Shepard and Jordan, 1984.

133 **experienced musicians are more sensitive:** McDermott, Lehr, and Oxenham, 2010.

134 **'Who Cares If You Listen?':** Babbitt, 1958.

137 **novelty conveys its own separate reward:** Guitart-Masip et al., 2010; Bunzeck and Düzel, 2006.

137 **many listeners don't recognize repetitions:** Margulis, 2010.

138 **become truly bored:** Schellenberg, Peretz, and Vieillard, 2008.

138 **carefully matched lists of letters:** Williamson, Baddeley, and Hitch, 2010.

138 **less powerful than visual memory:** Cohen, Horowitz, and Wolfe, 2009.

138 **'The 'special' power':** Schuylkind, 2009.

138 **Beethoven . . . is often praised:** Konečni and Karno, 1992.

138 **'If the movements':** Quoted in ibid.

139 **rearranged the order of the movements:** Konečni, 1984.

139 **Bach's *Goldberg Variations:*** Gotlieb and Konečni, 1985.

139 **carving musical compositions:** Tillmann and Bigand, 1996.

139 **preferred the bastardized combinations:** Tan, Spackman, and Peaslee, 2006.

139 **ended in keys that were inconsistent:** Cook, 1987.

141 **what the program has going for it:** http://research.microsoft.com/en-us/um/redmond/projects/songsmith/research.html.

142 **'plays merely with sensations':** Kant, 1790.

142 **'sonic wallpaper':** Kivy, 1993.

142 **Kant's argument was that music:** Kant, 1790.

143 **affiliative component:** Rentfrow and Gosling, 2006; Selfhout et al., 2009.

143 **us and them:** Berreby, 2005.

143 **Music also unfolds over time:** Kivy, 1993.

143 **two distinct neural systems:** Salimpoor et al., 2010.

144 **the brain pats itself on the back:** Pessiglione et al., 2006.

144 **thug-love duets:** Sanneh, 2006.

145 **directly tied to neural machinery:** Chen, Penhune, and Zatorre, 2008; Grahn and Rowe, 2009.

145 **'Music is a kind of kaleidoscope':** Payzant, 1986. Some philosophers have

taken Hanslick's kaleidoscope metaphor to be a pejorative dig against music, akin to Kant's perspective of music as empty decoration. Regardless of how it was intended, his characterization of music seems remarkably apt.

Knowing Without Knowing

148 **follow descending melodies:** Starr and Waterman, 2003.

150 **'When composing':** Tymoczko, 2011.

151 **something is slightly out of key:** Fujioka et al., 2004.

151 **how far apart two notes are:** Burns and Ward, 1999.

151 **detect deviations in a rhythm:** Honing and Ladinig, 2009; Vuust et al., 2009.

151 **identify the individual notes in a chord:** Marco, McLachlan, and Wilson, 2010.

151 **all expert *listeners:*** Bigand and Poulin-Charronnat, 2006.

152 **seemed to have much the same intuitions:** Bigand, 1990.

153 **'Telling More Than We Can Know':** Nisbett and Wilson, 1977.

155 **jazz almost always requires a kind of mixture:** Johnson-Laird, 2002.

155 **legendary improviser:** http://www.bbc.co.uk/radio3/bach/bachatozi. shtml.

155 **performers in the classical tradition improvised frequently:** Haynes, 2007.

158 **Zollo interviews James Taylor:** http://bluerailroad.wordpress.com/james-taylor-the-bluerailroad-interview/.

159 **'this [unusual] chord':** The exact identity of the chord in question is in dispute. James Taylor, who is in a good position to know, possibly having asked McCartney, claimed it was an F13, but on the basis of sound and video, Dominic Pedler, 2003, argues that the chord in question was instead an F7#9. Either way, the chord was not very common in the pop music of the time.

Take It to the Limit

164 **key of F-sharp:** http://www.historynet.com/irving-berlin.htm.

164 **special custom piano:** http://americanhistory.si.edu/collections/object.cfm? key=35&objkey=59.

165 **'As long as the two of us':** http://www.youtube.com/watch?v=ca_GcvApODg.

167 **alignment of ... representations:** Van Ee et al., 2009; Andersen et al., 1995.

168 **relearn mappings between visual and motor space bit by bit:** Ghahramani, Wolpert, and Jordan, 1996.

169 **generally an alignment problem:** Pfordresher and Brown, 2007.

169 **head and chest voices:** Clippinger, 1917.

170 **Such feedback can be extremely useful:** Welch, Howard, and Rush, 1989; Howard, 2005.

170 **digital pianos that had been electronically muted:** Repp and Knoblich, 2004.

171 **astonishingly complex choreography:** Ortmann, 1929.

171 **The articulators in our vocal tract do something similar:** Macneilage, 1969; Garrett, 1980.

171 **remarkable efficiency:** Palmer, 2006.

171 **the kinds of errors they make:** Ibid.

171 **anticipation error:** Garrett, 1980.

172 **other notes from the same key:** Palmer and van de Sande, 1993; Repp, 1996.

172 **listeners rarely even notice:** Repp, 1996.

174 **first scientific documentation:** Vernon, 1932.

174 **even experts aren't perfect:** Repp, 2005.

175 **is true around the globe:** Balkwill, Thompson, and Matsunaga, 2004; Balkwill and Thompson, 1999.

175 **power of subtle timing cues transcends ... expertise:** Honing and Ladinig, 2009.

175 **memorize complex pieces:** Chaffin and Logan, 2006.

176 **Roger Chaffin:** Chaffin's lab has an Excel spreadsheet called Study Your Music Practice that you can download for free at http://www.musicpsyc.uconn.edu/symp/intro.html.

177 **away from their instruments:** I thank Terre Roche for relating Ms. Abreu's advice.

177 **showmanship:** For more stage antics, see http://www.ultimate-guitar.com/columns/the_guide_to/stage_antics_the_good_the_bad_and_the_ugly.html.

178 **'The first thing I learned':** Barone, 2007.

178 **musical coordination between individuals:** Keller and Appel, 2010.

178 **divide one's attention:** Keller, 2008.

178 **auditory equivalent of mental imagery:** Keller and Appel, 2010.

180 **even-tempered system:** An exceptionally accessible discussion of the widely used even-tempered tuning system, and how it was developed, can be found in Isacoff, 2001; illustrative sound examples can be found at http://www.yuvalnov.org/temperament/.

181 **an entire realm of alternate tuning:** http://members.cox.net/waguitar-tunings/tunings.htm.

182 **recognize expressive timing differences:** Honing and Ladinig, 2009.

183 **removed the entire low bass string:** For a gallery of Keith Richards's guitars and alternate tunings, see http://members.tripod.com/~Blue_Lena/guitar.html.

183 **'I found I was getting sort of jaded':** http://www.youtube.com/watch?v=_QqsNIH9cio.

183 **earliest adopters of the Mellotron:** Emerick and Massey, 2006.

184 **Hendrix preferred Fender Stratocasters:** Henderson, 1981.

185 **'Hammond's Folly':** Shelton, 2003.

185 **Dylan's own account:** Dylan, 2005.

187 **The Beatles may have undergone a similar revolution:** Everett, 1999. According to Everett, 'Paperback Writer' was perhaps the first of Paul's character studies, after he was goaded by an aunt who wondered why all he ever wrote about was love.

Heavy Metal

193 **software that improvises jazz:** Johnson-Laird, 1987; Johnson-Laird, 2002.

193 **consisted entirely of robots:** http://www.patmetheny.com/orchestrioninfo/.

194 **Tristan Jehan's Swinger:** http://musicmachinery.com/2010/05/21/the-swinger/.

195 **better at learning foreign languages:** Marques et al., 2007.

195 **higher IQs:** Schellenberg, 2004.

195 **Nobel Prize winners:** Root-Bernstein et al., 2008.

195 **more effective than ... drama lessons:** Schellenberg, 2004.

195 **small number of carefully controlled studies:** Moreno et al., 2009.

196 **'almost all of the available data':** Schellenberg, 2009.

196 **show social advantages:** Goldstein, Wu, and Winner, 2009.

196 **grossed over three billion dollars:** Radosh, 2009.

197 **researchers have built robots:** http://slashbot.wordpress.com/ and http:// guitar heronoid.blogspot.com/.

197 **the illusion of control:** Langer, 1975; Wegner, 2002.

197 **famous set of studies:** Glass and Singer, 1972.

197 **learned helplessness:** Seligman and Maier, 1967.

199 **informal study:** http://multiplayerblog.mtv.com/2009/01/15/fender-survey-shows -music-games-drive-students-to-play-real-instruments/.

199 **the science of pleasure:** Gilbert, 2006.

199 **eudaimonia:** Waterman, 2008.

199 **'How can I live a balanced life':** Ryff and Singer, 1998.

200 **'self-actualization':** Maslow, 1946.

200 **a greater sense of purpose and personal growth:** Ryff and Singer, 2008.

200 **twenty-seven cultures:** Park, Peterson, and Ruch, 2009.

200 **A third used diary checklists:** Steger, Kashdan, and Oishi, 2008.

200 **room for both:** Peterson, Park, and Seligman, 2005; Steger, Kashdan, and Oishi, 2008; Huta and Ryan, n.d.

200 **'selfish gene':** Dawkins, 1976.

REFERENCES

Ackermann, Teresa F., Daniela S. Kempe, Florian Lang, and Undine E. Lang. 2010. Hyperactivity and enhanced curiosity of mice expressing PKB/SGK-resistant glycogen synthase kinase-3 (GSK-3). *Cellular Physiology and Biochemistry* 25 (6): 775–86.

Albouy, Geneviève, Virginie Sterpenich, Evelyne Balteau, Gilles Vandewalle, Martin Desseilles, Thanh Dang-Vu, Annabelle Darsaud, et al. 2008. Both the hippocampus and striatum are involved in consolidation of motor sequence memory. *Neuron* 58 (2): 261–72.

Alossa, Nicoletta, and Lorys Castelli. 2009. Amusia and musical functioning. *European Neurology* 61 (5): 269–77.

Andersen, Susan M., Noah S. Glassman, Serena Chen, and Steve W. Cole. 1995. Transference in social perception: The role of chronic accessibility in significant-other representations. *Journal of Personality and Social Psychology* 69 (1): 41–57.

Anderson, John R. 1992. Automaticity and the ACT* theory. *American Journal of Psychology* 105 (2): 165–80.

Anderson, John R., and Lael J. Schooler. 1991. Reflections of the environment in memory. *Psychological Science* 2 (6): 396.

Anderson, Michael C., and James H. Neely. 1996. Interference and inhibition in memory retrieval. *Memory* 22: 586.

Andreas, Jamey. 2005. *The principles of correct practice for guitar: The perfect start for beginners, and the answer to the problems of players*. Woodstock, NY: Jamey World.

Babbitt, Milton. 1958. Who cares if you listen? *High Fidelity* 8 (2): 38–40.

Baird, Amee, Sarah J. Wilson, Peter F. Bladin, Michael M. Saling, and David C. Reutens. 2004. The amygdala and sexual drive: Insights from temporal lobe epilepsy surgery. *Annals of Neurology* 55 (1): 87–96.

Baker, Mark C. 2001. *The atoms of language*. New York: Basic Books.

Balkwill, Laura-Lee, and William Forde Thompson. 1999. A cross-cultural investigation of the perception of emotion in music: Psychophysical and cultural cues. *Music Perception* 17 (1): 43–64.

REFERENCES

Balkwill, L. L., W. F. Thompson, and R. Matsunaga. 2004. Recognition of emotion in Japanese, Western, and Hindustani music by Japanese listeners. *Japanese Psychological Research* 46 (4): 337–49.

Ball, Philip. 2010. *The music instinct: How music works and why we can't do without it.* London: The Bodley Head.

Barone, Richard. 2007. *Frontman: Surviving the rock star myth.* New York: Backbeat Books.

Bavelier, Daphne, and Helen J. Neville. 2002. Cross-modal plasticity: Where and how? *Nature Reviews Neuroscience* 3 (6): 443–52.

Bengtsson, Sara L., Mihály Csíkszentmihályi, and Fredrik Ullén. 2007. Cortical regions involved in the generation of musical structures during improvisation in pianists. *Journal of Cognitive Neuroscience* 19 (5): 830–42.

Bennett, Dawn. 2007. Utopia for music performance graduates: Is it achievable, and how should it be defined? *British Journal of Music Education* 24 (2): 179–89.

Berreby, David. 2005. *Us and them: Understanding your tribal mind.* New York: Little, Brown.

Bickerton, Derek. 2009. *Adam's tongue: How humans made language, how language made humans.* New York: Hill and Wang.

Bigand, Emmanuel. 1990. Abstraction of two forms of underlying structure in a tonal melody. *Psychology of Music* 18 (1): 45.

Bigand, Emmanuel, and Barbara Poulin-Charronnat. 2006. Are we 'experienced listeners'? A review of the musical capacities that do not depend on formal musical training. *Cognition* 100 (1): 100–30.

Birdsong, David. 2009. Age and the end state of second language acquisition. In *The new handbook of second language acquisition,* ed. W. C. Ritchie and T. K. Bhatia, 401. Bingley, UK: Emerald Group Publishing.

Bornstein, Robert F. 1989. Exposure and affect: Overview and meta-analysis of research, 1968–1987. *Psychological Bulletin* 106 (2): 265–89.

Bouchard, Thomas J., David T. Lykken, Matthew McGue, Nancy L. Segal, and Auke Tellegen. 1990. Sources of human psychological differences: The Minnesota study of twins reared apart. *Science* 250 (4978): 223–28.

Browne, David. 1993. The unmade star. *New York Times,* October 24.

Bunzeck, Nico, and Emrah Düzel. 2006. Absolute coding of stimulus novelty in the human substantia nigra/VTA. *Neuron* 51 (3): 369–79.

REFERENCES

Burns, Edward, and Paul Ward. 1999. Intervals, scales, and tuning. In *The psychology of music,* ed. Diana Deutsch, 215–64. San Diego: Academic Press.

Buttram, Joe B. 1996. Learning theory and related developments: Overview and applications in music education and music therapy. In *Handbook of music psychology,* ed. Donald A. Hodges, 401–68. San Antonio: IMR Press.

Cage, John. 1961. *Silence: Lectures and writings.* Middletown, Conn.: Wesleyan University Press.

Cantalupo, Claudio, Dawn L. Pilcher, and William D. Hopkins. 2003. Are planum temporale and sylvian fissure asymmetries directly related? An MRI study in great apes. *Neuropsychologia* 41 (14): 1975–81.

Cantalupo, Claudio, and William D. Hopkins. 2001. Asymmetric Broca's area in great apes. *Nature* 414 (6863): 505.

Chaffin, R., and T. Logan. 2006. Practicing perfection: How concert soloists prepare for performance. *Advances in Cognitive Psychology* 2 (2): 113–30.

Chen, Jer-Ming, John Smith, and Joe Wolfe. 2008. How to play the first bar of 'Rhapsody in Blue.' *Journal of the Acoustical Society of America* 123 (5): 3123.

Chen, Joyce L., Virginia B. Penhune, and Robert J. Zatorre. 2008. Listening to musical rhythms recruits motor regions of the brain. *Cerebral Cortex* 18 (12): 2844–54.

– – – . 2009. The role of auditory and premotor cortex in sensorimotor transformations. *Annals of the New York Academy of Sciences* 1169: 15–34.

Clippinger, D. A. 1917. *The head voice and other problems: Practical talks on singing.* New York: Oliver Ditson Company.

Cohen, Michael A., Todd S. Horowitz, and Jeremy M. Wolfe. 2009. Auditory recognition memory is inferior to visual recognition memory. *Proceedings of the National Academy of Sciences of the United States of America* 106 (14): 6008–10.

Conard, Nicholas J., Maria Malina, and Susanne C. Münzel. 2009. New flutes document the earliest musical tradition in southwestern Germany. *Nature* 460 (7256): 737–40.

Cook, Nicholas. 1987. The perception of large-scale tonal closure. *Music Perception:* 197–205.

Coon, Hilary, and Gregory Carey. 1989. Genetic and environmental determinants of musical ability in twins. *Behavior Genetics* 19 (2): 183–93.

Copland, Aaron. 1957. *What to listen for in music.* New York: McGraw-Hill.

Cowansage, Kiriana K., Joseph E. LeDoux, and Marie-H. Monfils. 2010.

REFERENCES

Brain-derived neurotrophic factor: A dynamic gatekeeper of neural plas=ticity. *Current Molecular Pharmacology* 3 (1): 12–29.

Cowen, Tyler. 2007. *Discover your inner economist: Use incentives to fall in love, survive your next meeting, and motivate your dentist.* New York: Dutton.

Crain, Stephen. 1991. Language acquisition in the absence of experience. *Behavioral and Brain Sciences* 14 (4): 597–650.

Craske, Michelle, and Kenneth D. Craig. 1984. Musical performance anxiety: The three-systems model and self-efficacy theory. *Behaviour Research and Therapy* 22 (3): 267–80.

Crawley, Alisha M., Daniel R. Anderson, Alice Wilder, Marsha Williams, and Angela Santomero. 1999. Effects of repeated exposures to a single episode of the television program *Blue's Clues* on the viewing behaviors and comprehension of preschool children. *Journal of Educational Psychology* 91 (4): 630–37.

Creech, Andrea. 2009. The role of the family in supportive learning. In *The Oxford handbook of music psychology,* ed. Susan Hallam, Ian Cross, and Michael Thaut, 294–305. New York: Oxford University Press.

Csźkszentmihályi, Mihály. 1990. *Flow: The psychology of optimal experience.* New York: Harper & Row.

Cuddy, Lola, and Annabel J. Cohen. 1976. Recognition of transposed melodic sequences. *Quarterly Journal of Experimental Psychology* 28 (2): 255–70.

Curtis, Meagan E., and Jamshed J. Bharucha. 2010. The minor third communicates sadness in speech, mirroring its use in music. *Emotion* 10 (3): 335–48.

Curtiss, Susan. 1977. *Genie: A psycholinguistic study of a modern-day 'wild child.'* New York: Academic Press.

Dalla Bella, Simone, Isabelle Peretz, Luc Rousseau, and Nathalie Gosselin. 2001. A developmental study of the affective value of tempo and mode in music. *Cognition* 80 (3): B1–10.

Dalla Bella, Simone, Jean-François Giguère, and Isabelle Peretz. 2007. Singing proficiency in the general population. *Journal of the Acoustical Society of America* 121 (2): 1182–89.

Darwin, Charles. 1874. *The descent of man, and selection in relation to sex.* New York: A. L. Burt.

Davidson, L. 1985. Tonal structures of children's early songs. *Music Perception*

2 (3): 361–73.

Davidson, L., P. McKernon, and Howard Gardner. 1981. The acquisition of song: A developmental approach. In *Documentary report of the Ann Arbor symposium,* 301–15. Reston, Va.: Music Educators National Conference.

Dawkins, Richard. 1976. *The selfish gene.* Oxford: Oxford University Press.

Debaere, F., N. Wenderoth, S. Sunaert, P. Van Hecke, and S. P. Swinnen. 2004. Changes in brain activation during the acquisition of a new bimanual coordination task. *Neuropsychologia* 42 (7): 855–67.

Dehaene, Stanislas, and Laurent Cohen. 2007. Cultural recycling of cortical maps. *Neuron* 56 (2): 384–98.

Deutsch, Diana. 1983. The generation of two isochronous sequences in parallel. *Perception & Psychophysics* 34 (4): 331–37.

Deutsch, Diana, Trevor Henthorn, and Mark Dolson. 2004. Absolute pitch, speech, and tone language: Some experiments and a proposed framework. *Music Perception* 21 (3): 339–56.

Deutsch, Diana, Trevor Henthorn, Elizabeth Marvin, and HongShuai Xu. 2006. Absolute pitch among American and Chinese conservatory students: Prevalence differences, and evidence for a speech-related critical period. *Journal of the Acoustical Society of America* 119 (2): 719–22.

Dowling, W. J. 1982. Melodic information processing and its development. In *The psychology of music,* ed. Diana Deutsch, 413–29. San Diego: Academic Press.

Draganski, Bogdan, Christian Gaser, Volker Busch, Gerhard Schuierer, Ulrich Bogdahn, and Arne May. 2004. Neuroplasticity: Changes in grey matter induced by training. *Nature* 427 (6972): 311–12.

Dweck, Carole S. 2007. *Mindset: The new psychology of success.* New York: Ballantine Books.

Dylan, Bob. 2005. *Chronicles: Volume one.* New York: Simon & Schuster.

Eerola, Tuomas, Geoff Luck, and Petri Toiviainen. 2006. An investigation of pre-schoolers' corporeal synchronization with music. In *Proceedings of the 9th international conference on music perception & cognition,* Bologna.

Ehrlich, Cyril. 1990. *The piano: A history.* New York: Oxford University Press.Elbert, Thomas, Christo Pantev, Christian Wienbruch, Briggitte Rockstroh, and Edward Taub. 1995. Increased cortical representation of the fingers of the left hand in string players. *Science* 270 (5234): 305.

Embick, David, Alec Marantz, Yasushi Miyashita, Wayne O'Neil, and

REFERENCES

Kuniyoshi Sakai. 2000. A syntactic specialization for Broca's area. *Proceedings of the National Academy of Sciences of the United States of America* 97 (11): 6150.

Emerick, Geoff, and Howard Massey. 2006. *Here, there, and everywhere.* New York: Gotham Books.

Ericsson, K. Anders. 2008. Deliberate practice and acquisition of expert performance: A general overview. *Academic Emergency Medicine* 15 (11): 988–94.

Ericsson, K. A., et al. 2006. The influence of experience and deliberate practice on the development of superior expert performance. In *The Cambridge handbook of expertise and expert performance,* ed. K. Anders Ericsson, 683–703. New York: Cambridge University Press.

Ericsson, K. Anders, Michael J. Prietula, and Edward T. Cokely. 2007. The making of an expert. *Harvard Business Review* 85 (7–8): 114–21, 193.

Ericsson, K. Anders, Ralf Th. Krampe, and Clemens Tesch-Römer. 1993. The role of deliberate practice in the acquisition of expert performance. *Psychological Review* 100 (3): 363–406.

Fadiga, Luciano, Laila Craighero, and Alessandro D'Ausilio. 2009. Broca's area in language, action, and music. *Annals of the New York Academy of Sciences* 1169: 448–58.

Fernald, Anne. 1985. Four-month-old infants prefer to listen to motherese. *Infant Behavior and Development* 8 (2): 181–95.

Fisher, Charles W., David C. Berliner, Nikola N. Filby, Richard Marliave, Leonard S. Cahen, and Marilyn M. Dishaw. 1981. Teaching behaviors, academic learning time, and student achievement: An overview. *Journal of Classroom Interaction* 17 (1): 2–15.

Fisher, Simon E., and Gary F. Marcus. 2006. The eloquent ape: Genes, brains and the evolution of language. *Nature Reviews Genetics* 7 (1): 9–20.

Fitch, W. Tecumseh. N.d. Musical protolanguage: Darwin's theory of language evolution revisited. Unpublished manuscript, University of St. Andrews, http://www.st-andrews.ac.uk/~wtsf/DarwinLanguageEvolution.html.

Fitts, P. M. 1954. The information capacity of the human motor system in controlling the amplitude of movement. *Journal of Experimental Psychology* 47 (6): 381–91.

REFERENCES

Frega, Ana Lucia. 1979. Rhythmic tasks with 3-, 4-, and 5-year-old children: A study made in Argentine Republic. *Bulletin of the Council for Research in Music Education* 59: 32–34.

Friedrich, Andrea, Thomas Zentall, and Ronald Weisman. 2007. Absolute pitch: Frequency-range discriminations in pigeons (*Columba livia*): Comparisons with zebra finches (*Taeniopygia guttata*) and humans (*Homo sapiens*). *Journal of Comparative Psychology* 121 (1): 95–105.

Fritz, Thomas, Sebastian Jentschke, Nathalie Gosselin, Daniela Sammler, Isabelle Peretz, Robert Turner, Angela D. Friederici, and Stefan Koelsch. 2009. Universal recognition of three basic emotions in music. *Current Biology* 19 (7): 573–76.

Fujioka, Takako, Laurel J. Trainor, Bernhard Ross, Ryusuke Kakigi, and Christo Pantev. 2004. Musical training enhances automatic encoding of melodic contour and interval structure. *Journal of Cognitive Neuroscience* 16 (6): 1010–21.

Gall, Francis J. 1825. *Sur les fonctions du cerveau et sur celles de chacune de ses parties.* Paris: J.-B. Baillière.

Garrett, M. F. 1980. Levels of processing in sentence production. *Language Production* 1: 177–220.

Genesee, Fred. 1987. *Learning through two languages: Studies of immersion and bilingual education.* Rowley, Mass.: Newbury House Publishers.

Gervain, Judit, Iris Berent, and Janet Werker. 2009. The encoding of identity and sequential position in newborns: An optical imaging study. Boston University Conference on Language Development, 34.

Ghahramani, Z., D. M. Wolpert, and M. I. Jordan. 1996. Generalization to local remappings of the visuomotor coordinate transformation. *Journal of Neuroscience* 16 (21): 7085–96.

Giedd, Jay N., Jonathan Blumenthal, Neal O. Jeffries, F. X. Castellanos, Hong Liu, Alex Zijdenbos, Tomás Paus, Alan C. Evans, and Judith L. Rapoport. 1999. Brain development during childhood and adolescence: A longitudinal MRI study. *Nature Neuroscience* 2: 861–62.

Gilbert, Daniel T. 2006. *Stumbling on happiness.* New York: Vintage Books.

Gladwell, Malcolm. 2008. *Outliers: The story of success.* New York: Little, Brown, and Company.

Glass, D. C., and J. E. Singer. 1972. *Urban stress: Experiments in noise and social stressors.* New York: Academic Press.

REFERENCES

Goldstein, T. R., K. Wu, and E. Winner. 2009. Actors are skilled in theory of mind but not empathy. *Imagination, Cognition and Personality* 29 (2): 115–33.

Gordon, Edwin E. 1967. *A three-year longitudinal predictive validity study of the musical aptitude profile.* Iowa City: University of Iowa Press.

– – –. 1997. *Learning sequences in music: Skill, content, and patterns: A music learning theory.* Chicago: GIA.

Gotlieb, Heidi, and Vladimir J. Konečni. 1985. The effects of instrumentation, playing style, and structure in the Goldberg Variations by Johann Sebastian Bach. *Music Perception* 3 (1): 87–102.

Gould, Stephen Jay. 1980. *The panda's thumb: More reflections in natural history.* New York: Norton.

Grahn, Jessica A., and James B. Rowe. 2009. Feeling the beat: Premotor and striatal interactions in musicians and nonmusicians during beat perception. *Journal of Neuroscience* 29 (23): 7540–48.

Green, Barry, and W. Timothy Gallwey. 1986. *The inner game of music.* New York: Doubleday.

Green, C. Shawn, and Daphne Bavelier. 2003. Action video game modifies visual selective attention. *Nature* 423 (6939): 534–37.

Grill-Spector, Kalanit, Nicholas Knouf, and Nancy Kanwisher. 2004. The fusiform face area subserves face perception, not generic within-category identification. *Nature Neuroscience* 7 (5): 555–62.

Grodzinsky, Yosef. 2001. The neurology of syntax: Language use without Broca's area. *Behavioral and Brain Sciences* 23 (1): 1–21.

Grol, Meike J., Floris P. de Lange, Frans A. J.Verstraten, Richard E. Passingham, and Ivan Toni. 2006. Cerebral changes during performance of overlearned arbitrary visuomotor associations. *Journal of Neuroscience* 26 (1): 117–25.

de Groot, Adrianus Dingeman. 1965. *Thought and choice in chess.* New York: Basic Books.

Grout, Donald Jay, J. Peter Burkholder, and Claude V. Palisca. 2006. *A history of Western music.* New York: W. W. Norton.

Guitart-Masip, Marc, Nico Bunzeck, Klaas E. Stephan, Raymond J. Dolan, and Emrah Düzel. 2010. Contextual novelty changes reward representations in the striatum. *Journal of Neuroscience* 30 (5): 1721–26.

REFERENCES

Habib, Michel, and Mireille Besson. 2009. What do music training and musical experience teach us about brain plasticity? *Music Perception* 26 (3): 279–85.

Háden, Gábor P., Gábor Stefanics, Martin D. Vestergaard, Susan L. Denham, István Sziller, and István Winkler. 2009. Timbre-independent extraction of pitch in newborn infants. *Psychophysiology* 46 (1): 69–74.

Hakuta, Kenji, Ellen Bialystok, and Edward Wiley. 2003. Critical evidence: A test of the critical-period hypothesis for second-language acquisition. *Psychological Science* 14 (1): 31–38.

Hannon, Erin E., and Sandra E. Trehub. 2005. Tuning in to musical rhythms: Infants learn more readily than adults. *Proceedings of the National Academy of Sciences of the United States of America* 102 (35): 12639–43.

Hanslick, Eduard. 1986. *On the musically beautiful: A contribution towards the revision of the aesthetics of music.* Trans. Geoffrey Payzant. Indianapolis, Ind.: Hackett.

Harms, Kimberly J., Mengia S. Rioult-Pedotti, D. Rosy Carter, and Anna Dunaevsky. 2008. Transient spine expansion and learning-induced plasticity in layer 1 primary motor cortex. *Journal of Neuroscience* 28 (22): 5686–90.

Haynes, Bruce. 2007. *The end of early music: A period performer's history of music for the twenty-first century.* New York: Oxford University Press.

Henderson, David. 1981. *'Scuse me while I kiss the sky: The life of Jimi Hendrix.* New York: Bantam Books.

Hickok, Gregory, Kayoko Okada, and John T. Serences. 2009. Area Spt in the human planum temporale supports sensory-motor integration for speech processing. *Journal of Neurophysiology* 101 (5): 2725–32.

Hickok, Gregory, and David Poeppel. 2004. Dorsal and ventral streams: A framework for understanding aspects of the functional anatomy of language. *Cognition* 92 (1–2): 67–99.

Higuchi, Satomi, Thierry Chaminade, Hiroshi Imamizu, and Mitsuo Kawato. 2009. Shared neural correlates for language and tool use in Broca's area. *Neuroreport* 20 (15): 1376–81.

Honing, Henkjan, and Olivia Ladinig. 2009. Exposure influences expressive timing judgments in music. *Journal of Experimental Psychology: Human Perception and Performance* 35 (1): 281–88.

Houston, Scott. 2004. *Play piano in a flash: Play your favorite songs like a pro – whether you've had lessons or not!* New York: Hyperion Books.

REFERENCES

Howard, David M. 2005. Technology for real-time visual feedback in singing lessons. *Research Studies in Music Education* 24 (1): 40.

Howard, M. A., I. O. Volkov, R. Mirsky, P. C. Garell, M. D. Noh, M. Granner, H. Damasio, et al. 2000. Auditory cortex on the human posterior superior temporal gyrus. *Journal of Comparative Neurology* 416 (1): 79–92.

Huron, David Brian. 2006. *Sweet anticipation: Music and the psychology of expectation.* Cambridge, Mass.: MIT Press.

Huta, Veronika, and Richard M. Ryan. 2010. Pursuing pleasure or virtue: The differential and overlapping well-being benefits of hedonic and eudaimonic motives. *Journal of Happiness Studies* 11 (6): 735–62.

Hyde, Krista L., Jason Lerch, Andrea Norton, Marie Forgeard, Ellen Winner, Alan C. Evans, and Gottfried Schlaug. 2009a. The effects of musical training on structural brain development: A longitudinal study. *Annals of the New York Academy of Sciences* 1169: 182–86.

– – –. 2009b. Musical training shapes structural brain development. *Journal of Neuroscience* 29 (10): 3019–25.

Ingram, David. 1995. The cultural basis of prosodic modifications to infants and children: A response to Fernald's universalist theory. *Journal of Child Language* 22 (1): 223–33.

Isacoff, Stuart. 2001. *Temperament: The idea that solved music's greatest riddle.* New York: Alfred A. Knopf.

Ito, Masao. 2008. Control of mental activities by internal models in the cerebellum. *Neuroscience* 9 (4): 304–13.

Iverson, Paul, Patricia K. Kuhl, Reiko Akahane-Yamada, Eugen Diesch, Yoh'ich Tohkura, Andreas Kettermann, and Claudia Siebert. 2003. A perceptual interference account of acquisition difficulties for non-native phonemes. *Cognition* 87 (1): B47–57.

Jackendoff, Ray. 2007. *Language, consciousness, culture: Essays on mental structure.* Cambridge, Mass.: MIT Press.

– – –. 2009. Parallels and nonparallels between language and music. *Music Perception* 26 (3): 195–204.

Janata, Petr. 2009. The neural architecture of music-evoked autobiographical memories. *Cerebral Cortex* 19 (11): 2579–94.

Jäncke, Lutz, Susan Koeneke, Ariana Hoppe, Christina Rominger, and Jürgen Hänggi. 2009. The architecture of the golfer's brain. *Plos ONE* 4 (3): e4785.

REFERENCES

Johnson-Laird, Philip N. 1987. Reasoning, imagining, and creating. *Bulletin of the Council for Research in Music Education* 40: 71–87.

– – –. 2002. How jazz musicians improvise. *Music Perception* 19 (3): 415–42.

Jorgensen, H. 2002. Instrumental performance expertise and amount of practice among instrumental students in a conservatoire. *Music Education Research* 4 (1): 105–19.

Kant, Immanuel. 1790. *The critique of judgement*. Oxford: Clarendon Press, 1952.

Kastner, M. P., and R. G. Crowder. 1990. Perception of the major/minor distinction: IV. Emotional connotations in young children. *Music Perception* 8 (2): 189–201.

Katz, Jonah, and David Pesetsky. 2009. The recursive syntax and prosody of tonal music. http://web.mit.edu/jikatz/www/RecursionHandout.pdf.

Keenan, Julian Paul, Mark A. Wheeler, Gordon G. Gallup, and Alvaro Pascual-Leone. 2000. Self-recognition and the right prefrontal cortex. *Trends in Cognitive Sciences* 4 (9): 338–44.

Keenan, Julian Paul, V. Thangaraj, Andrea R. Halpern, and Gottfried Schlaug. 2001. Absolute pitch and planum temporale. *Neuroimage* 14 (6): 1402–8.

Keller, Peter E. 2008. Joint action in music performance. In *Enacting intersubjectivity: A cognitive and social perspective on the study of interactions*, ed. F. Morganti et al., 205–21. Amsterdam: IOS Press.

Keller, Peter E., and Mirjam Appel. 2010. Individual differences, auditory imagery, and the coordination of body movements and sounds in musical ensembles. *Music Perception* 28 (1): 27–46.

Kenny, D. T., and M. S. Osborne. 2006. Music performance anxiety: New insights from young musicians. *Advances in Cognitive Psychology* 2 (2): 103–12.

Kirschner, S., and M. Tomasello. 2009. Joint drumming: Social context facilitates synchronization in preschool children. *Journal of Experimental Child Psychology* 102 (3): 299–314.

– – –. 2010. Joint music making promotes prosocial behavior in 4-year-old children. *Evolution and Human Behavior,* doi:10.1016/j.evolhumbehav.2010.04.004.

Kivy, Peter. 1993. *The fine art of repetition: Essays in the philosophy of music*. Cambridge, England, and New York: Cambridge University Press.

Kleber, B., R. Veit, N. Birbaumer, J. Gruzelier, and M. Lotze. 2009. The brain of opera singers: Experience-dependent changes in functional activation. *Cerebral Cortex* 20 (5): 1144–52.

Klein, Richard, and Blake Edgar. 2002. *The dawn of human culture.* New York: John Wiley & Sons.

Knoch, Daria, Alvaro Pascual-Leone, Kaspar Meyer, Valerie Treyer, and Ernst Fehr. 2006. Diminishing reciprocal fairness by disrupting the right prefrontal cortex. *Science* 314 (5800): 829–32.

Knudsen, Eric I., and P. F. Knudsen. 1990. Sensitive and critical periods for visual calibration of sound localization by barn owls. *Journal of Neuroscience* 10 (1): 222–32.

Knutson, Brian, and Jeffrey C. Cooper. 2006. The lure of the unknown. *Neuron* 51 (3): 280–82.

Koelsch, Stefan, Thomas Fritz, and Gottfried Schlaug. 2008. Amygdala activity can be modulated by unexpected chord functions during music listening. *Neuroreport* 19 (18): 1815–19.

Konečni, Vladimir J. 1984. Elusive effects of artists' messages. In *Cognitive processes in the perception of art*, ed. W. R. Crozier and A. J. Chapman, 71–93. Amsterdam: North Holland.

Konečni, Vladimir J., and Mitchell Karno. 1992. Empirical investigations of the hedonic and emotional effects of musical structure. *Musik Psychologie* 11: 119–37.

Krashen, Stephen D., Michael A. Long, and Robin C. Scarcella. 1979. Age, rate and eventual attainment in second language acquisition. *TESOL Quarterly* 13 (4): 573–82.

Kraus, Nina, Erika Skoe, Alexandra Parbery-Clark, and Richard Ashley. 2009. Experience-induced malleability in neural encoding of pitch, timbre, and timing. *Annals of the New York Academy of Sciences* 1169: 543–57.

Kroodsma, Donald E. 2005. *The singing life of birds: The art and science of listening to birdsong.* Boston: Houghton Mifflin.

Kuhl, Patricia K., and Andrew N. Meltzoff. 1982. Bimodal speech perception in early infancy. *Journal of the Acoustical Society of America* 71: S77–S78.

Lang, Catherine E., and Marc H. Schieber. 2004. Human finger independence: Limitations due to passive mechanical coupling versus active neuromuscular control. *Journal of Neurophysiology* 92 (5): 2802–10.

Langer, E. J. 1975. The illusion of control. *Journal of Personality and Social Psychology* 32 (2): 311–28.

Leaver, Amber M., Jennifer Van Lare, Brandon Zielinski, Andrea R.

Halpern, and Josef P. Rauschecker. 2009. Brain activation during anticipation of sound sequences. *Journal of Neuroscience* 29 (8): 2477–85.

Lebedeva, Gina C., and Patricia K. Kuhl. 2010. Sing that tune: Infants' perception of melody and lyrics and the facilitation of phonetic recognition in songs. *Infant Behavior & Development* 33 (4): 419–30.

Lehmann, Andreas C., John A. Sloboda, and Robert H. Woody. 2007. *Psychology for musicians: Understanding and acquiring the skills.* New York: Oxford University Press.

Lehmann, Andres C., and K. Anders Ericsson. 1998. Historical developments of expert performance: Public performance of music. In *Genius and the mind: Studies of creativity and temperament,* ed. Andrew Steptoe, 67–94. New York: Oxford University Press.

Lerdahl, Fred, and Ray Jackendoff. 1983. *A generative theory of tonal music.* Cambridge, Mass.: MIT Press.

Levitin, Daniel J. 1994. Absolute memory for musical pitch: Evidence from the production of learned melodies. *Perception & Psychophysics* 56 (4): 414–23.

– – –. 2006. *This is your brain on music: The science of a human obsession.* New York: Dutton.

Lewkowicz, David J. 2002. Heterogeneity and heterochrony in the development of intersensory perception. *Cognitive Brain Research* 14 (1): 41–63.

Limb, Charles J. 2006. Structural and functional neural correlates of music perception. *The Anatomical Record Part A: Discoveries in Molecular, Cellular, and Evolutionary Biology* 288 (4): 435–46.

Linkenhoker, Brie A., and Eric I. Knudsen. 2002. Incremental training increases the plasticity of the auditory space map in adult barn owls. *Nature* 419 (6904): 293–96.

Luft, Andreas R., and Manuel M. Buitrago. 2005. Stages of motor skill learning. *Molecular Neurobiology* 32 (3): 205–16.

MacNeilage, P. F., and J. L. DeClerk. 1969. On the motor control of coarticulation in CVC monosyllables. *Journal of the Acoustical Society of America* 45: 1217.

McDermott, Josh, and Marc D. Hauser. 2005. Probing the evolutionary origins of music perception. *Annals of the New York Academy of Sciences* 1060: 6–16.

McDermott, Josh H., Andriana J. Lehr, and Andrew J. Oxenham. 2010.

REFERENCES

Individual differences reveal the basis of consonance. *Current Biology* doi:10.1016/j.cub.2010.04.019.

McKee, Robert. 1997. *Story: Substance, structure, style and the principles of screenwriting*. New York: ReganBooks.

McPherson, Gary. 2006. *The child as musician: A handbook of musical development*. New York: Oxford University Press.

Mannes, Elena. 2009. *The music instinct: Science & song*. PBS.

Marco, David J. T., Neil McLachlan, and S. J. Wilson. 2010. The role of familiarity in the perception of dissonance for musical chords. In *Proceedings of the 11th international conference on music perception and cognition (ICMPC11)*, ed. S. M. Demorest, S. J. Morrison, and P. S. Campbell, Seattle.

Marcus, Gary F. 2004. *The birth of the mind: How a tiny number of genes creates the complexities of human thought*. New York: Basic Books.

– – –. 2006. Cognitive architecture and descent with modification. *Cognition* 101: 443–65.

– – –. 2008. *Kluge: The haphazard construction of the human mind*. Boston: Houghton Mifflin.

Marcus, Gary F., Keith J. Fernandes, and Scott P. Johnson. 2007. Infant rule learning facilitated by speech. *Psychological Science* 18 (5): 387–91.

Marcus, Gary F., Steven Pinker, Michael Ullman, Michelle Hollander, T. J. Rosen, and Fei Xu. 1992. Overregularization in language acquisition. *Monographs of the Society for Research in Child Development* 57 (4, Serial No. 228).

Marcus, G. F., S. Vijayan, S. Bandi Rao, and P. M. Vishton. 1999. Rule learning by seven-month-old infants. *Science* 283 (5398): 77–80.

Margulis, Elizabeth H. 2010. Repetition detection across multiple exposures. In *Proceedings of the 11th international conference on music perception and cognition (ICMPC11)*, Seattle.

Marin, Oscar S. M., and David W. Perry. 1999. Neurological aspects of music perception and performance. In *The psychology of music*, ed. Diana Deutsch, 653–724. San Diego: Academic Press.

Marques, Carlos, Sylvain Moreno, São Luís Castro, and Mireille Besson. 2007. Musicians detect pitch violation in a foreign language better than nonmusicians: Behavioral and electrophysiological evidence. *Journal of Cognitive Neuroscience* 19 (9): 1453–63.

Maslow, A. H. 1943. A theory of human motivation. *Psychological Review* 50:

370–96.

Mead, David. 2004. *Crash course: Acoustic guitar.* London: SMT.

Mead, Virginia Hoge. 1996. More than mere movement: Dalcroze eurhythmics: Dalcroze techniques work with students of all ages. *Music Educators Journal* 82 (4): 38.

Meinz, Elizabeth J., and David Z. Hambrick. 2010. Deliberate practice is necessary but not sufficient to explain individual differences in piano sight-reading skill: The role of working memory capacity. *Psychological Science* 21 (7): 914–19.

Memmert, Daniel. 2006. The effects of eye movements, age, and expertise on inattentional blindness. *Consciousness and Cognition* 15 (3): 620–27.

Merzenich, Michael M., R. J. Nelson, M. P. Stryker, M. S. Cynader, A. Schoppmann, and J. M. Zook. 1984. Somatosensory cortical map changes following digit amputation in adult monkeys. *Journal of Comparative Neurology* 224 (4): 591–605.

Miller, G. A. 1956. The magical number seven plus or minus two: Some limits on our capacity for processing information. *Psychological Review* 63 (2): 81–97.

Miller, Geoffrey. 2000. Evolution of human music through sexual selection. In *The origins of music,* ed. N. L. Wallin, B. Merker, and S. Brown, 329–60. Cambridge, Mass.: MIT Press.

Miller, Leon K. 1989. *Musical savants: Exceptional skill in the mentally retarded.* Hillsdale, N.J.: L. Erlbaum.

Milner, G. 2009. *Perfecting sound forever: An aural history of recorded music.* London: Faber & Faber.

Mithen, Steven. 2005. *The singing Neanderthals: The origins of music, language, mind and body.* London: Weidenfeld & Nicolson.

– – –. 2009. The music instinct: The evolutionary basis of musicality. *Annals of the New York Academy of Sciences* 1169 (1): 3–12

Moon, C. M., and W. P. Fifer. 2000. Evidence of transnatal auditory learning. *Journal of Perinatology* 20 (8 Pt. 2), S37–44.

Moog, Helmut. 1976. *The musical experience of the pre-school child.* London: Schott Music.

Moors, Agnes, and Jan De Houwer. 2006. Automaticity: A theoretical and conceptual analysis. *Psychological Bulletin* 132 (2): 297–326.

Moreno, Nerea, and Agustín González. 2007. Evolution of the amygdaloid complex in vertebrates, with special reference to the anamnio-amniotic transition. *Journal of Anatomy* 211 (2): 151–63.

Moreno, Sylvain, Carlos Marques, Andreia Santos, Manuela Santos, São Luís Castro, and Mireille Besson. 2009. Musical training influences linguistic abilities in 8-year-old children: More evidence for brain plasticity. *Cerebral Cortex* 19 (3): 712–23.

Mozolic, Jennifer L., Satoru Hayasaka, and Paul J. Laurienti. 2010. A cognitive training intervention increases resting cerebral blood flow in healthy older adults. *Frontiers in Human Neuroscience* 4: 16.

Müller, Mira, Lea Höfel, Elvira Brattico, and Thomas Jacobsen. 2009. Electrophysiological correlates of aesthetic music processing: Comparing experts with laypersons. *Annals of the New York Academy of Sciences* 1169: 355–58.

Münte, Thomas F., Eckart Altenmüller, and Lutz Jäncke. 2002. The musician's brain as a model of neuroplasticity. *Nature Reviews Neuroscience* 3 (6): 473–78.

Nakamura, Jeanne, and Mihály Csźkszentmihályi. 2009. Flow theory and research. In *Oxford handbook of positive psychology,* ed. C. R. Snyder and S. J. Lopez, 195–206. New York: Oxford University Press.

Newport, Elissa L. 1988. Constraints on learning and their role in language acquisition: Studies of the acquisition of American Sign Language. *Language Sciences* 10 (1): 147–72.

– – –. 1990. Maturational constraints on language learning. *Cognitive Science* 14 (1): 11–28.

Nisbett, Richard, and Timothy D. Wilson. 1977. Telling more than we can know: Verbal reports on mental processes. *Psychological Review* 84: 231–59.

North, Adrian C., and David J. Hargreaves. 1995. Eminence in pop music. *Popular Music and Society* 19 (4): 41–66.

Ortmann, Otto. 1929. *The physiological mechanics of piano technique: An experimental study of the nature of muscular action as used in piano playing, and of the effects thereof upon the piano key and the piano tone.* New York: E. P. Dutton.

Palmer, Caroline. 2006. The nature of memory for music performance skills. In *Music, motor control and the brain,* ed. Eckart Altenmüller, Jürg Kesselring, and Mario Wiesendanger, 39–53. Oxford: Oxford University Press.

Palmer, Caroline, and Carla van de Sande. 1993. Units of knowledge in music performance. *Journal of Experimental Psychology, Learning, Memory, and Cognition* 19 (2): 457–70.

REFERENCES

Palmer, Robert. 1995. *Rock & roll: An unruly history*. New York: Harmony Books.

Pantev, C., L. E. Roberts, M. Schulz, A. Engelien, and B. Ross. 2001. Timbre-specific enhancement of auditory cortical representations in musicians. *Neuroreport* 12 (1): 169–74.

Park, N., C. Peterson, and W. Ruch. 2009. Orientations to happiness and life satisfaction in twenty-seven nations. *Journal of Positive Psychology* 4 (4): 273–79.

Patel, Aniruddh D. 2003. Rhythm in language and music: Parallels and differences. *Annals of the New York Academy of Sciences* 999: 140–43.

– – –. 2008. *Music, language, and the brain*. New York: Oxford University Press.

Patel, Aniruddh D., John R. Iversen, Micah R. Bregman, and Irena Schulz. 2009. Experimental evidence for synchronization to a musical beat in a nonhuman animal. *Current Biology* 19 (10): 827–30.

Pedlar, D. 2003. *The songwriting secrets of the Beatles*. New York: Omnibus Press.

Perani, Daniela, Maria Cristina Saccuman, Paola Scifo, Danilo Spada, Guido Andreolli, Rosanna Rovelli, Cristina Baldoli, and Stefan Koelsch. 2010. Functional specializations for music processing in the human newborn brain. *Proceedings of the National Academy of Sciences of the United States of America* 107 (10): 4758–63.

Peretz, Isabelle, Monique Radeau, and Martin Arguin. 2004. Two-way interactions between music and language: Evidence from priming recognition of tune and lyrics in familiar songs. *Memory & Cognition* 32 (1): 142–52.

Peretz, Isabelle, Régine Kolinsky, Mark Tramo, Raymone Labrecque, Claude Hublet, Guy Demeurisse, and Sylvie Belleville. 1994. Functional dissociations following bilateral lesions of auditory cortex. *Brain: A Journal of Neurology* 117 (Pt. 6): 1283–301.

Pessiglione, Mathias, Ben Seymour, Guillaume Flandin, Raymond J. Dolan, and Chris D. Frith. 2006. Dopamine-dependent prediction errors underpin reward-seeking behaviour in humans. *Nature* 442 (7106): 1042–45.

Peters, M., and S. Schwartz. 1989. Coordination of the two hands and effects of attentional manipulation in the production of a bimanual 2:3 polyrhythm. *Australian Journal of Psychology* 41 (2): 215–24.

Peterson, C., N. Park, and M. E. P. Seligman. 2005. Orientations to happiness and life satisfaction: The full life versus the empty life. *Journal of Happiness Studies*

6 (1): 25–41.

Pfordresher, Peter Q., and Steven Brown. 2007. Poor-pitch singing in the absence of 'tone deafness.' *Music Perception* 25 (2): 95.

– – – . 2009. Enhanced production and perception of musical pitch in tone language speakers. *Attention, Perception & Psychophysics* 71 (6): 1385–89.

Phelps, Elizabeth A., and Joseph E. LeDoux. 2005. Contributions of the amygdala to emotion processing: From animal models to human behavior. *Neuron* 48 (2): 175–87.

Phillips-Silver, Jessica, and Laurel Trainor. 2005. Feeling the beat: Movement influences infant rhythm perception. *Science* 308 (5727): 1430.

Pinker, Steven. 1994. *The language instinct.* New York: William Morrow.

Plantinga, Judy, and Laurel J. Trainor. 2005. Memory for melody: Infants use a relative pitch code. *Cognition* 98 (1): 1–11

Poldrack, Russell A., Fred W. Sabb, Karin Foerde, Sabrina M. Tom, Robert F. Asarnow, Susan Y. Bookheimer, and Barbara J. Knowlton. 2005. The neural correlates of motor skill automaticity. *Journal of Neuroscience* 25 (22): 5356–64.

Poremba, Amy, Megan Malloy, Richard C. Saunders, Richard E. Carson, Peter Herscovitch, and Mortimer Mishkin. 2004. Species-specific calls evoke asymmetric activity in the monkey's temporal poles. *Nature* 427 (6973): 448–51.

Radosh, Daniel. 2009. While my guitar gently beeps. *New York Times Magazine,* August 16.

Rainbow, E. 1981. A final report on a three-year investigation of rhythmic abilities of preschool aged children. *Bulletin of the Council for Research in Music Education* 66–67 (Spring–Summer): 69–73.

Ramus, Franck. 2004. Neurobiology of dyslexia: A reinterpretation of the data. *Trends in Neurosciences* 27 (12): 720–26.

Rauschecker, Josef P. 2005. Neural encoding and retrieval of sound sequences. *Annals of the New York Academy of Sciences* 1060: 125–35.

Rauschecker, Joseph, Biao Tian, and Marc Hauser. 1995. Processing of complex sounds in the macaque nonprimary auditory cortex. *Science* 268 (5207): 111–14.

Rentfrow, Peter J., and Samuel D. Gosling. 2003. The do re mi's of everyday life: The structure and personality correlates of music preferences. *Journal of Personality and Social Psychology* 84 (6): 1236–56.

– – –. 2006. Message in a ballad: The role of music preferences in interpersonal perception. *Psychological Science* 17 (3): 236–42.

Repp, Bruno H. 1996. The art of inaccuracy: Why pianists' errors are difficult to hear. *Music Perception* 14 (2): 161–83.

– – –. 2005. Sensorimotor synchronization: A review of the tapping literature. *Psychonomic Bulletin & Review* 12 (6): 969–92.

Repp, Bruno H., and Günther Knoblich. 2004. Perceiving action identity: How pianists recognize their own performances. *Psychological Science* 15 (9): 604–9.

Repp, Bruno H., and Meijin Bruttomesso. 2009. A filled duration illusion in music: Effects of metrical subdivision on the perception and production of beat tempo. *Advances in Cognitive Psychology* 5 (1): 114–34.

Reznikoff, I. 2005. On primitive elements of musical meaning. *Journal of Music and Meaning* 3, section 2.

Rémy, Florence, Nicole Wenderoth, Karen Lipkens, and Stephan P. Swinnen. 2008. Acquisition of a new bimanual coordination pattern modulates the cerebral activations elicited by an intrinsic pattern: An fMRI study. *Cortex* 44 (5): 482–93.

Rice, Timothy. 1994. *May it fill your soul: Experiencing Bulgarian music.* Chicago: University of Chicago Press.

Rogan, Michael, Ursula V. Stäubli, and Joseph E. LeDoux. 1997. Fear conditioning induces associative long-term potentiation in the amygdala. *Nature* 390 (6660): 604–7.

Root-Bernstein, R., L. Allen, L. Beach, R. Bhadula, J. Fast, C. Hosey, B. Kremkow, et al. 2008. Arts foster scientific success: Avocations of Nobel, National Academy, Royal Society, and Sigma Xi members. *Journal of Psychology of Science and Technology* 1 (2): 51–63.

Rosenbloom, P. S., and A. Newell. 1986. The chunking of goal hierarchies: A generalized model of practice. *Machine Learning: An Artificial Intelligence-Approach* 2: 247–88.

Ross, Alex. 2007. *The rest is noise: Listening to the twentieth century.* New York: Farrar, Straus & Giroux.

Ross, Deborah, Jonathan Choi, and Dale Purves. 2007. Musical intervals in speech. *Proceedings of the National Academy of Sciences of the United States of America* 104 (23): 9852–57.

Roth, N. 1986. Sigmund Freud's dislike of music: A piece of epileptology.

REFERENCES

Bulletin of the New York Academy of Medicine 62 (7): 759–65.

Ruthsatz, J., D. Detterman, W. S. Griscom, and B. A. Cirullo. 2008. Becoming an expert in the musical domain: It takes more than just practice. *Intelligence* 36 (4): 330–38.

Rüsseler, Jascha, Ckart Altenmüller, Wido Nager, Christine Kohlmetz, and Thomas F Münte. 2001. Event-related brain potentials to sound omissions differ in musicians and non-musicians. *Neuroscience Letters* 308 (1): 33–36.

Ryff, Carol D., and Burton Singer. 1998. The role of purpose in life and personal growth in positive human health. *The Human Quest for Meaning: A Handbook of Psychological Research and Clinical Applications,* ed. Paul T. P. Wong, and Prem S. Fry, 213–35. Mahwah, N. J.: Erlbaum.

Ryff, Carol D., and Burton H. Singer. 2008. Know thyself and become what you are: A eudaimonic approach to psychological well-being. *Journal of Happiness Studies* 9 (1): 13–39.

Sacco, K., F. Cauda, L. Cerliani, D. Mate, S. Duca, and G. C. Geminiani. 2006. Motor imagery of walking following training in locomotor attention: The effect of 'the tango lesson.' *Neuroimage* 32 (3): 144–49.

Sacks, Oliver W. 2007. *Musicophilia: Tales of music and the brain.* New York: Alfred A. Knopf.

Saffran, Jenny R., Michelle M. Loman, and Rachel R. Robertson. 2001. Infant long-term memory for music. *Annals of the New York Academy of Sciences* 930: 397–400.

Saffran, Jenny R., and Gregory Griepentrog. 2001. Absolute pitch in infant auditory learning: Evidence for developmental reorganization. *Developmental Psychology* 37 (1): 74–85.

Salen, Katie, and Eric Zimmerman. 2004. *Rules of play: Game design fundamentals.* Cambridge, Mass.: MIT Press.

Salganik, Matthew J., Peter Sheridan Dodds, and Duncan J. Watts. 2006. Experimental study of inequality and unpredictability in an artificial cultural market. *Science* 311 (5762): 854–56.

Salganik, Matthew J., and Duncan J. Watts. 2008. Leading the herd astray: An experimental study of self-fulfilling prophecies in an artificial cultural market. *Social Psychology Quarterly* 71 (4): 338–55.

Salimpoor, Valorie N., Mitchel Benavoy, Kevin Larcher, Alain Dagher, and Robert J. Zatorre. 2010. Anatomically distinct dopamine release during anticipation and experience of peak emotion to music. *Nature Neuroscience,*

REFERENCES

advance online publication, January 9, 2011, doi:10.1038/nn.2726.

Salthouse, Timothy A. 2009. When does age-related cognitive decline begin? *Neurobiology of Aging* 30 (4): 507–14.

Sanneh, Kelefa. 2006. The season of thug-love duets has begun. *New York Times*. June 1.

Sapolsky, Robert M. 2005. *Monkeyluv: And other essays on our lives as animals.* New York: Scribner.

Savion-Lemieux, Tal, Jennifer A. Bailey, and Virginia B. Penhune. 2009. Developmental contributions to motor sequence learning. *Experimental Brain Research* 195 (2): 293–306.

Schachner, Adena, Timothy F. Brady, Irene M. Pepperberg, and Marc D. Hauser. 2009. Spontaneous motor entrainment to music in multiple vocal mimicking species. *Current Biology* 19 (10): 831–36.

Scheinfeld, Amram, and Morton D. Schweitzer. 1939. *You and heredity.* Garden City, N.Y.: Garden City.

Schellenberg, E. Glenn. 2004. Music lessons enhance IQ. *Psychological Science* 15 (8): 511–14.

– – – . 2009. Music training and nonmusical abilities: Commentary on Stoesz, Jakobson, Kilgour, and Lewycky (2007) and Jakobson, Lewycky, Kilgour, and Stoesz (2008). *Music Perception* 27 (2): 139–43.

Schellenberg, E. Glenn, Isabelle Peretz, and Sandrine Vieillard. 2008. Liking for happy- and sad-sounding music: Effects of exposure. *Cognition & Emotion* 22 (2): 218–237.

Schellenberg, E. Glenn, and Sandra E. Trehub. 2003. Good pitch memory is widespread. *Psychological Science* 14 (3): 262–66.

Schiff, David. 1997. *Gershwin: Rhapsody in blue.* New York: Cambridge University Press.

Schlaug, Gottfried, Marie Forgeard, Lin Zhu, Andrea Norton, Andrew Norton, and Ellen Winner. 2009. Training-induced neuroplasticity in young children. *Annals of the New York Academy of Sciences* 1169: 205–8.

Schlaug, Gottfried, Luz Jäncke, Yanxiong Huang, Jochen F Staiger, and Helmuth Steinmetz. 1995. Increased corpus callosum size in musicians. *Neuropsychologia* 33 (8): 1047–55.

Schneider, Peter, Vanessa Sluming, Neil Roberts, Michael Scherg, Rainer Goebel, Hans J. Specht, H. Günter Dosch, Stefan Bleeck, Christoph Stippich, and André Rupp. 2005. Structural and functional asymmetry of lateral Heschl's gyrus reflects pitch perception preference. *Nature Neuroscience* 8 (9): 1241–47.

Scholz, Jan, Miriam C. Klein, Timothy E. J. Behrens, and Heidi Johansen-Berg. 2009. Training induces changes in white-matter architecture. *Nature Neuroscience* 12 (11): 1370–71.

Schulkind, Matthew D. 2009. Is memory for music special? *Annals of the New York Academy of Sciences* 1169: 216–24.

Schwartz, Charles. 1979. *Gershwin, his life and music.* Indianapolis: Bobbs-Merrill.

Selfhout, Maarten H. W., Susan J. T. Branje, Tom F. M. ter Bogt, and Wim H. J. Meeus. 2009. The role of music preferences in early adolescents' friendship formation and stability. *Journal of Adolescence* 32 (1): 95–107.

Seligman, M. E., and S. F. Maier. 1967. Failure to escape traumatic shock. *Journal of Experimental Psychology* 74 (1): 1–9.

Semaw, Sileshi, Michael J. Rogers, Jay Quade, Paul R. Renne, Robert F. Butler, Manuel Dominguez-Rodrigo, Dietrich Stout, William S. Hart, Travis Pickering, and Scott W. Simpson. 2003. 2–6-million-year-old stone tools and associated bones from OGS-6 and OGS-7, Gona, Afar, Ethiopia. *Journal of Human Evolution* 45 (2): 169–77.

Serafine, Mary Louise, Janet Davidson, Robert G. Crowder, and Bruno H. Repp. 1986. On the nature of melody-text integration in memory for songs. *Journal of Memory and Language* 25 (2): 123–35.

Shammi, P., and D. T. Stuss. 1999. Humour appreciation: A role of the right frontal lobe. *Brain: A Journal of Neurology* 122 (Pt. 4): 657–66.

Shelton, Robert. 2003. *No direction home: The life and music of Bob Dylan.* New York: Da Capo Press.

Shepard, R. N., and D. S. Jordan. 1984. Auditory illusions demonstrating that tones are assimilated to an internalized musical scale. *Science* 226 (4680): 1333–34.

Shipton, Russ. 2001. *The complete guitar player.* New York: Amsco.

Singh, Leher, James L. Morgan, and Catherine T. Best. 2002. Infants' listening preferences: Baby talk or happy talk? *Infancy* 3 (3): 365–94.

Slevc, L. Robert, Jason C. Rosenberg, and Aniruddh D. Patel. 2009. Making psycholinguistics musical: Self-paced reading time evidence for shared processing of linguistic and musical syntax. *Psychonomic Bulletin & Review* 16 (2): 374–81.

Sloboda, John A. 1996. The acquisition of musical performance expertise: Deconstructing the 'talent' account of individual differences in musical expressivity. In *The road to excellence: The acquisition of expert performance in the arts and sciences, sports and games,* ed. K. Anders Ericsson, 107–26. Mahwah, N.J.: Erlbaum.

Smith, J. David, Deborah Nelson, Lisa Grohskopf, and Terry Appleton. 1994. What child is this? What interval was that? Familiar tunes and music perception in novice listeners. *Cognition* 52 (1): 23–54.

Smith, M. D., and C. J. Chamberlin. 1992. Effect of adding cognitively demanding tasks on soccer skill performance. *Perceptual and Motor Skills* 75 (3 Pt. 1): 955–61.

Smith, Patti. 2010. *Just kids.* New York: Ecco.

Snyder, Bob. 2000. *Music and memory: An introduction.* Cambridge, Mass.: MIT Press.

Soley, Gaye, and Erin E. Hannon. 2010. Infants prefer the musical meter of their own culture: A cross-cultural comparison. *Developmental Psychology* 46 (1): 286–92.

Soska, K. C., M. A. Galeon, and K. E. Adolph. In press. On the other hand: Overflow movements of infants' hands and legs during unimanual object exploration. *Developmental Psychobiology*.

Standley, Jayne, and Clifford K. Madsen. 1990. Comparison of infant preferences and responses to auditory stimuli: Music, mother, and other female voice. *Journal of Music Therapy* 27 (2): 54–97.

Starr, Larry, and Christopher Alan Waterman. 2003. *American popular music: From minstrelsy to MTV.* New York: Oxford University Press.

Steger, Michael F., Todd N. Kashdan, and Shigehiro Oishi. 2008. Being good by doing good: Daily eudaimonic activity and well-being. *Journal of Research in Personality* 42 (1): 22–42.

Stein, Barry E., and M. Alex Meredith. 1993. *The merging of the senses.* Cambridge, Mass.: MIT Press.

Stein, Barry E., and Terrence R. Stanford. 2008. Multisensory integration: Current issues from the perspective of the single neuron. *Neuroscience* 9 (4): 255–66.

Sugimoto, Tasuku, Hiromi Kobayashi, Noritomo Nobuyoshi, Yasushi Kiriyama, Hideko Takeshita, Tomoyasu Nakamura, and Kazuhide Hashiya.

REFERENCES

2010. Preference for consonant music over dissonant music by an infant chimpanzee. *Primates: Journal of Primatology* 51 (1): 7–12.

Summers, Jeff. 2002. Practice and training in bimanual coordination tasks: Strategies and constraints. *Brain and Cognition* 48 (1): 166–78.

Suzuki, Shinichi. 1969. *Nurtured by love: A new approach to education.* New York: Exposition Press.

Szpunar, Karl K., E. Glenn Schellenberg, and Patricia Pliner. 2004. Liking and memory for musical stimuli as a function of exposure. *Journal of Experimental Psychology: Learning, Memory, and Cognition* 30 (2): 370–81.

Tallerman, M. 2007. Did our ancestors speak a holistic protolanguage? *Lingua* 117 (3): 579–604.

Tan, Siu-Lan, Matthew P. Spackman, and Christy Peaslee. 2006. The effects of repeated exposure on liking and judgments of musical unity of intact and patchwork compositions. *Music Perception* 23 (5): 407–21.

Theusch, Elizabeth, Analabha Basu, and Jane Gitschier. 2009. Genome-wide study of families with absolute pitch reveals linkage to 8q24.21 and locus heterogeneity. *American Journal of Human Genetics* 85 (1): 112–19.

Thompson, Clive. 2007. Halo 3: How Microsoft Labs invented a new science of play. *Wired* 15 (9), 140–47, 184, 192.

Thompson, William Forde, E. Glenn Schellenberg, and Gabriela Husain. 2004. Decoding speech prosody: Do music lessons help? *Emotion* 4 (1): 46–64.

Thomson, William. 1991. *Schoenberg's error.* Philadelphia: University of Pennsylvania Press.

Tiihonen, Jari, J. Kuikka, J. Kupila, K. Partanen, P. Vainio, J. Airaksinen, M. Eronen, T. Hallikainen, J. Paanila, and I. Innunen. 1994. Increase in cerebral blood flow of right prefrontal cortex in man during orgasm. *Neuroscience Letters* 170 (2): 241–43.

Tillmann, Barbara, and Emmanuel Bigand. 1996. Does formal musical structure affect perception of musical expressiveness? *Psychology of Music* 24 (1): 3.

Tindall, Blair. 2004. Better playing through chemistry. *New York Times,* October 17. http://www.nytimes.com/2004/10/17/arts/music/17tind. html?_r=1&pagewanted=print&position=.

Tomaino, Concetta M. 2010. Recovery of fluent speech through a musician's use of prelearned song repertoire. *Music and Medicine* 2 (2): 85.

Trainor, Laurel J., Christine D. Tsang, and Vivian H. W. Cheung. 2002. Preference for sensory consonance in 2- and 4-month-old infants. *Music Perception* 20 (2): 187–94.

Trainor, Laurel J., Xiaoqing Gao, Jing-jiang Lei, Karen Lehtovaara, and Laurence R. Harris. 2009. The primal role of the vestibular system in determining musical rhythm. *Cortex* 45 (1): 35–43.

Trainor, Laurel J., and Sandra E. Trehub. 1994. Key membership and implied harmony in Western tonal music: Developmental perspectives. *Perception & Psychophysics* 56 (2): 125–32.

Trehub, Sandra E. 2001. Musical predispositions in infancy. *Annals of the New York Academy of Sciences* 930: 1–16.

Trehub, Sandra, Glenn Schellenberg, and D. Hill. 1997. The origins of music perception and cognition: A developmental perspective. In *Perception and cognition of music,* ed. Irène Deliège and John A. Sloboda, 103–28. Hove, UK: Psychology Press.

Trehub, Sandra E., Laurel J. Trainor, and Anna M. Unyk. 1993. Music and speech processing in the first year of life. *Advances in Child Development and Behavior* 24: 1–35.

Turner, Leslie M., Adrian R. Young, Holger Römpler, Torsten Schöneberg, Steven M. Phelps, and Hopi E. Hoekstra. 2010. Monogamy evolves through multiple mechanisms: Evidence from V1aR in deer mice. *Molecular Biology and Evolution* 27 (6): 1269–78.

Twain, Mark. 1880. *A tramp abroad.* London: Chatto & Windus.

Tymoczko, Dmitiri. 2011. *A geometry of consonance.* New York: Oxford University Press.

Ukkola, Liisa T., Päivi Onkamo, Pirre Raijas, Kai Karma, and Irma Järvelä. 2009. Musical aptitude is associated with AVPR1A-haplotypes. *Plos ONE* 4 (5): e5534.

Uszler, Marienne. 2003. *Play it again, Sam: What, why, and when to repeat.* Fort Lauderdale, Fl.: FJH Music Co.

Uszler, Marienne, Stewart Gordon, and Elyse Mach. 1991. *The well-tempered keyboard teacher.* New York: Maxwell Macmillan International.

van Ee, Raymond, Jeroen J. A. van Boxtel, Amanda L. Parker, and David Alais. 2009. Multisensory congruency as a mechanism for attentional control over perceptual selection. *Journal of Neuroscience* 29 (37): 11641–49.

Vanstone, Ashley D., Lola L. Cuddy, Jacalyn M. Duffin, and Elizabeth Alexander. 2009. Exceptional preservation of memory for tunes and lyrics: Case studies of amusia, profound deafness, and Alzheimer's disease. *Annals of the New York Academy of Sciences* 1169: 291–94.

Vernon, Leroy Ninde. 1932. Synchronization of chords in artistic piano music. PhD dissertation, University of Iowa.

Vinkhuyzen, Anna A. E., Sophie van der Sluis, Danielle Posthuma, and Dorret I Boomsma. 2009. The heritability of aptitude and exceptional talent across different domains in adolescents and young adults. *Behavior Genetics* 39 (4): 380–92.

Vogel, Harold L. 2004. *Entertainment industry economics: A guide for financial analysis.* Cambridge and New York: Cambridge University Press.

Vuust, Peter, Leif Ostergaard, Karen Johanne Pallesen, Christopher Bailey, and Andreas Roepstorff. 2009. Predictive coding of music – brain responses to rhythmic incongruity. *Cortex* 45 (1): 80–92.

Vygotsky, Lev Semenovich. 1978. *Mind in society: The development of higher psychological processes.* Cambridge. Mass.: Harvard University Press.

Ward, Paul, Nicola J. Hodges, A. Mark Williams, and Janet L. Starkes. 2004. Deliberate practice and expert performance: Defining the path to excellence. In *Skill acquisition in sport: Research, theory and practice,* ed. A. Mark Williams and Nicola J. Hodges, 231–58. New York: Routledge.

Watanabe, Donald, Tal Savion-Lemieux, and Virginia B. Penhune. 2007. The effect of early musical training on adult motor performance: Evidence for a sensitive period in motor learning. *Experimental Brain Research* 176 (2): 332–40.

Waterman, A. S. 2008. Reconsidering happiness: A eudaimonist's perspective. *Journal of Positive Psychology* 3 (4): 234–52.

Watson, John B. 1925. *Behaviorism.* New York: W. W. Norton.

Wegner, D. M. 2002. *The illusion of conscious will.* Cambridge, Mass.: MIT Press.

Weisberg, Robert W. 1999. Creativity and knowledge: A challenge to theories. In *Handbook of creativity,* ed. Robert J. Sternberg, 226. New York: Cambridge University Press.

Welch, G. F. 2008. A developmental view of children's singing. *British Journal of Music Education* 3 (3): 295–303.

REFERENCES

Welch, Graham, Desmond C. Sergeant, and Peta J. White. 1998. The role of linguistic dominance in the acquisition of song. *Research Studies in Music Education* 10 (1): 67.

Welch, Graham, D. M. Howard, and C. Rush. 1989. Real-time visual feedback in the development of vocal pitch accuracy in singing. *Psychology of Music* 17 (2): 146.

Werker, J. F., and R. C. Tees. 1992. The organization and reorganization of human speech perception. *Annual Review of Neuroscience* 15: 377–402.

Wickelgren, W. A. 1977. Speed-accuracy tradeoff and information processing dynamics. *Acta Psychologica* 41 (1): 67–85.

Williamson, Victoria J., Alan D Baddeley, and Graham J. Hitch. 2010. Musicians' and nonmusicians' short-term memory for verbal and musical sequences: Comparing phonological similarity and pitch proximity. *Memory & Cognition* 38 (2): 163–75.

Wilson, Marlene A., and Lorain Junor. 2008. The role of amygdalar mu-opioid receptors in anxiety-related responses in two rat models. *Neuropsychopharmacology* 33 (12): 2957–68.

Wilson, Sarah J., Dean Lusher, Catherine Y. Wan, Paul Dudgeon, and David C. Reutens. 2009. The neurocognitive components of pitch processing: Insights from absolute pitch. *Cerebral Cortex* 19 (3): 724–32.

Wilson, T. D. 2002. *Strangers to ourselves.* Cambridge, Mass.: Harvard University Press.

Winkler, István, Gábor P. Háden, Olivia Ladinig, István Sziller, and Henkjan Honing. 2009. Newborn infants detect the beat in music. *Proceedings of the National Academy of Sciences of the United States of America* 106 (7): 2468–71.

Wright, Beverly A., and Andrew T. Sabin. 2007. Perceptual learning: How much daily training is enough? *Experimental Brain Research* 180 (4): 727–36.

Xu, Tonghui, Xinzhu Yu, Andrew J Perlik, Willie F. Tobin, Jonathan A. Zweig, Kelly Tennant, Theresa Jones, and Yi Zuo. 2009. Rapid formation and selective stabilization of synapses for enduring motor memories. *Nature* 462 (7275): 915–19.

Yust, Jason. 2010. Diatonic categorization in the perception of melodies. In *Proceedings of the 11th international conference on music perception and cognition (ICMPC11),* ed. S. M. Demorest, S. J. Morrison, and P. S. Campbell, Seattle.

Zacks, J. M., B. Tversky, and G. Iyer. 2001. Perceiving, remembering, and communicating structure in events. *Journal of Experimental Psychology: General* 130 (1): 29–58.

Zajonc, R. B. 1968. Attitudinal effects of mere exposure. 1. *Journal of Personality and Social Psychology Monograph Supplement* 9 (2 Pt. 2).

Zann, Richard A. 1996. *The zebra finch: A synthesis of field and laboratory studies.* Oxford: Oxford University Press.

Zatorre, Robert J., and Jackson T. Gandour. 2008. Neural specializations for speech and pitch: Moving beyond the dichotomies. *Philosophical Transactions of the Royal Society of London B: Biological Sciences* 363 (1493): 1087–104.

INDEX

INDEX

Bonham, John, 101
'Boots of Spanish Leather', 135
'Borderline', 174
'Both Sides Now', 109
brain, 218
  of adults vs. children, 91–92
  amygdala, 32, 33, 211
  auditory cortex, 46, 211
  basal ganglia, 154, 212, 218
  benefits of music for, 195, 196
  Broca's area, 32, 55–56, 57, 62, 212
  cerebellum, 20, 154, 212
  cerebral hemispheres, 212
  corpus callosum, 20, 21, 212
  evolution of, 33
  facts vs. actions coded in, 154
  fusiform gyrus, 32, 213
  grey matter in, 33, 52, 91, 95
  Heschl's gyrus, 21, 213
  hippocampus, 42, 52, 57, 213
  and language, 32, 61
  learning irregularities, 42
  and learning to play an instrument, 18–19
  mapping, 167–69
  medial temporal lobe, 154
  and memory, 57–58, 168
  motor cortex, 214
  multisensory links in, 30
  of musician vs. nonmusician, 19–21, 195
  planum temporale, 20, 32, 33, 215
  plasticity of, 3, 215
  and practice, 21, 94
  prefrontal cortex, 32, 42, 56, 216
  primary motor cortex, 19
  proceduralization and, 52
  rewiring, 18, 19, 22
  sensorimotor cortex, 18n, 19
  and singing, 59
  somatosensory cortex, 20
  specialized functions in, 57–58
  speed-accuracy trade-off, 51
  superior temporal gyrus, 32, 33, 217
  temporal lobe, 217
  Wernicke's area, 32, 217
  white matter, 52, 91
brain damage, 55, 56

brain-imaging techniques, 18
Braxton, Anthony, 155
Brecht, Bertolt, 186, 187
bridge (transition), 147
Broca's area of the brain, 32, 55–56, 57, 62, 212
Brown, James, 147
'Brown Sugar', 183
Bruner, Jerome, 82
Bryant, Kathena, 203
Buckley, Jeff, 101
Buckley, Tim, 101
Bunnell, Dewey, 156
'Burden of Proof', 149
Byrd, Bobby, 147

cadenzas, 156
Cage, John:
  4'33", 134
  randomly generated pieces, 134
  and repetition, 135n
calibration between representations, 167, 169–70
calluses, 47
Capretto, Carla, 203
Carey, Mariah, 109
Cash, Rosanne, 100
cave paintings, 112
Chaffin, Roger, 176
chants, 117, 214
Charles, Ray, 164
Cherry, Rebecca, 162–63
children:
  brains of adults vs., 91–92
  chord recognition in, 26
  comparison with animals, 27–28
  general learning by, 92–94, 96
  language acquired by, 2, 25, 27, 38–39, 46, 54, 60
  music acquired by, 25–28, 31, 45, 54, 56, 60
  neural changes with practice, 20–21, 91–92
  overregularization by, 38–39
  and pitch, 25–26, 45–46, 60
  and rhythm, 26–27, 31, 75
  teaching music to, 70–77, 81
  and tempo, 75–76
Chomsky, Noam, 24, 61
chords, 13

INDEX

minimalism, 58
minor scale, 16, 17, 26, 214
'Mr Sellack', 149–50
Mitchell, Joni, 109, 181
Mithen, Steven, *The Singing Neanderthals,* 58–59
Moby (band), 130
modular theory, 55
'Money for Nothing', 17
monophony, 214
moods, musical expression of, 64
Moog Guitar, 201–2
Morello, Tom, 3, 69, 71, 74, 81–82, 184–85
'most unwanted music', 124–25
motherese, 59
motivation, 66, 81–82
motor control, 43, 78
Mozart, Wolfgang Amadeus, 110, 117n
Mozart family, 101
Mull, Martin, 63
Murphy, Jessie, 178–79, 203
muscle memory, 57
muscles, coordination of, 43, 78
Muscle Shoals Rhythm Section, 149
music:
    addiction to, 17
    capacity for acquisition of, 30, 192
    children's acquisition of, 25–28, 31, 45, 54, 56, 60
    cognitive benefits of, 195–96
    cohesion in, 138–40
    cultural selection of, 118
    and dance, 31
    descriptions of, 63, 134, 142, 145
    ear training for, 45–46
    emergence in childhood of, 54
    evolution of, 108–11, 118
    finger strength in, 43, 46–47
    and genes, 102–3
    genres of, 181–82
    health benefits of, 200
    hearing, 166–68
    human desire to create, 9, 17
    inner structures of, 84
    instinct for, 24, 25–28
    and language compared, 24, 25, 30–31, 53–64
    liking for familiarity in, 126–30
    listening to, 29–30
    memorizing, 83–84, 175–77
    minimalist, 58
    as mnemonic device, 138
    moods expressed in, 64
    and motion, 31, 76, 145
    muscle control in, 43, 78
    neural overlap of language and, 56, 61
    optimum time to learn, 6
    pattern recognition in, 43
    perceived rewards of, 199–201, 203
    playing together, 96, 107, 178–79
    prenatal influence of, 23
    reading, 164–65
    repetition in, 135, 136
    rules of, 54
    streams of notes, 131
    systematic, 26
    technology of, 114–18, 137, 193, 194–95
    time required to learn, 11
    universals in, 28–29
musical achievement, studies of, 80–82
musical aptitude, 104
musical instruments:
    learning to play, 18–19
    modifications to, 183–85
music education, 70–71, 80–84
    Dalcroze method, 75–76
    knowledge acquired via, 30, 66–67
    as optional, 69
    and students' parents, 73, 81
    Suzuki method, 11, 71–72, 74–75
    teaching teachers, 83–84
    see also teachers of music
musicians:
    becoming expert, 167
    brains of nonmusicians vs., 19–21, 195
    listening, by nonmusicians vs., 151–52
    making a living, 110
    self-marketing, 98
    self-taught, 69
Musicophilia (Sacks), 55

INDEX